HF5823.S364 1976

SCHWARZ
THE SUCCESSFUL PROMOTER

# The Successful Promoter

# The Successful Promoter

### 100 SUREFIRE IDEAS FOR SELLING YOURSELF, YOUR PRODUCT, YOUR ORGANIZATION

## TED SCHWARZ

Henry Regnery Company • Chicago

Library of Congress Cataloging in Publication Data

Schwarz, Theodore.
　　The successful promoter.

　　Includes index.
　　1.　Advertising.　　2.　Sales promotion.　　I.　Title.
HF5823.S364　　1976　　　659.1　　　76-6285
ISBN 0-8092-8090-6

Copyright © 1976 by Ted Schwarz
All rights reserved
Published by Henry Regnery Company
180 North Michigan Avenue, Chicago, Illinois 60601
Manufactured in the United States of America
Library of Congress Catalog Card Number: 76-6285
International Standard Book Number: 0-8092-8090-6

Published simultaneously in Canada by
Beaverbooks
953 Dillingham Road
Pickering, Ontario L1W 1Z7
Canada

# Contents

*Introduction* vii
1 Understanding the Communications Media 1
2 Reaching the Public without Cost 11
3 Becoming an Instant Celebrity 55
4 Advertising 69
5 Writing Newspaper and Magazine Advertising 91
6 Direct Mail and Mail-order Advertisements 111
7 Nonprofit and Charitable Organization Promotion 135
8 The Window Display 173
9 Shopping Center Promotions 185
10 Outdoor Advertising 189
11 Using Newsletters 195
12 Printing 213
*Index* 219

# Introduction

Fenster Freebush built a better mousetrap. It came in three finishes and seventeen decorator colors and could lure a mouse hiding anywhere within a five-mile radius of the trap. In addition, it played stereo music and, when it was not otherwise occupied, could be used as a combination beer cooler and fondue pot for parties. Freebush had 1,000 of these units constructed, then waited for the world to beat a path to his door. Nobody came!

Contrary to what we would like to believe, few people, products, or businesses are instant successes. The fact that a person has talent and ability means little if no one is aware of those characteristics. A store can offer quality merchandise for the lowest possible price yet go bankrupt when no one comes inside to examine the wares. And products like Freebush's better mousetrap gather dust on dealers' shelves if no one knows to look for them. The only way for anything to succeed is for the public to be aware of it, and that means promotion.

The purpose of this book is to teach you how to handle the promotion that is so vital to success. It will discuss the various communications media and explain how to utilize them to best advantage. It will show you how to obtain free publicity as well as how to create advertisements, newsletters, and other promotional vehicles. In short, if you have personal abilities, a product, or a business you want others to know about, this book will tell you how to communicate the information in the most effective manner and at the lowest possible cost.

# The Successful Promoter

# 1

# Understanding the Communications Media

Everyone knows something about how to use the communications media: Newspapers are meant for housebreaking dogs and lining birdcages. Magazines are excellent for attacking houseflies. And television sets offer the cheapest baby-sitting service ever devised.

But obviously there is more to the news media than that. A newspaper, for example, is made up of various sections that reach different audiences. Unless you truly understand radio, television, newspapers, and magazines—what they are and how they can be most effectively utilized—you will never be able to effectively promote your cause. It is therefore essential that we start our discussion of promotion with a basic explanation of the various communications media.

For generations newspapers have been one of the most effective ways to reach lots of people at very low cost. Most American families read at least one newspaper a day. In addition, newspapers are the only effective medium for running many types of promotions.

Take the owner of a supermarket. If he advertises on television he can hope to leave a fleeting impression at best. Food prices will be forgotten by the viewer long before he or she can compare the values with competing stores. And what if the owner wants to offer coupon specials? Anyone trying to remove a coupon from the television screen will be frustrated at best and might even be electrocuted, an occurrence that will not promote good customer relations. With a newspaper advertisement, however, the reader can easily tear the coupon from the page, hurting no one except the family member who was trying to read the article printed on the back.

While newspapers are excellent promotion vehicles, the specific section you choose will determine how many people read about you or your product. The front page, obviously, is read by more people than any other. Unfortunately you can appear on the front page only if you have a story of great importance or exceptional reader interest.

Some people make headlines by shooting their spouses. Reporters interview them, photographers take their pictures, and their names become familiar to everyone. But such actions do not generate business, improve your reputation in the community, or keep you on good terms with your in-laws. That is why most people seeking favorable promotion choose to avoid this most popular page.

The second greatest readership can be found with the radio and television section. Even people who buy newspapers only to housebreak their dogs tend to read the television listings. Reader surveys show that people read related articles and advertisements found on this page as well.

The comics pages also have a strong appeal. Advertising in this section will reach men, women, and children of all ages and all backgrounds.

Certain columns and features have a strong following, though these will vary from newspaper to newspaper. "Martha Mudpie's Household Hints" might be number one in some papers while "Malicious Millicent's Rumor Round-up" captivates readers in others. Often the most popular feature will be a locally produced consumer help column—the type that might be called "Action Line," "Action Please," "The Ombudsman," or something similar. However, it has been found that few columns attract a regular following unless they appear on the same pages day after day. If people cannot turn to the same spot to locate a feature, they do not tend to read it regularly.

Once you get past the areas of greatest mass popularity, a newspaper actually becomes a compilation of special interest sections that generally have a limited but loyal following. There are the women's pages, once the domain of cooking, sewing, and homemaker hint columns.

These features are still staples but today most women's sections also run articles on the expanding role of women in society. The large number of women who are achieving their greatest personal fulfillment outside the home are no longer being neglected by the editors.

Sports pages, once considered an all-male attraction, are luring both sexes. Professional women's golf, tennis, and other popular sports are as likely to be featured as are articles on football teams and boxing champions.

Business pages also are expanding in many areas. They still carry "hard" business news such as the stock market report, corporate executive promotions, and information concerning "sophisticated" investing. However, they are also carrying such general information as how the average family can stretch its buying power in these inflationary times. Many lower income readers who once skipped the business section now read many of the articles featured there.

Real estate sections attract the person interested in buying a home as well as those do-it-yourselfers who follow the home improvement features often carried there. The readers are generally family people, perhaps more stable in their lifestyle than the readers of some of the other sections.

Book sections are increasingly popular, and many larger papers, such as the *New York Times*, devote a large amount of space to the literary world on a weekly basis. Despite the popularity of television, book sales are greater than ever. People who read these sections can be assumed to be interested in education, personal advancement, and entertainment. They can also be assumed to have more money than average, for many new books cost $10 or more.

Automotive sections sell cars, of course, but in many communities these sections include items relating to oil, steel, rubber, and similar products. In the East and Midwest, where a city's economy might relate directly to the manufacture of automobiles, such sections will attract wide reader interest.

There are other sections, of course. Religion often is covered in depth on Saturday. Special feature stories may appear in a locally produced Sunday magazine, and there will be special editions for certain holidays.

This book will concentrate on three areas of newspaper use. We will discuss advertising in newspapers, of course, but, of more importance for those with little or no budget, we will discuss how to be written-up by columnists and how to make your own news story. The latter two areas require no money and can be the most effective forms of promotion.

Magazines must be broken down into several categories. The days when a magazine tried to be of interest to everyone in the family are just about gone. Such publications as *Life*, *Look*, and *Collier's* have disappeared. The few that remain, such as the revived *Saturday Evening Post*, are quite different from what they were in the past.

News weeklies reach extensive audiences but their advertising rates are as high as their readership is large. Few businesses can afford an advertisement that will appear in all issues of *Time* or *Newsweek*, for example. Even when advertising sections are sold on a regional basis, the fee can be quite high.

Free publicity in news weeklies is difficult to obtain. These publications are concerned only with writing about people and businesses that are of interest throughout the nation. If you find a way to generate electricity by utilizing the hot air emitted during congressional speeches, every reporter in the nation will rush to your door. But if you merely want people to know what a nice person you are so that you can be elected mayor of your town, you probably will be ignored by the national news magazines.

Special interest publications can be quite another matter. A photography magazine might not care about the person who has harnessed congressional hot air. However, that small town mayoral candidate could be headlined if in his spare time he developed a way to photograph a black cat in a coal bin at midnight.

Trade journals limit themselves to features and news about events in specific fields. *Modern Tire Dealer* is concerned with the sales of tires by service stations, specialized companies, and others. *Veterinary Economics* deals with the financial side of being a veterinarian. The *Rangefinder Magazine* is concerned with professional photographers who are employed by studios. No matter what field of endeavor someone is in, there probable is a publication related to it. In fact, it would not surprise me to learn that there is a magazine called *Mugger and Bank Robber Monthly* offering advice on what stockings are least likely to run when pulled over the head, which getaway cars get the best mileage, and which leading mouthwashes will keep your breath from being offensive to the victim.

Editorial write-ups can be effective means of promotion in any type of magazine. However, many people feel that advertisements have a better future in monthlies than they do in magazines that appear more frequently. A weekly publication must be read in seven days, for example: when the new issue arrives, the old issue is discarded.

A monthly, on the other hand, will sit around at least four times longer. The reader will return to it again and again, often passing it on to others. Monthlies are also likely to carry articles which have less immediacy than an item in *Time* or *Newsweek*, for example. Someone reading the monthly six months or a year from the date of issue conceivably will receive as much enjoyment from an article as the person who reads it when it first arrives. Thus, monthlies are more likely to be stored away for reading during one of those periodic attic-cleaning binges that never seem to get off the ground. Obviously advertising carried in these magazines will have an impact far longer than just 30 days.

Radio is an often misunderstood medium. Many people relate it to television, but its audience is quite different. Prime time for radio is not in the evening, as it is for television. A radio is a highly mobile means of getting information and entertainment. It can be carried in a pocket or purse, taken to the beach, or left in a car. People tend to listen to radio while engaged in some other activity; their eyes do not have to be glued to a screen. As a result the largest audience comes during periods of peak activity.

For example, a radio audience is extemely large during the hours of 6 to 10 in the morning. During this period people listen while getting ready for school or work, fixing breakfast, or commutingby car. Regardless of what they are doing they are likely to have a radio playing in the background.

The second largest audience comes in the afternoon rush hours from 4 to 6 P.M. Once again you have commuters as well as children relaxing after school and people fixing their meals. Commercials, special programs, and guest interviews all get an unusual degree of attention during these periods. Lunchtime shows are also popular on radio.

How valuable radio might be for you will depend upon what you are trying to promote. Commercials generally require repetition to be successful because people do not usually listen intently enough to catch them the first time through.

The success of an interview will depend upon many factors. The average person listens to the radio for just 20 minutes during prime time. A guest on a show aired during this period may not reach as many people as he would during a weekend special program unless he is on the air during the entire rush hour period. This may be easier than it seems, though, because most stations use a single disc jockey during each prime time period, and you have only to convince the station personnel that what you have to say will interest the audience.

Prime time radio varies in format from city to city. Most large cities want "personalities" handling the shows aired during these periods. Humor might be used extensively or the disc jockey might interview community leaders concerning topics of local interest. Occasionally there will be call-in shows during which the listening audience can telephone the disc jockey or his guest and ask questions. Some stations prefer to put their call-in shows in a midday time slot, however, because the audience is more stable.

A good personality costs a lot of money compared with someone like Stuttering Stanley Shuttleworth, newly graduated from the Monty Mushmouth School of Radio Braodcasting and Bus Station Announcing. Stuttering Stanley is heard on stations that run nothing but prerecorded taped music—either rock or "middle-of-the-road." Stuttering Stanley is paid a tiny sum to make certain the tape doesn't break and to read the time and temperature, which he sometimes does incorrectly. This gives him the experience he needs to move on to a station where he can be a "personality." In this way the station owner gets the greatest return on his money and the person attempting to promote something is left out in the cold. Interviews are aired only as obligatory public-service spots buried in the midnight to 1 A.M. slot every third February 29.

Once again, what makes a person, product, or business worth mentioning will vary with the audience a particular radio station happens to reach. My wife and I once drove through a tiny, isolated community in New Mexico. We turned on the local radio station and happened to hear the news broadcast. A feature story concerned the previous night's birth of a baby and an important part of the program involved telling which local citizens had entered the hospital and which ones were well enough to go home. With so little happening, it is hard to imagine any action of a local person that would not be of interest to the station.

Every station tends to specialize in a certain approach to the broadcast day. Some stations aim for the youth market by featuring rock music and young disc jockeys whose vocabulary is limited to the phrases "right on," "groovy," and "too much" with an occasional "far out" used for variety. A disc jockey who actually is able to complete an intelligible sentence is banished to a station playing less raucous music such as the "middle-of-the-road" (M.O.R.) variety.

M.O.R. can cover a wide range of approaches. For some stations M.O.R. means a combination of rock music, soft sounds popular in the '40s and '50s, and even light classical. Others favor the "easy listening" music of Mantovani, Peter Nero, Henry Mancini, and similar musicians.

Generally either a rock or an M.O.R. station will take first place in the ratings. Often this is the result of intensive promotions and giveaways just before the rating surveys are conducted rather than an indication of the year-round popularity of a station. However, advertising rates will increase as a station approaches the number one position, regardless of how it accomplishes this feat.

A third type of station features country-western music. The "Nashville Sound" can be heard in cities such as New York as well as in Memphis. It has an extremely loyal audience.

A much smaller audience follows the classical music stations. These often exist only in larger cities and then only on FM. Although the number of listeners is often minimal, they are generally wealthier than average. They had to spend extra money to buy an FM receiver and many have quite elaborate stereo equipment. Such stations are often good vehicles for raising money or selling high-priced items.

Finally there are the stations that feature talk shows. Sometimes these are all-news stations. Other times they follow audience participation formats with special guests appearing regularly.

Whenever you consider radio, you must give thought to the type of person you are trying to reach as well as to the number of listeners a station has. Sometimes a small station will have an audience whose tastes and buying habits relate to the item you are trying to promote. Utilizing such a station will get you a far better response than if you use a more popular station whose audience's buying habits are quite different.

Television is the most dramatic of all approaches to promotion. Television offers sight and sound, color, movement, and excitement unmatched by the other media. It also offers high costs and an audience that can be surprisingly limited.

Television is divided into several time periods. From 7 to 10 P.M. is prime time—when the largest audience is watching. However, various studies have shown that prime time is really best for reaching men and children. Women tend to be engaged in some activity while the television is on rather than giving it their full attention. They are least likely to be influenced by commercials during this period, for example.

The next largest audience comes during the hours just before and just after prime time. These are periods when some people are eating or getting ready for bed so the audience is greatly reduced. In fact, until 6 P.M., television will be dramatically behind radio in terms of audience size.

Television's third greatest audience comes between 4 and 6 P.M., often attracting a large number of children, and 11 to 12 P.M., a period considered "all-adult." Programs such as the *Tonight Show* attract a loyal following during the later hour.

The last audience of any size can be found gathered around their television sets from 9 A.M. until 4 P.M., Monday through Friday. This is a period during which programming is aimed at women. Game shows, soap operas, and women-oriented variety programs abound. Some viewers sit glued to their sets. Others consider the programming dull and seldom turn on the set during this period.

The poorest audience, and one which few stations try to analyze, can be found during the remaining time. Saturdays usually have children's programming throughout the morning, and Sundays often have a combination of religious programs and public-service broadcasts. Charges for air time are often low during these off periods primarily because the audience is relatively unpredictable.

Television stations can be broken down into three categories. There are the network owned and affiliated stations, the nonnetwork commercial stations, and the nonprofit or educational channels. The network stations attract the largest audiences and charge the most money for their air time. The educational channels do not accept normal advertising.

The nonnetwork commercial station is a unique entity. Such a station, often found in the Ultra-High Frequency (UHF) range of channels 14 to 83, may charge no more for advertising than the leading radio station. This can be quite a bargain even with the station's relatively limited audience.

Nonnetwork commercial stations have several problems, though. The first is the fact that so many are located in the UHF frequencies while network stations use the standard Very High Frequency (VHF) range of channels 2 through 13. Although all television sets sold in the past several years have had to be able to receive both VHF and UHF stations, there are numerous older sets that will not receive UHF broadcasts. Converters are available to modernize the sets but few owners feel they are worth the trouble.

UHF tuning is different from VHF. Tuning VHF involves clicking the dial into place. UHF tuning requires you to slowly rotate a knob to reach your station. If you turn a little too fast you will go right past your station. Even when you find it, you have to work fairly hard to get it tuned in exactly. Many people feel that such effort is more trouble than it is worth. As a result they never bother watching the UHF channels.

Most nonnetwork commercial stations are limited in the type of programming they can have. With the exception of local programming, such as high school and/or college sports, there is little they air that is original. Most of their shows are popular reruns such as the early *I Love Lucy* and the original *Dick Van Dyke Show*. The movies they run are often the same ones the other stations showed 10 to 15 years ago. They do attract viewers, sometimes in fairly large numbers, but rarely are they considered competition for the network affiliates.

The only advantage to the nonnetwork commercial station is the cost of advertising. Most have rates that are competitive with a higher priced radio station. However the cost must be weighed against the potential audience you are trying to reach.

A fairly new phenomenon is cable television. With a cable hookup, subscribers can receive numerous channels in addition to the ones normally available in their cities. A subscriber pays a monthly fee for having his set converted to receive an additional 10 to 15 stations.

In some communities the cable television service includes a locally produced channel that features original, amateur programming and local sponsors. Commercials for area merchants might be run or perhaps the camera will just show a sign mentioning the sponsor's name. This is more of a novelty than a serious method of promotion. For the moment it is not worth considering.

Larger cities are liable to have locally produced talk shows featured during their weekly programming. Some of these are syndicated. Others are strictly for the city. But all of them are interested in people and products in which the audience might be interested.

All the communications media discussed so far have one thing in common. They are interested in any person, product, or business that their readers or listeners will find newsworthy, informative, or entertaining. If you can slant what you are trying to promote to fit one of these categories, you will be desired by the media representatives.

# 2

# Reaching the Public without Cost

Before you can begin promoting anything, you must first decide who you are trying to reach. Just because a particular communication medium reaches a large audience does not mean it will be effective for you. For example, if you use television promotion to sell stocks and bonds, it does you no good to reach an audience of 20-million viewers if those viewers are children watching a Saturday morning cartoon show.

The first stage in any promotion is to sit down and analyze who can use what you are promoting and how you can best reach that audience. For example, I once worked for a builder who was interested in promoting his ability to handle "turn-key" housing. The turn-key program was one in which private builders constructed low-income housing in an area approved by the Department of Housing and Urban Development (HUD). When the housing was completed satisfactorily, it was purchased by the government—the builder "turned the key" over to HUD.

The head of the family firm was a rising young black contractor. For years the company had been successful in the field of single family housing but this project, done in conjunction with a more established contractor, was his first major construction job. He wanted to obtain similar jobs in the future but to do so he had to become better known. It was my job to solve this problem.

In order to promote someone who is in the housing field, it is important to determine just what is important to the people who will be authorizing such construction. Price is one factor, but when bids are close there may be other reasons for making the final selection.

One consideration is the type of construction. The builder was using a new type of prefabricated concrete paneling that was cheaper than other approaches yet extremely sturdy and adaptable to a wide variety of building designs. I did a photo story on the technical side of the project that eventually found its way onto the pages of *Engineering News-Record,* a magazine read by technical experts in the field. This helped to establish the builder's professional expertise even though this was his first project.

Another consideration when a community authorizes construction of low-income housing units is the impact on the immediate neighborhood. Before living conditions can be improved, people must be moved from the housing located on the land on which the project is to be built. The homes are generally substandard, but they are all the people have. They do not want to leave, they do not know where to move, and they generally resent the entire situation. This can lead to anything from a riot to a lawsuit unless matters are handled with extreme tact.

In the case of the construction firm for which I was working, the head of the company worked with the local city councilwoman to help relocate the families before the project began. They helped parents find someone to watch their children, then took them to other homes in their price range. The contractor went so far as to have some of his staff use trucks to help move families when they found new homes. The people were delighted to learn that somebody cared about them enough to go out of their way to help. There were no complaints.

When the project was started, local people were used whenever possible. Some worked as skilled and unskilled laborers. Others served as watchmen. The project became a community affair as well as a means for the builder to make money. As it neared completion, people in the neighborhood were so proud of the way it looked that they began taking an interest in their own property. Private homes and small apartments that had been neglected for years were suddenly being repaired and repainted. The area had developed a pride it had not known for years.

Two more stories emerged from this neighborhood change. One appeared in the local newspaper as a feature. It was written by a reporter who had housing as his "beat" and who had been kept apprised of the project.

The second article appeared in *Nation's Cities,* a publication that goes to mayors, city managers, city council personnel, and others. The article featured the local councilwoman's work during the relocation phase of the project but there were many photographs of the builder's staff and the construction project. Without spending one cent for advertising, the builder's work was exposed to people in the fields that could most utilize his services. He received inquiries from communities planning turn-key projects in several different states.

In this particular example the builder had new business as his objective. He had neither a "name" nor extensive experience in the type of construction his firm wanted to do in the future. He was not interested in being known by the community at large except where it would help him with his business. The objectives were quite clear.

What are you trying to promote? If you have a company or product, there may be one or more objectives. Perhaps you are attempting to get people to buy a new laundry detergent. You are going to want to reach housewives and others who regularly do the wash. This means utilizing such mass media as radio, television, newspapers, and family oriented magazines.

Or perhaps you are trying to improve your company's image in the eyes of the public. Oil companies, for example, are constantly trying to justify their rising prices to the average person. They try to stress the constant, expensive research and exploration they regularly undertake. They show the many public benefits their efforts have produced over the years. They might even show the community service projects in which their personnel are engaged from time to time. The only thing they do not want to stress is the rising profit picture that has been all too common for them.

If you are running for political office you must actually promote several different things. The elderly will be interested in your views concerning health care, low cost recreation, and housing. Mass transportation might also be of concern. These same subjects might arouse the anger of a group of middle-aged workers with families, however. They mean an increased tax burden for these people who already feel themselves trapped to the limit.

When talking with middle-aged family people, a politician might want to stress the job market, the economy, and education. These subjects are of immediate concern to such a group.

Jobs are also important to young people just out of high school and college. They want an opportunity to prove themselves and politicians who work to help them gain that chance will get their support. But they seldom care about retirement communities or old age health benefits.

Thus we come to the first and most important rule for promoting anything. You must know your audience! You must understand who you are trying to reach and then locate the medium that will do it most effectively.

As was noted earlier, newspapers are perhaps the most effective means for promoting just about anything. A newspaper reaches more people than any other single medium. More important, it is so arranged that you can use different sections and features to reach various audiences.

There are several ways to use a newspaper. The first is through a news story.

News stories can be divided into three categories. The first is spot news—an unexpected situation of importance to the newspaper's readers. A fire in a department store is spot news. A bank holdup is spot news. Both events are considered chance happenings for which no one can prepare.

Few people or businesses are involved in spot news stories except as unwilling participants. If you own a factory that is the scene of union violence during a strike, this will be spot news that gets your business name in the newspaper but perhaps not in a way you desire. If you promote an aerosol product that explodes in the mayor's face, that's spot news you would definitely prefer to do without.

Promotion is the attempt to gain public support for yourself, your product, or your business. You put yourself or your product on public display where you hope that a critical examination will reveal more good points than bad. Since spot news generally works against this end, be happy if it doesn't come your way.

Occasionally you can originate spot news that will help you achieve your goals. For example, if you are planning to run for political office you will want to consider the timing of the start of your campaign carefully. You could write a speech making the announcement and outlining your platform, take it to a printer, and have copies made. Then you could "unexpectedly" hold a press conference, make your announcement, and pass out copies of the speech so you can be quoted exactly if the editors see fit to do so. Weeks of planning may have been involved, but the actual announcement is quite sudden. As spot news, it might well be used on the next radio broadcast or in the next edition of the newspaper.

Planning spot news stories can help you get maximum coverage for your announcement. Contrary to what many people think, the actual importance of a news story may be secondary to its timing in determining how much space it is given. Take a look at a week's newspaper. Study the types of stories run each day, the number of stories used, and the amount of space devoted to each. Saturday's paper usually contains less news space than any other day of the week simply because a Saturday paper goes unread by many people. Newsstand sales generally are the lowest for the week, and many community papers do not even bother to publish that day. If you can control the timing of a news event, try to avoid scheduling it at a time when it is likely to make spot news on a Saturday—unless your town happens to have a Saturday paper with an unusually large circulation.

The greatest number of stories customarily appear the day the newspaper has maximum store advertising. Usually there is one day of the week—Wednesday, Thursday, or sometimes Friday—when supermarkets and other stores do their heaviest advertising. This day will vary from community to community but will be consistent in any individual newspaper. The increased advertising means extra pages for additional news space. There seems to be a place for almost any story on the peak advertising day.

Even so, some experts feel that the peak advertising day is a poor time to try and place anything. There are so many articles appearing that many get just a passing glance.

What is really the best time for a news story? Monday morning's edition! The Monday morning paper must rely on news breaking on Sunday, traditionally a slow day in the city room. As a result, matters that might be considered trivia, suitable for burying on an inside section the rest of the week, might become page one headlines when the story is released in time for Monday morning's edition.

If you are planning to make an announcement, stage a publicity stunt, or do anything else that might be considered newsworthy, doing it on a

Sunday could enable you to capture Monday morning's headlines. At least you should get far more space than would be likely at any other time of the week.

Sunday news stories generally get radio and television exposure for the same reasons. Since Sunday is slow for news, the stations tend to give more air time to less important matters just because there is little competition. However, radio and television newscast audiences are drastically reduced on Sunday, so if you want the greatest impact on the broadcast media's audience, you should probably time the event for a weekday when there are more listeners. It is only with daily newspapers that the Sunday news event is so beneficial.

Naturally any Sunday news story must be tempered with common sense concerning your cause and your community. If you are a minister who is planning a news conference to announce your entrance into politics, Sunday may be the worst possible day regardless of the headlines you could generate in Monday morning's paper. Many of your potential constituents may feel that you, of all people, should revere Sunday as the Lord's day. For you to be engaged in nonclerical activity on Sunday will be considered sinful by some people even if the extent of your activity is an afternoon press conference. You could gain headlines at the expense of votes.

A second type of news is called "feature" news. A feature is generally an in-depth look at a person, event, or product. It is not as timely as spot news, though it might be run alongside a spot news story. It is usually similar to a magazine article that is selected because it will be of interest several months hence.

As an example of a spot news and feature news combination, let us suppose that you are head of the Wonder Widget Works, a company that makes left-handed widgets. Your firm has decided to expand into the field of inflatable gee-gaws, an action which will require you to construct a second factory and add hundreds more employees. When you announce the expansion of your firm, news of the boom to local employment is immediate or spot news. Additional jobs are of great interest to area readers, and the editor probably will give the story major play.

The spot news story about the jobs might be accompanied by a second article detailing the history of Wonder Widget Works, including when it was founded, what it makes, and the number of people it employs. Such a story is usually run next to the spot news story as a "side-bar."

However, it could be placed anywhere in the paper or might be saved for a day or two later. It is timely in so far as it relates to a spot news event, yet timeless in that it can be run at anytime over the next few days or weeks and still be of reader interest.

Sometimes several stories can be generated by the controlled announcement of related newsworthy events. Wonder Widget first made news by announcing its expansion. This was followed by a feature on the history of the company and its present number of employees. A few weeks pass and the firm is ready to begin hiring people to construct the second plant. William Wonder, a widget production expert from Wisconsin, is being brought to town to take over the building and management of the gee-gaw factory. His arrival means increased employment opportunity, a fact that makes the spot news category. Once that story has been run, the Wonder Widget Works' president alerts the reporters that William Wonder is an area native who grew up in the community, went to high school there, moved away to make his name, and is returning as a success. This is feature material, so a fourth story appears in the paper.

There will be additional items as time passes. When the plant is opened, a ribbon cutting ceremony attended by the mayor fits the spot news category. There may be yet another feature recapping the plant's history and discussing the boost in area employment.

There are other types of newspaper feature stories as well. Sometimes they stand alone, unrelated to the news of the day. They are run because they happen to be of ongoing reader interest. For example, there might be a feature concerning new advances in birth control or one on home canning and food preservation. Such "one-shots" unrelated to the news can be excellent promotion vehicles.

For example, Indian jewelry is extremely popular in the Southwestern United States. Unfortunately its popularity has meant that many unscrupulous dealers are trying to take advantage of the market. They offer fake jewelry, machine-made items, and/or low quality turquoise and silver. Hundreds of thousands of dollars are taken from people who buy junk, assuming that it's a good investment.

One Arizona newspaper decided to do an in-depth study of the Indian jewelry problem as a feature story. The reporter interviewed several local dealers, who discussed ways to avoid being taken. They told how to determine the true value of any item offered for sale.

The jewelry feature story was in the public service area because it could save money for many readers who might otherwise be taken. However, it might also boost the business of the cooperating dealers who were interviewed. After all, if your knowledge of Indian jewelry is limited to what you have read in the article, you are going to be extremely concerned about being cheated. When you make your next purchase, where will you go? To one of the dealers quoted in the feature, of course! Although the paper never intended the feature to be a promotion piece, that is precisely the effect it will have for those dealers.

The third type of news is created news. This can be any type of event staged strictly for the publicity. The incident must be newsworthy to get into the papers, but it will not occur at all unless the people involved are certain that it will make the paper.

For example, if a mailman bites a dog on his route, that would be spot news. If the paper did an article of the background of the dog-biting mailman, discussing his years with the postal service, his family, and his motivations for attacking the dog, that would be feature news.

But what if the mailman was head of a union that wanted to dramatize to the public the problems carriers have with dogs that are allowed to roam freely? These men and women are constantly being bitten because the dog owners do not keep their pets fenced in the yard or attached to a leash. The union head decided that the only way to get public attention was to do the unusual—attack and bite a dog roaming loose in front of a house along his route. He then called the various news media, told them of his intentions, and explained when and where he would do the biting. He then went to the home at the prearranged time, made certain reporters and camera crews were present, and bit the dog. His action would unquestionably be news even though it was created especially for the publicity.

Keep in mind that a newsworthy event will be reported regardless of whether or not it was planned specifically for publicity. Timing and the type of event, of course, will determine the space given to it.

**Press Releases**

There are two ways to get a newspaper write-up. The first is through the kind of activity just described. The second is through the release of written information. This is meant to give the paper a degree of flexibility in determining when and how much they publish.

Press releases are not as difficult to write as people often think. They are not meant to win literary prizes but solely to provide information to the newspaper. Usually an editor or reporter will rewrite the statements contained in the release—either to improve your prose or to make himself feel creative. In any event, you do not have to be a literary genius to handle this method of promotion.

The simplest release is an announcement for an event, such as a hospital fund raising dinner or a meeting of the county Democratic or Republican party. Whatever the activity, each newspaper has a set approach it uses for such items. This approach is part of a paper's "style."

For example, suppose you are promoting an art exhibit in a local gallery. Your area newspaper will probably carry a weekly listing of such events, perhaps on the Sunday pages when space is frequently given to the arts. This listing may be called "At the Galleries" or something similar. Every item listed will follow the identical pattern or style. Thus an announcement might read: "Paint-By-Number Art Gallery, 1354 Main St., Daily 1 to 6. Sunday 12 to 6. Toothpick sculpture by Belinda Birdwell through Sept. 15."

The announcement has everything the reader must know. It contains the name and address of the gallery, the hours it is open, the show being featured, and the period during which the exhibit will be on display. In short, it completely answers the essential questions—Who, What, When, Where, and How?

However you word your announcement, it will wind up in the paper's style. If the additional information you supply is of sufficient interest, a story might be considered as well.

You can save yourself considerable time by recognizing that an announcement must be limited to the style and information the paper or broadcasting station will be likely to use. If you are uncertain about the paper's style, call the city desk and ask what form should be used for the release. The radio and television stations generally have announcements handled through the Community Affairs Director, Public Service Director, or Program Director, depending upon the station. If you tell the person on the switchboard what you are trying to learn, you will be placed in contact with the proper party. Then, when you know the style desired, use it every time. The courtesy will be appreciated and you are more likely to get the space you are seeking.

Be certain to include all facts in the announcement. Give full addresses including driving aids if appropriate. For example, suppose a meeting is being held in the home of Mathew Dimwiddy who lives on a tiny, poorly marked dirt road called Delgado Street. You know that the average person, given just the Delgado Street address, might spend all night trying to find the road. To make things clear, relate the address to a better known, nearby road. You might say something to this effect: "The meeting of the Loyal Order of Muskrats will be held at the home of Mathew Dimwiddy, 349 Delgado St., one block north of Main Ave." If this slight addition to the address is kept short and simple, most newspapers will include it. Just be certain you don't get carried away and say something like: ". . . 349 Delgado St., a small dirt road that can be reached by traveling west on 40th St. to the third traffic light past the grocery store with the busted window. Then turn east on Pritchard for 1.735 miles, north on Cromwell until you reach a house with a red light in the window where you will turn east . . . ." You get the idea.

Never try to combine an announcement with what amounts to a news story. You should use a separate release for that or you may find the information is overlooked.

For example, take the announcement for the Paint-By-Number Art Gallery. It might have been written to include the information that Belinda Birdwell's sculpture includes a life-size, toothpick statue of Jesse James, which she made while holding the toothpicks with her toes. That might well be a news story and many papers would even run a photo feature on Belinda at work. However, if the information is sent as part of the announcement there is a good chance nothing will be done about it.

Some newspapers have an editor who reads announcements before having them rewritten in proper style. If the announcement concerning Belinda Birdwell reaches such a person, a reporter may be assigned to do an interview.

Other newspapers routinely turn press releases over to a lower echelon person without the editor bothering to read them. Sometimes they are given to the newest reporter on the staff. Other times they are tossed into a basket where they are allowed to pile up. Any reporter with a free moment is expected to pull out a stack, rewrite them in proper style, and pass the rewritten material over to the copy desk. The original is either filed or discarded. Under these circumstances, few reporters are going to bother mentioning Belinda's talented toes. They might find the information interesting or amusing, but few will bother mentioning it to someone who could give the go ahead for a story.

To gain news space, your press release must cover something the paper considers news. This sounds rather simplistic but it is not. For example, I live in a part of the country where tourism is a major industry, giving employment directly or indirectly to over 35,000 people. If an airline is thinking of eliminating its flights to the local airport, the information might or might not make the front page elsewhere. But here, where I live, such information probably would be the day's headline. That airline is a major carrier of tourists from several parts of the country. If it stops traveling to the local airport, thousands of people may plan their vacations and conventions for other, more convenient cities. The entire local economy would be threatened.

Perhaps you are trying to promote a new children's cereal that has all the nutritional value of 27 different fruits and vegetables and is endorsed by dentists because it contains no sugar and by doctors because it helps children grow. If you attempt to gain publicity for this new breakfast sensation in the *Golden Acres Daily Constitutional*, a newspaper serving a retirement community, the editor will probably toss it in the wastebasket. However, if the same release went to a newspaper with a large circulation among growing families, the editor might want to do a story about it.

Certain general items should go directly to the city desk, where they will be handled as the editor sees fit. The story about the gee-gaw factory is of general interest since it will mean new jobs and a boost for the local economy. Anything that will affect, interest, or amuse a large percentage of the readers should be sent through the city desk.

But suppose the interest is specialized. Sending a release to the city desk might result in its being forwarded to the right department—or it might be discarded. Thus you should address it to the person who is most likely to use it.

If you feel a particular columnist could use the information, then that is the person to whom you should address your release. But if you have only a department in mind, such as society, business, entertainment, or real estate, then just address the release to the editor for that department. Your envelope will read: "Aviation Editor, *The Daily Bleat*, 1345 Fairwell St., Dead-At-Night, Ohio, 00300."

How do you prepare a release? The first consideration is timeliness. A paper must have the information in plenty of time to rewrite it and fit into available space in advance of an event. A meeting at a local restaurant of the corporate heads of the 20 largest companies in the United States is important news. If the paper learns about the event far enough in advance, it will be played for all it is worth. This usually means one or two days notice at the very least. Thus, if you want the news story to appear on Thursday, getting it to the paper by Tuesday at the latest is advisable. That meeting will lose most of its news value when it is over. If your release does not arrive until after the luncheon meeting has been held, it will probably be discarded.

When sending a story in advance, it is considered permissable to request that the material be used on a particular day. To do this, simply mark the material "For Release August 25" or whatever date is desired. Most newspapers honor such release dates if at all possible.

Occasionally you will send a press release to a paper and the item will appear in advance of the release date, a fact that can cause some problems. It is important to understand why this occurs.

If you send an important announcement, such as the one concerning the Wonder Widget Works expansion, it may be a major news story. However, despite its importance, you want the paper to wait to run the item. The Wonder Widget Works' president, Percival Barnstable, is planning to announce the expansion on April 15, the same day he and his wife, Elvira, will celebrate their 50th Wedding Anniversary. Thus the story may arrive on April 12 with the notation "For Release April 15" so that it will appear at the same time the formal announcement is made.

Unknown to the person sending the release, the paper's business editor has learned about the expansion through his personal sources. He put all the facts together, wrote an article, and scheduled it for the April 14 edition of the paper—one day before the city editor would have run the story based on the release.

Not all newspapers cross-check departments to make certain that no two reporters are covering the same story. It is almost never necessary since stories with a limited audience are routinely assigned to the person covering that "beat." Crime stories are handled by the police reporter. Weddings go to the society editor. But sometimes things do not work the way they normally do; when that happens, a paper may run a story you would have preferred to delay. Unfortunately there is little you can do about such a situation; complaining only jeopardizes your ability to successfully place future stories.

A news release must be factual and contain all essential information. If someone's name is mentioned, give the full name. Include complete, correct addresses. Supply all other details the paper might need. If a reporter has to call a half dozen places to obtain details you omit, the project may become so involved that the editor may not feel the time is warranted. He may discard the release altogether.

A news release must be concise. Details must be given without opinionated description. You must never say: "Congressman Blowhard Windbag's speech before the City Club was the finest the members have ever heard." That expresses an opinion. However, the same point can be made by citing facts. The line might then read: "Congressman Blowhard Windbag's speech before the City Club received a 37-minute standing ovation." Obviously the group enjoyed it but you are not making an editorial opinion.

Start with the most important and interesting information, adding details in succeeding paragraphs. For example, take a typical release concerning a new photographic product. The camera is introduced by the company president during the stockholders' meeting. It is only one of several matters brought to the attention of those in attendance, but it is by far the most dramatic. The camera's success or failure will determine the company's future profits.

The release might read: "A new camera capable of taking a three-dimensional, life-size, color portrait of the person holding it was introduced today by Webly Bixby, president of the InstaSnap Camera Corporation. The camera, shown at the company's annual stockholders' meeting in Dead-At-Night, Iowa, will retail for $129.50.

"The camera, as yet unnamed, has been developed over the past five years at a cost of $30 million. It is expected to be placed on the market in time for Christmas sales.

" 'We feel this camera will start a revolution in the photographic industry,' said Bixby. 'No longer will couples have to settle for tiny enlargements in wedding albums. They can now get life-size, three-dimensional photographs of everyone in attendance. Parents can have images of their children as they grow. It is an idea whose time has definitely arrived!'

"Processing laboratories are being established in several cities around the United States. These laboratories will be able to process and enlarge the photographs in three days. Currently it costs $3,750 to have a 36 exposure roll of the new film processed and printed, but Bixby says he expects the price to drop drastically in the weeks ahead."

Notice how this news release is written. It starts with the most important facts. It tells what has been developed—the new camera. It tells how it works—it takes three-dimensional, life-size, color pictures. It tells where the announcement was made—the InstaSnap Camera Corporation's annual stockholders' meeting in Dead-At-Night, Iowa. It tells who introduced it—Webly Bixby, corporation president. And it tells the retail price, $129.50.

Less important information follows. The second paragraph tells a little about the development time and costs of the camera, as well as when it will be available to the public.

The third paragraph gives extra color in the form of a quote from Bixby. There is an opinion here—the camera "will start a revolution in the photographic industry"—but it is attributed to a particular person. Under such a circumstance it is perfectly acceptable.

The final paragraph provides more specific information about other aspects of the camera. The information is important but not to the degree of the facts that preceded it.

To be usable, a release of this type must be received in the newsroom no later than two days prior to the meeting. Naturally it will bear a release date coinciding with the meeting. If it could not be used until a day or two after the formal announcement, it would be stale news.

Where would such a release be sent? One copy would go to the Business Editor of the newspaper. A second, identical release would go to the city desk. A third would go to the person responsible for a local photography column, if any. It's often a good idea to let each know that releases are being sent to the others.

Most likely an announcement of this type would warrant a feature story. If the paper was located in the same city as the stockholders' meeting, a reporter would probably attend and write a complete review. At the very least, one of the departments is likely to do a feature on the new product and its development.

The news release might be accompanied by illustrations. Perhaps a professional photographer would use one of the cameras to photograph a scantily clad young woman wearing a sash marked "Miss InstaSnap." The portrait could be enlarged to life-size and a second photograph taken showing Miss InstaSnap looking at herself. A black-and-white copy would go to the newspapers and radio stations. A color copy would be sent to television stations and magazines that might be able to use the color.

Some companies like to generate editorial interest prior to the day an announcement will be made. They want to arouse public curiosity and get as much coverage of an event as possible. If the InstaSnap people used this approach, an earlier release might read:

"A totally new concept in photographic equipment will be revealed at the annual stockholders' meeting of the InstaSnap Camera Corporation, Webly Bixby, Corporate President, announced today. A specialized camera, 5 years and $30 million in the making, will be unveiled before the stockholders' meeting in the corporation's conference room at 2 P.M., August 17.

" 'The camera is a major technological breakthrough,' said Bixby. 'It will revolutionize the photographic industry.' "

This type of release is short and provides enough information to interest an editor. The second paragraph is all quoted opinion but the opening provides specific facts. We know what the product is, as well as the fact that it involved a major commitment in time and money. We are also told when and where the camera will be introduced.

Such a release is meant to interest the press, not to be used as news. The general public is apparently not invited to the meeting and details are too general for a story. Only the wording of the later item is adequate for the paper to go ahead with a news item on the basis of the release alone.

No matter how much may be happening at an event, your press release should be limited to the information that is of genuine, widespread public interest. The InstaSnap stockholders' meeting involved far more than just the introduction of the camera. There was a financial report and such corporate business as voting on whether or not to give aged Hawley Roberts, company janitor, a 12-cents an hour raise. But such information is important only to the people in attendance and the stockholders who could not attend. The average newspaper reader would be bored.

Some of the investment information might be news, however. If the

InstaSnap Corporation was going to hire 300 new workers to build the cameras, this would be of great interest to the immediate community. Such information would belong in every release sent to the local news media. Newspapers in other cities would not mention the new job openings because their readers would live too far away to apply. Thus, material might have to be added to or subtracted from a basic release, depending on where it will be sent.

Many experts feel that when you have sufficient time it is best to phone the news media to alert them to a story. In the case of the InstaSnap Corporation, at least three different departments would have to be contacted at the newspaper. There would also be a need to contact the news and program directors of radio and television stations as well as members of the editorial staffs of magazines.

The type of reception your telephone call receives will depend upon when you place it and how you handle yourself. Newspapers have certain periods when the staff is under great pressure to meet deadlines. This happens shortly before each edition change and is consistent from day to day. It would be wise for you to check with the paper to learn when slack periods occur. If you try to telephone a story during rush hour, you will be given very little time or consideration.

Television and radio station news people are busiest shortly before the news broadcasts. Check your newspaper listings and time your call so it does not interfere with last minute preparations.

Magazines, for the most part, do not have such regular periods of peak activity. The main exception is the weekly periodical—either newspaper or magazine. Such publications usually have one day of the week when they are busiest. In the case of magazines, this will probably be the day immediately before the publication is scheduled to reach the stands. It is also likely that the day immediately following publication will be somewhat slow because the staff is under less pressure.

When you call, be polite, businesslike and to the point. Giving rambling details over the telephone will "turn off" the staffer just as quickly as putting inconsequential matter in your press release. Always make certain that you are not calling at a busy time before launching into a lengthy conversation. If it is a busy time, leave your name and number but be sure to check back yourself if you fail to hear from the reporter within a reasonable time. Again, time your calls so that there are at least a couple of days between when you provide the information and the time you want a news story to appear.

Have a list of important details in front of you when you call. The reporter may wish to ask questions that you must be prepared to answer. You should have all the facts at hand so that you do not waste the person's time.

*Newspaper Columns*

Occasionally you will want to obtain a mention in a local column. Newspaper columnists working on a local level generally fall into specific areas. They might be gossip columnists, filling their space with items about people of prominence and interesting events occurring in your area.

Other columnists use humorous items to fill their space. Some of these are taken from wire service copy flowing into the paper around the clock. Other items are provided by local people and businesses, which receive a credit line. Sometimes the items are true. Sometimes they are simply meant to be entertaining. The main criteria are that the items be humorous and that the columnist knows whether or not they actually occurred.

A few columnists write general commentary on anything that moves them. Sometimes they must do this on a daily basis. More likely such a column will be used weekly, perhaps in one of the sections of Sunday's paper.

The other locally produced column found regularly throughout the country is the public service column, usually consumer oriented. These are the "Action Line" type columns mentioned earlier.

Columnists are different from the rest of the editorial staff in that they want an exclusive on the material they use. They have plenty of trouble filling space over the years and they do not want to have to "kill" an item because it duplicates what some other department or a rival newspaper is using. However, the exclusive can be a sidelight on a story released elsewhere.

For example, suppose that the press release for the InstaSnap Camera Corporation generated several stories. A feature on the product was prepared by the camera columnists. A second feature on the company earnings, profit picture, and estimated earnings from the new product would be handled by the business editor. And a general story highlighting the additional employment the camera's production would generate would make one of the general news pages. It might seem that just about everything has been done to promote the situation that is possible. But wait!

Suppose the president, Webly Bixby, and his wife are leaving for Europe shortly after the meeting. This item might delight the gossip columnist. Or perhaps the society columnist would be given that tidbit and the gossip columnist would be told that the Bixby's are planning to visit the orphanage where a foster child they have supported for five years is living. Each of these items would be given to one person only. They are exclusives concerning someone who is making the news.

Now what if there is a humorous incident connected with the making of the new camera? Suppose one of the technicians thought the camera prototype was no good because every photograph had a large blob in the center regardless of where the lens was pointed. Then, when the camera was about to be sent back to the development department for improvement, someone discovered that the technician had been holding the camera incorrectly. The big blob on each picture was actually his thumb! This story would be a perfect exclusive for the local humor columnist.

Some newspapers have a column featuring new products of reader interest. A set of photographs of the new camera and some general facts about what it can do, information lacking in other stories, would fit perfectly in this feature.

Finally, a guide for camera shoppers might be prepared under Welby Bixby's name. This would tell the average person how to determine his or her needs and budget when making a camera purchase. It would be a general item that would neither promote nor even mention InstaSnap products. The only reference to the company would be in the by-line, "By Welby Bixby, President of InstaSnap Camera Corporation." This short feature would be sent to the consumer oriented column's editor, perhaps with a covering note reading to the effect:

"Camera prices are climbing into the luxury class. Our latest model will sell for $129.50 when it is released, quite a sizable investment for the average person. But many people need not spend so much money if they are realistic about their desires. A $20 or $30 camera may be all they will ever really need. The enclosed guide to choosing the right camera at the lowest price may be of interest to your readers."

Will such a release get into the paper? Perhaps. It will depend upon the paper policy, the policy of the editor of the consumer affairs column, and the conciseness of the release. Just remember that it is always best to promote every aspect that you can rather than relying on just the most likely areas.

It is a wise idea to contact a columnist directly to learn how he or she wants to receive material. Unlike regular staff members, most columnists do not have set periods when they are busiest. Most try to work one or more days ahead so they do not have a last minute rush. However, when the columnist actually sits down to work, a phone call may be a nuisance. Always ask if the person you contact is busy before going ahead and discussing the reason for your call.

The subject of photographs included with press releases is always a touchy one. Everyone has an idea of what is best, but few people attempting self or business promotion ever take the time to learn what editors want to see.

*Using Photographs*

No editorial mention is ever so effective as when an illustration is included. People may skim an article, read the opening paragraph, or skip the print item entirely. But most people are drawn to a photograph with its short caption. Often you will be successful only because the reader took the time to look at the illustration.

Unfortunately picture space is limited with most papers and top priority is given to staff photographers—one or more full-time employees on the staff whose job it is to take news photos. Because their salaries must be justified, their work gets the greatest play.

Then there are the wire services and picture syndicates. They are constantly sending their subscribers humorous, unusual, or dramatic photographs that can be run with brief captions. These might be pictures of people leaping from a building engulfed in flames or of children and animals. The work is excellent, interesting, and used by editors to fill holes on the page. After all, they are paying for the service to supply them with material and the more items they use, the better they can justify the expense of the service.

Only after the best work has been gleaned from all these sources will the photographs you submit with your press releases be considered. Obviously, they must be special.

The first criteria for a newspaper photograph is that it be newsworthy. Just as your press release must involve a timely situation of genuine community interest, so must your photograph fit this category. So many people fail to recognize this basic fact that one editor with whom I discussed the matter told me that he discards all but two of every 100 prints he receives with press releases.

Even when a picture is newsworthy it must not be static or dull. A portrait of H. R. Smitherson, corporation executive, staring solemnly into the camera is of little interest, even if the press release may be considered worthy of news space. The same is true of the trite photos of two people shaking hands, receiving a check or award, or any of the other dull photographs you've been bored by a thousand times. Yet somehow people tend to think that including something like this is important. In reality it is a needless expense. A photograph must be visually exciting. It must "grab" the editor or it will never get before the readers.

Some newspapers have a photo "style" in the same way they have a writing "style." Certain approaches or rules must be followed to ensure that a photograph will even be considered for usage. For example, some papers have a policy of showing no more than three people in any one photograph. An exception might be made in illustrating a story concerning masses thronging to the beach on the hottest day of the year. But in general the rules must not be broken. If the editor is truly a "by-the-rules" person, the most dramatic photo ever taken may be discarded if there are too many people in it.

The editor should be contacted well in advance of sending photographs. You should talk with the editor concerning the paper's picture requirements as well as its picture style. That way you will not waste valuable time by sending the wrong photograph.

I once was promotion director for a large metropolitan rock type radio station. My employer was interested in getting the station's call letters mentioned in both radio and teen-oriented columns. Since the station was constantly having contests and giveaways to boost ratings, the person in charge felt that a photograph of each winner being congratulated by a disc jockey should be sent to each paper. I argued against this but, overruled, dutifully sent releases and photographs at the conclusion of every contest. Most of the releases resulted in at least a brief mention. Not one of the photographs was used. They were too static and meaningless. The expense involved had been totally unnecessary.

When photographs seem useful, both vertical and horizontal photographs should be included. This makes it simpler for the editor to fit the picture into a particular slot.

News photographs might be reproduced in almost any size, but only 8" x 10" photos should be submitted. Although some papers can accept Polaroids or color slides, most want 8" x 10" photos because these are the easiest to handle when it comes to cropping, retouching, and reproduction.

Newspapers prefer black-and-white glossy photographs though they can reproduce color in black-and-white. At this stage in reproduction technique, very few papers can afford to run color. When they do, the work is almost always a carefully planned staff production.

Another problem with color use in newspapers is that many papers have yet to master reproduction techniques. Photographs often appear to be triple printed, each print a different color and shifted slightly from the other two. It is a little like the effect you used to get when you looked at one of the old 3-D movies without the special glasses. Poor reproduction destroys the value of any photograph.

Television stations and magazines are the best places for color work. TV can handle both 8" x 10" color and color slides. However, all prints submitted to television stations should have a surface known as "matte" so the lights do not create glare.

Magazines can use color prints and most will accept slides. However, because a few reject the most popular size slide, the 35mm, do not submit slides until you are certain what is desired. If you must submit material without being certain of the requirements, have prints made from your slides and submit both so that the magazine has a choice.

Photographs must be timely—but that can mean more than you think. Different newspaper sections have different lead times for the preparation of material. Some departments have deadlines for photographs as much as a week in advance of publication date. If you bring a photograph to the editor two or three days before publication date, it may be rejected because all available space has been filled. Learn your area newspaper's deadlines for each section. The editor will be glad to help you.

Make certain the photograph is appropriate to the story, the paper, and the community. If your release is about the opening of a political campaign and the photograph has a pretty girl as the focal point, she may be eye-catching but the print may be considered inappropriate.

The photograph should be adequately captioned even if you feel that everything is covered in the release. The photograph and the release might get separated. The release might be discarded. In fact, many times a photograph is submitted with the caption typed on a piece of paper, which is taped to the back of the print. Again be certain you have all details necessary, including full names and addresses of subjects and time, date, and location of events.

Keep the subject matter to a minimum and be certain that it fills the picture. Small images will disappear when the print is reproduced on the page.

Is there just one focal point of interest? People going in all directions make for a confusing photograph. The reader should be drawn to only one part of the picture. If many areas seem to be vying for attention, the picture will probably be rejected. When showing people, move in close. Let them fill the picture if possible.

Make certain that everyone is properly lighted so that all details will reproduce. Also learn about the tonal range a newspaper can reproduce. Some publications prefer what is known as a high contrast photograph—one with limited gray areas. If you take the photographs yourself or have some nonprofessional do it, you may wish to submit the strip of negatives with it. If your print is the wrong tonal range, a staff member can use the negative to make a new print that will reproduce properly. Just be certain to tell the staff if you want the negatives returned. Never expect the return of a photograph, however.

How socially important are the people or other subject matter in the photograph you submit? A picture of a family being aided by a doctor in a recently completed wing of the hospital might be used with a release discussing the hospital's opening. But if it is the mayor's family, you can be almost certain the photograph will be printed.

A good photograph might have drama. A photograph of a doctor receiving a check for $100,000 as a part of a heart research grant is dull to an editor. But if the same doctor is shown performing heart surgery as a result of the $100,000 grant mentioned in the caption, there is every likelihood it will be used.

The same is true for a politician. Suppose you are an incumbent city council member. One of your successes was the establishment of a recreation center for the elderly. The news release you are sending out discusses an awards dinner honoring your accomplishment. That's hardly earthshaking. But you are certain that it will result in a news item and you would like to have a photograph run with it. If you are egocentric, you are going to send a picture of yourself being honored. You will delight in posing, then curse when the picture never appears. However, if you let yourself be slightly humble and send in a photograph of happy senior citizens enjoying the recreation facilities, it most likely will be used.

Does the photograph depict something that is within the reader's area of immediate concern? Suppose you head a manufacturing company and you want to promote your latest branch in Sioux City, Iowa, 2,000 miles from your headquarters. You send a release to newspapers in Sioux City as well as to those in your immediate area. The Sioux City papers will naturally run the story with photographs. The plant is good for the community's economy. Local people had jobs building it and other local people will be employed by it. The company will be paying taxes and generally benefiting everyone there.

The papers serving the home office area, on the other hand, will see little of interest to use. Perhaps the expansion will be mentioned, though undoubtedly the item will be buried in a small space on the business pages. No photograph, no matter how dramatic, is likely to be used because the item lacks local interest. The people of the community will not work for the plant, nor will they benefit from its taxes. The new plant is simply not within their area of concern.

If your photographs involve something for which there are legal requirements, be certain they show the law being obeyed. A person in a car should be wearing seat belts. A person on a motorcycle must have a crash helmet and the cycle must be properly equipped for the area in which it is used. A motorcycle meant for off-road use, for example, lacks equipment required on a cycle meant for the highway. When people are shown violating laws, the photograph will be rejected unless the release deals with the subject of lawbreaking.

If at all possible photographic coverage should always be handled by a photographer from your local paper. This might be as an assignment when covering a news story or the photographer might be moonlighting. Whatever the case, he or she will know what the paper is likely to use and will record accordingly. Just be certain you let the photographer guide you. Do not insist on having certain poses taken when they are quite likely to be the type of images the editor is certain to reject.

Finally, use your creativity when planning photographs for newspaper use. Improvise situations, isolate interesting activities, and stay alert for the unusual. A picture is one of the best promotion techniques available but photographs are of no value unless the editor sees fit to use them.

Often you can get a newspaper to provide photographic coverage of an event when the story might not warrant a reporter. A photographer has to stay only a few minutes at most meetings, conferences, or speeches and, if you plan ahead, the principle people can be in positions that relate to the activity being photographed. The photographer works quickly, makes notes as to names and other relevant data for captions, then leaves. A reporter, on the other hand, must stay around until the event is over. He or she must hear what is going on, observe the people involved and the audience reaction, then carefully compose a story. This can take several hours of time, a luxury the paper may not have. This is why a request for photographic coverage is far more likely to be honored than is a request for news or feature coverage.

*Press Release Forms*

Every news release should follow a general form that will be readily understood from paper to paper. All news releases must be typed on one side of the paper only. Hand printed or written releases are both difficult to read and unimpressive.

If you are making several copies of the same release, either with a photocopier or a mimeograph machine, check each one to make certain it is clean and clear. Smeared duplicates should be discarded. They make a poor impression and might even be illegible.

Leave a lot of white space on your release. There should be fairly wide margins and a large amount of space at the top. Triple space between lines if your machine can handle this. If your typewriter will not triple space, then use double spacing. The editor will use all this space for making changes or adding notations for the person who will set it in type.

Another reason for so much space between sentences is the way in which newspapers edit copy. Often they will feel that material can be used "as-is" though it is a little longer than they can handle. Sentences or paragraphs will be literally cut out with a scissors. Then the remaining work will be pasted together. The extra spacing makes this type of cut and paste journalism much easier.

The upper right-hand corner of the first page should have the name, address, and telephone number of whomever a reporter can call for more information. This may be the name of the person who wrote the release, the president of a company, or anyone else who is intimately familiar with the material being covered.

The upper left-hand corner should have a one word title that relates to the story. This might be "InstaSnap" in the case of our camera company example. The word selected is just to help the printer keep everything together since the same word will appear at the top left corner of every sheet of the release. You never include a full headline or title for your copy. It will be neither used nor appreciated. When the paper decides how and where a release will be used, a headline is created to fit both the space available and the paper's style.

Assuming that your release runs more than one page, be certain to stop writing on a page at the end of a paragraph. There should not be any continuation of paragraphs from one page to the next, even if you must leave an abnormally large margin at the bottom of the page.

Before you go on to the next page, mark the bottom of the page completed with the word "more." Then, when you start the next page, put the page number next to your one word headline. Thus, the camera company story might have "InstaSnap-2" at the top of the second page.

When you reach the end of the release, write "-30-" at the bottom. Some people prefer to use a series of crosshatches such as ###. Either approach will make it clear that the story is complete.

If you are including pictures, write the word "Pix" below the headline so the editor knows to look for them. Photographs have a way of getting separated from the copy. The person handling the rewrite may have no other way of knowing that illustrations do exist.

It is a wise idea to put the date on the first page of your release, plus a notation as to when it should be used. If the news can be used at any time, put the words "for immediate release" at the start. If you would like the information held, put "for release _____."

## The Press Conference

Another method for disseminating information to the news media is through the use of the press conference. Reporters and photographers are brought together to hear an announcement and to ask questions about the information under discussion. This is a technique that is used by the heads of major corporations, politicians, and, of course, the President of the United States. It is often dramatic and exciting for the people staging the press conference. It can be an overused, monumental bore for the reporters asked to attend.

When is a press conference effective? When news must be given out quickly, when you are attempting to change what in theory is a routine announcement into spot news, or when you wish to clarify a situation or to quell rumors.

The problem with press conferences is that the people holding them tend to think more of themselves than the event they are attempting to promote. It is most enjoyable to stand in front of a podium, floodlights illuminating your face, television cameras whirring, microphones thrust in your face, and reporters scribbling notes at a fevered pitch. You are the center of attention and you want to enjoy such moments again and again.

Typical in many areas is the case of one Hawley W. Farthinbottom, owner of the Farthinbottom Poultry Farms, a major producer of chickens in Cowslip, Kansas. Farthinbottom has been interviewed from time to time by reporters for area newspapers and radio stations since his problems are reflected in the prices consumers will pay for his chickens in the stores.

One day Hawley read his name in the evening paper. He had been asked about what a feed shortage would do to his operating costs and his answer was printed that night. He smiled, clipped the item for his scrapbook, then turned on the evening news, wondering if the networks had picked up the item. Naturally there was no mention of Hawley's chicken feed woes on national news, but Hawley did see the President holding a press conference on the South Lawn of the White House.

"By golly, that's for me," said Hawley. "I've got something to tell the folks and that's the way to do it. I'll get my name in the papers again and that'll be good promotion for my chicken business."

The next day Hawley called the news media and invited them to a press conference at 2 P.M. that day. His mention of an important announcement aroused the curiosity of reporters. Half a dozen men and women arrived for the event, including the area editor of a major daily

50 miles away. It was assumed that Hawley was going to talk about a drastic change in food prices that would further devastate the economy. Or perhaps rumors of chemical contamination of the soil killing off chickens were true and Hawley was going to discuss that problem.

"The reason I called you all here today is because I got the most important announcement I ever made," Hawley began. The reporters waited breathlessly, sharpened pencils at the ready. "Today my son, Philbert Farthinbottom, has graduated from Benedict Arnold High School and will be joining me in raising chickens. From now on this place will be known as Farthinbottom and Son Poultry Farms."

Does this sound absurd? I wish it were. Hawley Farthinbottom is a composite of a number of people every newspaper reporter runs across during the course of his career. I met three such characters the first six months I was a reporter for an eastern newspaper.

We thus come to the first consideration when contemplating using the press conference for promoting yourself, your product, or your business. The announcement must be of genuine value to the news media. The subject matter must be important to the readers, viewers, and listeners of the newspapers and television or radio stations represented. It should also be information that could not be given out in a simpler way.

For example, suppose you are planning to run for public office. Holding a press conference to announce this decision has definite value. First, it gives you a chance to release the information simultaneously to all media. Everyone has an equal chance to get it before their audience at the same time.

Second, it gives all reporters an opportunity to question the person holding the conference so that they can provide a complete understanding of the reasons behind the announcement. The political candidate can explain where his or her views differ from those of the opposition. He or she can fully explain the reasons behind personal stands on various matters. A great deal of time and trouble can be saved for everyone through the open question and answer session.

If you are interested in holding a press conference there are several considerations. First is the location of the conference. Sometimes there is no choice. For example, suppose an airplane crashes on a rural highway. Reporters rush to the scene trying to obtain information from investigators at the site. Finally the head of the investigating team agrees to meet with the news people. An impromptu conference is held at the site, a location that is unplanned and not desirable but absolutely essential under the circumstances.

In your case such problems will not exist. You are using the press conference as a promotional tool and it can be planned well in advance. So the location should be considered carefully.

The convenience of the press is a prime consideration. You are seeking a favorable reaction from the news media so conditions should be as relaxing and as trouble free for them as possible.

Locate the press conference as close to the news media as possible. A rural factory owner might hold the conference in a hotel room in the downtown section of the nearest big city if that is where it would be most convenient for the majority of reporters. Invariably someone will have to drive farther than he or she might like, but the majority should be served.

Newspaper and magazine reporters have different needs from the staff members of radio and television stations. Broadcasters need quiet areas for follow-up interviews and recording general commentary summarizing the event. This will be used along with material recorded during the conference.

Some experts feel that two rooms, with simultaneous briefings, are best. One room is for newspaper and television personnel, the other for newspaper and magazine reporters. However, this is usually impractical and there may be resentment if everyone is not briefed by the same people. There may even be a feeling that each group is receiving different information, causing considerable resentment.

Are there plenty of electrical outlets in the room? Radio and television personnel carry equipment that can be battery operated. But life is easier for them if they can save this portable power for when it is absolutely essential.

*Caution! Check union regulations concerning electrical usage in the room you are using.* I once attended a conference in a large hall that had a contract with the electrical workers' union requiring members to be on hand to do any wiring. This included turning on the power to the various outlets and plugging in extension cords. No one other than authorized union members could do this. The television crews could not plug in their own equipment, for example, without an angry reaction. It was a silly stipulation, but it was also a period of rising unemployment when the union was trying to insure work for its members. Find out in advance if anyone special must be present to handle this sort of situation.

Most press conferences include soft drinks, coffee, and, perhaps, some food. This does not mean a sit-down meal, though, unless the conference is specifically a luncheon or dinner gathering. Sweet rolls in the early morning and small sandwiches around lunchtime are all that are necessary.

Liquor is seldom served at press conferences. One exception is the introduction of a new product. Many times manufacturers will unveil a new line and offer cocktails to those in attendance. This might happen when showing new cars, for example. However, it is not a necessity at any time and is usually best avoided.

Depending upon a reporter's deadline, the importance of a story and the distance that must be traveled to return to the newspaper, telephones may be needed. These must be available, and, if they are connected to a switchboard, the operator should be warned that there may be unusually heavy use of the facility shortly after the conference.

There are other niceties as well. You may want to have a place where the reporters can check their coats. You may want to have special transportation available. When the news media is shown a manufacturing plant or other large complex as part of the conference, electric carts are often rented for conveying everyone around the grounds. Again this is for their comfort and to keep impressions as favorable as possible.

Having been a reporter, I know that someone is most often likely to claim he was misquoted when he said something he did not want known or did not mean to say. When a person's exact words are used in a story, and those words make him out to be the buffoon he is, he will suddenly start screaming "biased press." He remembers his speech the way he wants to remember it, not the way it actually happened.

This is not to say that the press is perfect. Reporters can be mistaken about what was said. They can misquote either intentionally or by accident. As a result, it is best for everyone if a tape recording of the press conference is made for the files. Not only is there a cross-check should someone feel there was a misquotation, but copies can be supplied to any reporter requesting one for use in writing his story.

Every person who plans to use a press conference as one aspect of a promotional campaign should develop a media list containing the names of reporters who should be invited to such briefings. This does not mean just those who are favorable to your cause, product, or business. It means all those people whose readers either need to know about the conference or will definitely be interested in what is said.

For example, suppose Baxter Dalrymple calls a press conference to introduce his new invention—the Dalrymple 2000, a car that can get 60 miles to a gallon of alcohol, orange juice, and ammonia. All the local newspapers, radio, and television stations will be interested in the invention because: 1) Dalrymple is a local person with an invention that may be of national importance. 2) If the car is a dud, the humorous aspects of the story will amuse readers and listeners. 3) The success of the car will mean increased employment when it is manufactured; since jobs are scarce this bit of news is most important.

Who else might be interested? If the car works, there will be national interest. Major networks can probably pick up the story from their area affiliates, but Dalrymple may want to contact the major newspaper services—the Associated Press and United Press International. The local representative can be found by checking the white pages of the telephone directory. If there is no listing, talk with area newspapers to learn how to reach them.

The people concerned with the automotive industry will be interested. This means the editors of trade journals and special interest magazines devoted to cars.

The fact that the car runs, in part, on orange juice means that orange growers and sellers of juice will be interested. Trade journals for these people should be contacted as well.

If you do not know the names of specific reporters who have been assigned to cover your field in the past, contact the city editor of local papers and the managing editor for out-of-town papers and all magazines. The news directors of radio and television stations should also be notified.

How do you contact these people? This will depend upon your time. Sometimes a conference is called on the spur of the moment. A situation arises suddenly, and as many members of the news media as possible must be gathered immediately. In such a case the telephone is the most convenient tool. Naturally the invitations will then be limited to local media who can realistically send someone to attend in the time available. However, if there is an out-of-town publication of major importance that will be interested, contact the editor by long-distance. There is a chance the publication will know a local writer who has supplied the magazine with features in the past and who can be assigned to cover the conference if the editor feels it is important enough.

The telephone might also be used as a follow-up vehicle when there is plenty of lead time. The telephone call serves as a reminder.

Telegrams are usually more rapid than letters but not as fast as a telephone. They are little used today, and partly for that reason they can be impressive.

Normally a letter or press release informing the editors of the conference will be all that is necessary. The letter should be concise, covering in a general way what will be happening. For example, suppose a political candidate is going to announce that he is running for office. A letter inviting reporters to the press conference might say that the politician will "have an important announcement to make regarding his/her role in the upcoming Senatorial election." Everyone may know that the person intends to run but there is no formal word of this fact given anywhere in the release. There is even a chance that the politician may have decided to drop out of the race. In either case, the formal announcement of a final decision is important news and the event will be covered by the news media. The release tells enough to warrant sending staff members to cover it but does not give away what will be said at the conference.

Or take the case of the InstaSnap Corporation. The release might say that the conference is being held to introduce "a product that has been 5 years and $30 million in the making." Again, enough facts are given to justify a reporter's time but not enough information is provided for the news media to put the story together from the release.

Periodically someone tries to combine the release with a publicity stunt. For example, a bikini clad woman will personally deliver the invitation to the press conference on the theory that she will arouse the editor's interest (whatever *that* means!). Supposedly he will not only get the release, he might also bring in a photographer to record the woman.

Reality seldom works that way. First, there is a chance that the editor will prove to be a woman. Second, bikini clad females of nubile proportions sitting on a male editor's lap do not make for the kind of photographs most papers will run. Third, the approach is so obviously a publicity stunt that some editors will assume that the press conference cannot be of much value if this is the only way reporters can be attracted.

A news conference should be a carefully planned, carefully orchestrated event. Nothing should be left to chance. Start with the people involved. Who is going to speak? In the case of a political announcement or similar action involving one or two people, the principal participants must also be the ones who talk. If they utilize an outside spokesperson, the reporters may feel cheated, in which case they will either react unfavorably or will seek private interviews at a later time. Private interviews are time-consuming and are the very kind of activity the news conference is supposed to prevent.

If a conference is being held to introduce a product or to announce a corporate action, the company's top officials should do the talking. They may not be the most knowledgeable in such a case but they represent the firm in the public's mind. Anyone less important seems to downgrade the value of the announcement.

The person who will be meeting with reporters should be briefed prior to the conference. A formal announcement will be carefully planned, then written for presentation to the reporters. However, the question and answer session cannot be controlled. It is important for the speaker to be properly prepared to handle anything that might arise.

For example, suppose you are planning to announce your candidacy for political office. You and your staff should get together and consider every question that could be asked. What issues are important in the election? Taxation? Zoning? A change in the school system? Funds for social welfare? Go over every item that you know will be part of the campaign and review how you will handle it.

*Do not memorize a series of set answers!* Just be certain you are familiar with the topics and have your general position clear in your own mind. If there are any areas in which you have limited knowledge, be prepared to say something to the effect of: "That topic is one of personal concern and is currently undergoing study by myself and my staff. In a few days I hope to be able to propose some solutions but any comment at this time would be premature." Naturally such a comment is effective only if the topic is one of relatively minor importance in the election. If you are running for mayor of a city that has been torn apart by violence caused by school busing attempts and you use that answer to a question about busing, it will hurt your chances in the campaign. That would be considered an issue about which you are expected to have an opinion *before* announcing your candidacy.

Next consider possible questions that do not directly relate to the issue involved with the conference. In the political candidate example, you might be asked about your divorce, the fact that your son was arrested for speeding, or almost anything else of a personal nature. If you head a corporation, you might be questioned about charges of discrimination against women in management positions, product safety, or anything else that has been in the news recently. In other words, anticipate both the obvious and the unusual and think about how you would handle the matter should it arise.

Few people are relaxed when giving a press conference. There is excitement and tension involved in such events. It is easy to become flustered precisely when you most want to appear in full control. That is why it is important for the spokesperson to be thoroughly prepared. Policy positions should be decided in advance so that, although the answers may come off the top of your head, they are based on a carefully considered review of the issue.

A press conference should start promptly. Time is critical for the news media. Generally a conference must start within five minutes of the designated time. If the event is extremely casual you might delay an additional five minutes but that is all.

Decide how you will handle the matter of photography before the event. Often the still photographers are allowed to move in for a minute or two of picture taking as the speaker first steps to the microphone. During this period they can use flash. After the designated time they must move back, working with available light so they do not disrupt matters. The television crews will be kept toward the back, provided they can maintain a clear view of what is happening.

If you are going to handle questions from radio and television personnel separately from those of the print media, explain this at the beginning. It is not as important how you handle these matters as that you have a previously considered plan that is announced at the start. A conference must be as organized as possible to be effective.

Many press conferences are held by people who want to talk "off the record." Sometimes there seems to be a legitimate reason for this. Other times such an announcement just makes the person feel important—as though he or she is about to release some important, still secret information. *Do not do it!*

A press conference is designed to provide information the news media can use. "Off the record" statements might be made in private interviews but not in press conferences. In fact, such a request is liable to be ignored. Reporters frequently have the attitude that anything said before a group can be used because, if the information really had to be kept secret, it would not be said to so many people. Such an attitude is quite valid.

Assuming there is time, various releases and other items can be prepared for distribution to the reporters present as well as to those representatives of the news media who could not attend. What should these include? News releases giving the same general information covered in the announcement would be appropriate. If a prepared speech is given at the start of the conference, prepare copies.

The photographers will have action photographs of the participants. However, it is a good idea to have individual portraits of the people involved in case they are desired. These can be head shots that can be run small or filed by papers for future use.

In the case of the political candidate, short position papers might be included. A business might provide background information on the firm, the products, or whatever else relates to the announcement. If a new product is introduced, additional material might include a biography of the inventor, researcher and/or developer.

Plans should also be made for follow-up information. Once you begin going public with your promotion, there are going to be contacts to be maintained.

For example, if a new product is announced, editors are going to have to know who they can contact for follow-up information. When the public reads about the item, many people will start calling to learn where they can buy it.

In the case of a politician, the announcement of candidacy means constituents, clubs, fraternal organizations, lobbyists, and others are going to be seeking more information and interviews. They must be able to contact someone who can supply facts and arrange for interviews with the principals involved.

Before the press conference decide who should be the contact person and how the person can be reached. Perhaps this will be yourself and the number used will be your home telephone. Perhaps it will be a public relations person working for the firm or from an agency office. This number should be supplied. Manufacturers may have to expect queries from individuals a considerable distance away. It might be helpful to their image to establish a Wide Area Telephone Service (WATS) line with the phone company to receive calls at their expense.

If you cannot be certain that someone will be reachable during the normal business day, you must use either a telephone answering service or a recording machine that answers your telephone. People must feel that even when you are not available you care enough about their interests to be certain that you can respond to their inquiries.

**Magazine Promotion**

Obtaining mention in magazines is somewhat more difficult than obtaining newspaper coverage. Magazines tend to have either a wider audience or an audience with special interests. They also run in-depth articles rather than spot news. An announcement with an immediate impact will be stale by the time a magazine goes to press.

If you are promoting a product it is relatively easy to get free space in one or more magazines. However, this aspect of promotion will be discussed in the chapter covering advertising campaigns. For now let us look at how you or your company can obtain editorial mention without expense.

The first step towards getting into a magazine is to decide which publications will be beneficial. In the case of the builder for whom I once worked, I decided that magazines read by people involved in the low income housing field, both as builders and community planners, would prove most beneficial. The builder was interested in obtaining additional work for his company. Any personal promotion was secondary.

My approach was to determine what aspects of his business would be of public interest. From a totally personal standpoint, the success of his construction company might be of interest to magazines, such as *Ebony*, that are aimed at a black audience. Here was a black man competing successfully in a white-dominated field. Even more interesting was the fact that the man's father, who had died only recently, had had to struggle through the depression to obtain even the most menial of construction assignments. Often prejudice was so strong that he was subjected to violence wherever he worked. On one job he was forced to carry a revolver in his work apron pocket for protection.

The personal history of the family had drama, suspense, and a tale of success through hard work and determination. Some day the builder may want personal publicity and he will have an easy time arousing editorial interest in himself. But when he hired me, his family's story was not something he cared to promote. He wanted his company to grow and I was to do everything I could to help him achieve that end.

What else did the builder have to offer that would be of interest to others? One area was his unusual construction technique. It was not original with him, nor was the project the first of its kind. But the contractor who had developed the approach and who was working in partnership with my client had had very little exposure. I was able to do an article on the new technique as it was used in the joint project. Thus I gave exposure to both contracting firms, in no way implying that my client was the inventor of the process. All I did was show that the process was cheaper than many others—easy to use, fast, efficient, and practical—and that my client was one of the few builders in the country with experience in using it. The article was a cover story in a magazine for engineers and others in the building trade. The result? Instant recognition of my client's name all across the country by people who read the article.

Next I wanted to reach the city council members, mayors, city managers, and other city officials who seek bids for low income housing and award contracts to various builders. Of course, this is a somewhat specialized field, and construction jobs are not awarded locally only. Some builders do nothing but this type of work, handling projects in numerous communities around the United States. City government leaders are accustomed to seeking bids from builders outside their communities.

The subject of mass, low-income housing is a touchy one in most areas. Such projects can have many ramifications, as I mentioned earlier. How a builder reacts to a low income community and how the people living near the project site respond to its construction are of great interest to politicians. If violence or mass protests occur, the government leaders may not get reelected. They are thus concerned not only with their constituents' feeling but also with their own careers. If I could reach them with the story of how well my client worked with the community in which the project was being constructed, I reasoned, they would certainly be interested in talking with him about their community's needs.

I began checking periodicals aimed at city officials. Finally I settled on *Nation's Cities* as being the most logical. I knew that I had a story of interest to others. I also knew that I could base the story on the work of the city councilwoman in the area who had joined with the builder in helping the people. The magazine's readers would be far more interested in the councilwoman's role, but since her efforts were joined with those of the builder, a story about one would be a story about both. The editor was delighted when I sent the heavily illustrated article.

What was the result? The builder received inquiries from many cities around the country. Whether or not he got the additional work was a matter of his own salesmanship. The important aspect, from my viewpoint, had been accomplished: He had become a "name" through the promotion. His firm had developed instant recognition and respect in the field. His business suddenly had a good chance of achieving the growth he was seeking.

Magazine editors are constantly seeking articles of interest to their readers. The articles must have either entertainment or informational value, or both. The fact that the appearance of an article may prove beneficial to the subject, either directly or indirectly, is not important. Such benefit is of concern only if the article is obviously what is known as a public relations "puff" piece. A "puff" piece is meant to play up the individual, company, or product without regard for objectivity or, occasionally, the truth.

Your first step in getting magazine publicity for your company or yourself is to sit down and analyze your objective. For example, the InstaSnap Camera Corporation wants to introduce its product to the widest possible *buying* audience. The initial promotional efforts were local. Because the product is unique, news weeklies might possibly run an item about the camera. Newspaper wire services such as the Associated Press and United Press International might also convey the information to their subscribers.

But news stories reach a very general audience. Many of the people reading about the camera will have no interest in the product. Many others will not have the money to pay for it. Still others will not be able to afford the current high cost of processing. The InstaSnap president needs to get his camera's story before an audience that *is* interested in photography, that has money to spend, and that spends it on luxury items.

The first place the company will look is the obvious one. The firm will get in touch with the editors of the various photography magazines. A release might be sent outlining the new product and offering any material, sample cameras loaned for testing, or actual photographs the editors might desire. If enough of the publications are located in the same city, a company spokesman or the president himself might travel to that city to hold a press conference specifically for them. Such an approach is sure to result in several articles because the product will be of greater reader interest in those specialized publications.

What about not so obvious publicity? Travel and leisure magazines are potential outlets for stories. An article might tell how effective the new camera is on a holiday or perhaps play up the unusual aspect of being able to take life-size photographs of people and places you want to remember. People who read travel magazines have wanderlust at the very least, and usually they have more spare capital than the average person.

Other interested readers might include those who follow the airlines' magazines. If they can afford a plane ticket, they can afford the camera. And since the readers are in flight, it means that they travel for one reason or another.

The camera might have technological applications that could boost sales. Police departments might be able to use it to photograph people being booked after arrest. Perhaps the editors of publications such as *Police Chief*, the magazine of the International Association of Chiefs of Police, would be interested.

A politician might use a city magazine for self promotion. There are numerous such independent and Chamber of Commerce publications throughout the country. These include *Atlanta, Cleveland, Chicago,* and *San Francisco.* Such publications always consider the possibility of doing in-depth studies of candidates, but be prepared to grant them a long interview.

Keep in mind that magazines are not necessarily going to praise you, your product, or your business when you get editorial mention. In most cases they are interested only in presenting an unbiased report to the readers, and that may not always be in your candidate's favor.

In theory someone running for office has a clean record and stated goals that are fairly high minded. What that same person plans to do once he or she settles in the office and has attained some power may not be so admirable. But few people run for office with a tainted past that will return to haunt them. Even a truly penetrating study, if objective, probably will be somewhat favorable to the candidate.

The same is true for a product. A company is not going to introduce something it does not feel is safe and desirable. However, suppose you are producing an aerosol deodorant similar to one your company stopped manufacturing ten years ago. The reason the older product had been discontinued was because the cans were faulty. One of them was held near the flame of a gas stove and it exploded, killing an individual. The resulting publicity was so bad that the line had to be dropped; the company took serious financial losses. Now you believe that you can take a chance with the same type of product in an improved container that cannot explode.

If there is some reason for a magazine to do a story on the new deodorant, a reporter worthy of the name will probably get some background on your company. If newspaper files are checked, the reporter will learn about the death and will most certainly ask about it. How you handle this inquiry will determine the outcome of the interview.

Never deny something that happened. Do not lie or be evasive. Be straightforward and honest, telling the whole truth and supplying necessary data if applicable. If you are running for sheriff despite the fact that ten years earlier you served time for grand larceny, be honest about your past. Say that it was through your own mistakes that you developed a respect for the law and a determination to keep others from being victimized by someone with your former proclivities. Talk about rehabilitation and how you hope to repay society.

If a product was once faulty, talk about the knowledge you gained from the experience. Discuss changes in your research department and how the new product no longer offers a hazard. Use the mistake to show how your company has gained. Not only will it help your cause, it will also indirectly imply that another firm that has not faced adversity might have an as yet undetected faulty product.

Remember, you have no business promoting something that can be destroyed by having the full truth known to the public. If an object, business, or person has no chance of success with all the warts showing, the public will be better off never hearing about it. Nothing is perfect. Flaws are quite acceptable so long as they are not major.

There are basically two ways to approach an editor with personal or business promotion in mind. The first is to prepare an article or query letter for an article that you feel will interest the publication's readers.

There are several types of articles you might send. The first is an opinion piece, which is quite effective if your opinion is considered important. For example, if you are an incumbent politician anything you say on the pages of a magazine going to people in your field will be potentially usable. A mayor, for example, will have valid statements to make concerning large or small cities and their problems. Editors of magazines ranging from *Nation's Cities* to general interest publications concerned with urban affairs will be interested.

A congressman or senator can go to publications that are concerned with his or her committee assignment. A member of the House Banking Committee might have salable articles for financial journals, investment journals, and even numismatic publications such as the hobby press. A member of the Senate Armed Services Committee might have material of interest to veterans' publications, military magazines, perhaps some history magazines, and general interest magazines.

The "name" syndrome works outside of politics as well. The by-line of the president of a major corporation will be readily salable to a trade journal aimed at people in his field.

Then there are specialized promotions. A lawyer is not supposed to advertise, but the attorney can advertise in effect by writing for publications whose readers might be able to utilize legal services. Thus an attorney might write an article on malpractice from the lawyer's view and send it to a medical magazine. Or an accountant might write about tax laws for an investment publication. Or a pediatrician can write about the diseases that affect children for a family magazine.

If your name is not enough to ensure sales, you must be careful that your article is both interesting and factual, even if this means that your product, business, or cause is played down somewhat. For example, an editor for a small publishing company specializing in automotive and motorcycle related books did an article for a magazine read by motorcycle enthusiasts. The article was on books of value to cyclists. He gave a good cross section of the field, mentioning his company's books, where applicable, as well as those by several other publishing houses. The illustrations showed his company's books as well as those of others.

The publishing house editor gave his books an obvious plug, but the magazine published the article because the plug was a minor one. The article had been both objective and of value to the readers. He never said that his company's books were best, nor did he give them undue emphasis. He said that they were among several titles of value.

If you are uncertain what the magazine will be interested in, it is best to send a query letter first. Let's look at how to do this in general. For more specific information, you should check a copy of the annual *Writer's Market* published by Writer's Digest Books.

At the InstaSnap Corporation, Webly Bixby has decided that he wants more publicity than his firm has been receiving. He decides to do an article for one of the photography magazines but has been advised to query first. The article must mention his new camera line but it cannot be an obvious plug. The query might go this way:

Dear Editor,

Photography is an ever-changing medium of artistic expression. At one time equipment was cumbersome, exposures were long, and photographs were limited to staid, stiff portraits taken in the blazing sun or scenics recorded for several minutes at a time. As technology improved, so did cameras. They became smaller, lighter, and easier to operate.

In the past few years photography has seen more advances than at any time in its history. There have been computerized lenses, Polaroid pictures in a minute, Pocket Instamatics, and even our own new InstaSnap camera that takes life-size, three-dimensional pictures.

"New Developments in Photography" is an article I would like to send you on speculation. It tells of the many advances, what they mean to the average photographer, and what can be expected in the future. It will be well illustrated with examples of items discussed as well as with reproductions of designs our company's creative department has considered for tomorrow's cameras.

Thank you for your consideration.
Sincerely,
Webly Bixby, President
InstaSnap Camera Corporation.

The query letter is not a promotion piece for InstaSnap, and it will be obvious to the editor that the article will not be either. It is a general piece that will interest the readers. The fact that InstaSnap will receive a plug does not matter because the company really deserves one. The new camera belongs in this discussion and, so long as the article follows the approach mentioned in the letter, the editor may well be inclined to use it.

But what if you cannot write an article? No problem. Let someone else do it.

Webly Bixby is a third grade dropout who reached his present position by marrying the unattractive, ill-mannered daughter of InstaSnap's founder, who was so delighted to get the girl off his hands that he rewarded Bixby with the job. The company is managed by marketing and business experts with Bixby acting as a front man. He has enough personal charm and basic intelligence to handle the tasks assigned to him but has never mastered the art of learning to write. In fact, he spells his name a different way each time he has to sign a document. The article is being prepared by a public relations expert, but it is Bixby's name that is important and Bixby who will receive by-line credit.

Perhaps you cannot write and do not know anyone who can. There is another way to approach a magazine editor.

The second method for getting your company's name in print is to offer to tell your story to a writer. Plan an article just as you would if you were going to write it. Think about markets and what approaches you could use to achieve your desired ends. Then contact the editor with a slightly different approach. This time your letter might read:

Dear Editor,

After introducing our new InstaSnap camera capable of taking life-size, three-dimensional photographs, I began thinking about the many advances in camera technology in recent years. We have computer designed lenses, compact Pocket Instamatics, Polaroid photographs, and our new line, among numerous others. It seems there might be an article here for one of your staff members or a contributor. I would be happy to supply the writer with material on our new product as well as designs our people have considered for tomorrow's cameras. I'm certain other companies would be happy to do the same and the information would be of great interest to your readers.

Please let me know if you are interested in having me send the material to you or to the party you designate. I will be most happy to cooperate in any way I can.

Sincerely,
Webly Bixby, President
InstaSnap Camera Corporation

A letter of this nature is especially appreciated by editors. Any number of articles can be generated from your offer, each assigned to a different staff person or free lancer of the publication's choice. The editor feels as though he or she is earning the paycheck while you receive extensive publicity that would not be possible with a different approach.

Generating publicity is seldom difficult providing you meet the needs of the publication in which you want to receive mention. By analyzing who your audience is and which publications are likely to reach it, you can plan a viable promotion campaign without spending any more than the price of postage or the cost of a telephone call.

# 3

# Becoming an Instant Celebrity

Continuing with the concept of no-cost promotion, let us explore radio and television to a greater degree. The majority of your opportunities will come from the various talk shows so it might be beneficial to review the types of programs commonly found around the United States.

One approach to talk shows is used by Brendon Beetlebrow, a high school dropout who has been involved with broadcasting since he was 16. Brendon is a self-educated man in his late 30's. He prides himself on having read and memorized every book in his local public library, yet remains ashamed of his lack of schooling. He feels inferior and tries to use his acquired knowledge to constantly prove to others that he is as intelligent as they are. His talk show is liable to go something like the following:

BRENDON: This afternoon I am pleased to have as my guest, Mr. Milton Smitherman, the author of the book *I Was an Astronaut for the FBI.* Tell me, Milton, when you were an astronaut, did you feel as Plato did that the Karma of the planets gives one a sense of cosmic oneness with the forces of Zen?

MILTON: Well, actually I never gave it much thought and to tell the truth, I'm not certain just what you're asking. I mean I just started flying planes as a kid when my daddy taught me how to handle an old tri-wing crop duster on our farm. Then, after high school, I joined the Air Force and . . .

BRENDON: Fascinating, Milton. I understand that the earth takes on a pattern not unlike that of Dadaism when you view it from outer space. Do you feel that God is a surrealist at heart?

MILTON: . . . in the Air Force I began flying jets. I did some combat missions in Vietnam, then got involved with the space program. Pretty soon I . . .

BRENDON: Did I mention I was reading Da Vinci's notebooks in the original Italian the other day? His comments about the nature of flight seem most appropriate. He said . . .

And so it goes through one of the most boring and confused programs on radio. It sometimes seems to me that the only reason such talk shows stay on the air is that both the station manager and the sponsor are afraid to admit they can't comprehend what Brendon is saying. Rather than risk being called uneducated, they continue the program and hope that its listeners have more understanding than they do.

The second type of talk show host is the eternal adversary. This person thinks that the public likes nothing better than a good fight. He insults every guest, the sponsors, the station that employs him, his mother-in-law, and his wife. He has usually been married to four women, arrested a dozen times, and is missing three of his teeth from the time he walked into a bar and called an Eighth Degree Karate Black Belt a "sawed-off runt." The host, Freddie Fatlip, usually runs his show like the following:

FREDDIE: Good afternoon all you lazy goof-offs who are listening to me when you should get off your fat butts and do some work. My guest is Dr. Fenster MacNamara, a squinty-eyed, intellectual creep who's written a book entitled *Meadowlarks of the Wilderness*, a sissy name if I ever heard one. Tell me, doc, why didn't you write about sex if you wanted to make some bread?

FENSTER: You see, Mr. Fatlip, I'm an ornithologist. Studying our feathered friends is my life's work.

FREDDIE: Don't be so formal, doc. Call me Freddie like all the guys do. That is, if you're one of the guys. Man, you creeps at home should see this runt. He looks like one of the birds in his book—which I didn't read, I might add. I can tell all I need to know by looking at the cover. If there aren't any broads, I stick the thing in the trash. I'm a star. I don't got time for such nonsense.

Then there is the host who is trying for a network job despite the fact that he or she is currently working at a tiny station in Upsandowns, Utah, population 473. Typical is Millicent Merridew.

MILLICENT: Good afternoon, ladies and gentlemen. I am Millicent Merridew, probing interviewer, lightning wit and available as anchor person for the *Today Show* if anyone from the network is listening. Today I have as my guest the Reverend Lemuel Pious who has written the book *Heaven Is an Equal Opportunity Employer*. Tell me, Reverend Pious, although your book depicts you as a humble man of the cloth, isn't it true that you were once known as the most notorious post office player of 43rd Street? And didn't you once give little Janie Finklemeyer a special delivery that left a hickey that took two years to fade?

LEMUEL: What . . . Janie Finklemeyer? 43rd Street? I haven't lived there since I was 9 years old, just before my parents became missionaries and took me to heathen lands to spread the word of God. Like it says in my book . . .

MILLICENT: The year doesn't matter. We're only here to uncover the facts. Remember, Pious, you wrote this so-called autobiography. If you didn't want people probing into your past, you shouldn't have let yourself become a public figure. Now, let's look at something more recent. On July 23, 1972, after delivering a sermon on respect for the law, did you not receive a parking ticket that you tried to get out of paying?

LEMUEL: That's true. But there was a good reason for my overstaying the time. I had parked my 15-year-old, conservative black sedan in a space outside a hospital where I had gone to pray for a dying parishoner. While I was there, the woman in the next bed started to give birth and no one answered her call. I immediately delivered the baby for her which she named after me. Then, when I was starting to leave, fire broke out and I had to wheel 27 patients through the flames to safety. My clothing was destroyed and my skin suffered third-degree burns. The staff insisted upon my staying for treatment despite my protests that I had to put another dime in the meter. They said it was less important than my being treated so I accepted their advice on the condition they would let me donate a pint of blood to their blood bank at the same time they were cleaning my burns.

MILLICENT: But the truth is that you do not have an untainted past as your book would have us believe. I do my homework, Pious, that's why I'm known as "Probing Millicent, the Ms. with the Nose for News." Now, my next question is . . .

There are other kinds of interviewers as well. Countless men and women handle such shows with good taste and a respect for the people who appear as guests. Hopefully you live where one of these dedicated entertainers is working. Appearing on such a show is both a pleasure and an excellent means of self-promotion. But no matter what type of person conducts an interview, it may be worth your time to get such exposure. Let us now look at how you can appear on radio and television.

I will start by assuming that you are not connected with a charitable cause. If you are, you can often arrange for large segments of air time to be given over to you and your staff as a public service. This is especially true during fund raising programs. Many stations choose to satisfy some of the Federal Communication Commission's public service requirements by doing features on United Appeal member agencies and other worthwhile, nonprofit organizations. Getting air time under such circumstances is not a problem as will be shown in the section on promoting such groups.

To appear on a radio or television program you obviously have to be of interest to the audience. This means one of two things. Either you must be a "name" or you must be able to offer entertainment of value to the listener.

For example, if you are President of the United States or the richest man in the world, it does not matter what you have to say. A station is going to give you air time. The same is true if you are a famous actor or other celebrity. Political figures of importance in the community generally are welcome almost any time, though usually the topic for such an interview will be considered carefully.

The average person has a more difficult time appearing on a program though it probably can be accomplished with a little advanced planning. For example, take the case of Ptomaine Tillie's Grocery Emporium, a chain of supermarkets known for their low prices and equally low quality goods. The only reason the health department has not closed the stores is that the health inspectors are afraid to go inside.

Ptomaine Tillie advertises fairly heavily. She has a weekly, full-page advertisement in the local newspapers and she periodically uses a rather catchy jingle as part of a radio campaign. However, business remains poor and she is anxious to find new methods of promotion. She decides to seek exposure on radio and television talk shows produced locally. The only question is how to do it.

The majority of people are not interested in Ptomaine Tillie as a person. She has body odor, smokes thick cigars, constantly has curlers in her hair, shows a hint of a mustache, and is 55 pounds overweight. She also has a sixth grade education and her knowledge of most subjects is rather limited. Fortunately Ptomaine Tillie is an expert on one topic—buying groceries.

What makes Ptomaine Tillie an expert on groceries? The fact that she sells them. She knows what they cost, what quantities can result in discounts, how to get best buys, and numerous other facts of interest to everyone during times of economic hardship. With very little effort she could sit down and outline a talk on "How to Save Money in the Supermarket." Moreover, she has a reasonably attractive voice.

So Tillie becomes excited about her area of expertise. She calls the producer of the Manly Mushmouth talk show and tells him who she is. "I've put together some facts on how families can save money when grocery shopping," she says to him. "I can tell people how to make the best buys *regardless of where they shop!*"

Note the emphasis at the end of her second sentence. She is not offering self-serving advice about how to shop in *her* stores. She wants to tell the world how to save money *regardless of where they buy their food*. Naturally, if Manly wants to mention the fact that she heads the Ptomaine Tillie chain of stores, she would not object. But that is left unsaid.

What does the producer think of Ptomaine Tillie? Probably not much. The last time his wife bought a steak from her meat department the entire family had to have their stomachs pumped. However, Manly Mushmouth is on the air from 10 A.M. until 2 P.M. His show is heard mainly by housewives who do the family grocery shopping. Tips on saving money in the food store will be of great interest, regardless of who gives them.

Then there is the case of Lazlo Rafferty, the jeweler. He wants to sell more wedding and engagement rings but is not doing enough business to allow for anything more than a small advertisement in the newspaper. He would like to appear on radio and television to talk about his business but he runs a tiny, one-man shop in a fairly isolated area. Who would take an interest in him? Plenty of people.

Lazlo can get air time not by talking about his business but by talking about the customs that are symbolized by the jewelry he sells. After all, who wouldn't be fascinated by such facts as the meaning of the wedding ring? At one time couples engaged in "marriage by capture" during which the prospective groom would sneak up on a woman, bind her, and carry her off. Later the wedding ring was used to symbolize the bondage rather than continuing to tie her hands with rope.

Or what about the honeymoon? When the groom/kidnapper carried off his bride, her family was usually upset by the action. They would seek the couple who went into seclusion until the family realized it was too late to stop the marriage. This period of time was generally a month or one full phase of the moon. During this period the couple would become better acquainted while drinking a honey wine called mead. These two actions were combined and developed into our concept of the honeymoon.

Armed with tales like these, suddenly the jeweler is no longer promoting himself. He is entertaining the radio or television audience with facts of general interest. He becomes a welcome guest, and, depending upon how well he expresses himself, he may be invited back. It *could* happen.

Every other field has something to offer. Someone working for a loan company might talk about handling credit, the abuses of credit, or just general money management. Someone working for a music store might discuss ways to select an instrument for a child. The manager of the local movie theater might talk about changes in the industry, the history of film, or a similar topic.

No matter what it is you do, it is possible to find one or more areas of general interest related to it. Remember that what you discuss is not intended to be a direct plug for your company. It is going to be entertainment that only indirectly includes mention of who you are and where you work. However, this is to the good.

When you are a guest on a radio or television program, you immediately take on a special importance in the eyes of the audience. The public, more often than not, admires someone who is heard on the air. You become an expert in your field, someone to be consulted and, with luck, trusted. You may have the highest prices and poorest merchandise selection in town. But once you have been interviewed, your business stands to increase significantly, even if your business was mentioned only in the opening and closing of the interview.

Once you have decided upon a topic you could intelligently discuss, either from your own knowledge or with the help of some study in the public library, you will have to decide which shows you want to go on. Television offers three opportunities—network commercial stations, nonnetwork commercial stations, and public broadcast stations. These have been discussed in earlier chapters.

Check the week's listings carefully to determine if any programs originate in or near your community. Some stations take pride in their locally produced talk and information programs. Others lack the budget, the staff, and/or the inclination to go with anything other than "canned" material produced in the major broadcast centers.

If there are local programs, you must watch the ones that seem most likely. Study their format, who their guests are, and how they are interviewed. You may have to watch for a month or more to learn about a weekly program and at least five days for a daily show. If it is daily, watch from the *middle* of one week through the middle of the next. Occasionally a show will have a theme approach for a special broadcast week. If you watched the programs during the five days of the theme specials you might have felt that everything on the show has to revolve around that theme. Yet if you were to approach the producer with a similar subject, your idea would be rejected since the viewing audience had already been saturated with the theme during the special week.

Radio stations generally have one of three approaches. Either they are all music, all news, or have one or more talk shows. Sometimes the talk show will be an audience participation format. Other times the station personality handles all the questioning.

Listen to the various talk programs during the course of the broadcast day to learn where their emphasis happens to be. Midday shows generally are aimed at the housewife but they also have listeners who are sales people, office workers, and others who tune in regularly. Some stations aim more towards general interest programming during this period just as they do during rush hours.

Rock stations will have a strong teen audience in the evening with a surprising number of adults during the day. Country-western stations have a well mixed listening audience regardless of the hour. If you are uncertain who is listening when, the advertising department of the station can give you a statistical breakdown based on surveys.

Decide which time and which type of station is most likely to reach the people who can benefit you or your business. Then listen to the various disc jockeys on different stations during that period. Determine which one has an approach with which you would feel comfortable.

Finally sit down and outline just what it is you feel you have to offer. Research any aspect of the subject you may not know and generally prepare yourself for your appearance. Remember that station personnel will interview you concerning the topic before they decide whether or not to let you go on the air. In effect you are going to have to give a full show before you have a chance to be heard by the public.

When you are properly prepared, call the station, explain that you are interested in appearing on a particular program, and ask whom you should contact. You will be referred to the show's host, the show's producer, or the program director depending upon the size of the station and the degree of management control. Large stations or programs that generate both high listener interest and substantial revenue are likely to have a producer. His or her job will be to coordinate the program, screen possible guests, and generally prepare for each day's program.

The person to whom you talk will either invite you to the station for an interview or request that you send a resume of what you propose to discuss. The interview will be no problem if you have done your homework and have a reasonably pleasing personality. The resume may present some difficulty the first time out, though.

The best approach is to outline a situation of listener concern, tell what information you can provide, then tell the reason for your expertise. For example, let's look at the type of resume Ptomaine Tillie might have one of her better educated employees write for her.

"Inflation has been robbing the pockets of the American consumer for far too many years. Prices, especially for such necessities as food and shelter, have been rising even higher with no end in sight. Even with raises in pay many workers find that they cannot afford as much as they were able to purchase just one year ago. People living on fixed incomes are hurt even more.

"Fortunately there are ways to stretch your food dollar. There are approaches to shopping that can save a family large sums of money over the course of the average year. There are unusual cuts of meat, for example, that are remarkably inexpensive yet extremely tasty when properly prepared. I have information about such meat as well as details of how to save money on almost every purchase. I feel it would be of interest to the listeners of (name of program) and wonder if it might be possible for me to appear on the show?

"I am the owner of a chain of grocery stores and the mother of four children. Food has been a prime concern of mine for many years, both as a business person and a consumer. I feel I have valuable information to offer your listeners."

Such a resume tells very little but it gives enough information to let the station know whether or not Ptomaine Tillie's appearance might draw a favorable listener response. The producer knows the topic, the general approach that would be taken, and a little of the background of the person involved. In other words, he knows enough to decide whether to ask for more details.

Sometimes all arrangements will be handled during the initial telephone call. Perhaps the station is familiar with the person involved, either from general reputation or a previous appearance. Or perhaps the person seeking an appearance speaks so effectively that the call convinces the station personnel to provide air time. Regardless of the reason, when this occurs a short memo should be sent to the station staff member involved giving a brief summation of the call. The memo will repeat the topic to be discussed and the general approach to be taken. Mention whatever agreement was reached and confirm the proposed air or recording time.

Clothing is never a consideration when appearing on radio. No matter how intently people stare at their set, they are not likely to be able to see you. A television appearance is quite another matter, however. What you wear and how you hold yourself will make an impression on the audience—perhaps more of an impression than what you say. Ptomaine Tillie, for example, is going to have to remove those curlers, take a bath, and iron a dress.

There was a time when television had strict guidelines for clothing. A man had to wear a blue shirt since the cameras of the day could handle it better than a white one. This was a universal standard in the industry, and, for a while, it became a status symbol for a man to go to his office wearing a blue shirt. The person wearing it was saying, "I'm so important I have to dress to be ready to go on television at any moment."

Today the cameras have improved and there is more freedom of dress. However, white is still not desired, nor are distracting checkered patterns. Jewelry, including watches, should be kept to a minimum and care should be taken that nothing highly reflective is worn. The bright studio lights are liable to reflect from shiny metallic objects causing distracting flashes to appear on the screen. When in doubt ask the producer or director about what to wear prior to the day of the show.

A man should avoid going on the air with a new, short haircut. Let a few days elapse between the visit to the barber and the television appearance if possible. Newly cut, short hair often makes a man look scalped. Recently trimmed long hair seldom causes problems.

Shave shortly before air time. This will keep the lights from exaggerating any beard.

Makeup for women should be used sparingly. If a professional job is demanded by the station, someone on the staff will have the skill to apply it. Usually a light foundation is all that is necessary. Such special effects as long eyelashes or dramatic eye shadowing do nothing but deepen and darken the eyes under the harsh studio lights. Instead of looking beautiful, a woman wearing such makeup is going to appear to have two hollow, black sockets where her eyes should be.

A day or two before the television appearance do an in-depth review of the material you will be discussing. You should know your subject matter backwards and forwards. This does not mean memorizing a list of set responses to anticipated questions, however. It means being familiar enough with the material to be able to discuss it while under the intense pressure of the studio setting. Even veteran television performers get nervous on the air. If you are not thoroughly prepared for your appearance, the normal fright you will experience when facing the camera may cause you to forget what you wanted to say.

Some veteran television guests believe you should prepare a list of possible questions the interviewer could use when discussing your field of expertise. Such a list is to be taken to the station and given to the interviewer if requested. Some interviewers pride themselves on their advance preparation for a guest. They familiarize themselves with the guest's background and the field they will be discussing, then prepare their own questions. Other interviewers have neither the time nor the inclination for such a task. In that case, the assistance you give them in the form of a list of possible questions they can use probably will be greatly appreciated.

Television is a visual medium. It thrives on color, movement, and visual excitement. Your appearance will be enhanced by visual aids that can be shown from time to time while you talk. If you have pictures, charts, models, or other objects, talk with the producer about using them on the program. Sometimes these are greatly desired. Other times the director chooses to create the visual interest by the way the cameras change positions.

Always check in with the producer a week before scheduled air time for a last minute review of what is expected. You want all arrangements confirmed well before the show.

Try to arrive at the station at least 30 minutes before you are scheduled to appear. This will allow for last minute preparations and give you ample time to nibble your nails while nervously waiting to make your appearance. If you have a way of relaxing, such as chewing gum or standing on your head for meditation, this is the time to do it. You want to be as calm as possible when facing the camera.

The television host is king. No matter how prominent you might be, no matter how much interest there is in you or your field, the majority of the viewers are tuned in because of the host. Most will love him. Some will hate him. But all will be involved with him and want you to be the same way. Therefore it is important that you talk looking at the host rather than staring into the camera.

It is the television director's job to make certain that the show is visually interesting. When he or she wants to show you looking into the camera, and thus directly at the viewing audience, one of the cameras will be positioned behind the host, filming over his shoulder. The only time you should deliberately look into the camera is when you want to make a special point directly to the audience. All other times you should talk with the interviewer or the other program guests, if any.

How do you know which camera is "live"? It is the one with the red light on it. However, be careful that you don't get so involved looking for the light that you stop looking at the host.

Be prepared for the unpredictable. Assume the worst—that someone is going to ask you an annoying, overly personal, or downright nasty question and be prepared to reply with grace and humor. On the air you must appear to be a good sport who remains unruffled. After the show you can throw a rotten banana cream pie in the interviewer's face.

Television and radio are carefully timed media. They do not allow you the luxury of endless discussion. When the interviewer says time is up and you are in the middle of the funniest or most important story you have related during the program, do not try to finish it. Simply shut your mouth, smile, and inwardly curse the medium. When it is time to end the show or break for a commercial you will not have the luxury of even a few seconds.

If you think you might like to appear on the program a second time it will be important to know how you fared the first time around. Friends or a spouse watching the program make generally unreliable critics. They will either think you did no wrong or that you made a fool of yourself when the truth is probably somewhere in between. Discuss your appearance with the producer and/or host immediately after the show. If they are pleased you have nothing to worry about. If they are not, try to learn where you need improvement.

Television news programs offer special opportunities for publicity. Generally there are two types of news programs—spot news and feature stories. These fall into the same categories as newspapers and magazines discussed earlier. The only difference is that television features must be visually interesting.

For example, a person who has the ability to mentally work mathematical problems faster than a computer could easily be the subject for a magazine article. However television stations would assign a low priority to such a newsworthy person because the action is not very visual.

On the other hand, if you are seeking publicity for your hand-carved, animated, miniature circus that you exhibit at shopping centers, television news departments could be interested in producing a feature story. The cameras can take close-ups of the miniature people, animals, and buildings. The audience will be able to see acrobats performing and aerialists on the tiny "high wire." It is a story that will get as much air time as other news events allow.

News stories are generally handled by each station regardless of whether they are in the spot news or feature category. All you can do is make suggestions to the news director in a manner similar to that used when approaching a magazine editor. The main difference is that you will be working locally and probably using the telephone.

There are ways you can help the television news people and thus increase your chances of in-depth coverage. One is to provide any visual aids to which you have access. These would include short film clips, slides, photographs, or similar objects.

A second method is to make arrangements for the news department to film that which you are promoting. This might mean renting a large meeting room or arranging for the station's special lighting to be brought in.

Have background material prepared. This should include full names, addresses, descriptions, history, and everything else that is remotely involved. Such material helps the station personnel prepare the broadcast. Naturally you must have information concerning who can be contacted for additional facts that might be overlooked.

If you are staging an event for the news media, give them plenty of advance notice. Then keep them posted regularly so they are aware of any special restrictions or changes in what will be happening.

Keep in mind that getting radio and television publicity is sometimes much easier than you think. So long as what you are promoting has either news value or interest for the majority of the station's audience, you have a good chance of being welcomed with open arms. Remember, it is not so much who you are as what you know and how you plan to convey the information over the air. With a little thought and advance preparation, it's possible that air time literally will be yours free for the asking.

# 4

# Advertising

No matter how much free publicity you can obtain in the news media, there will probably come a time when you want to start a carefully controlled promotional campaign. This might be anything from a minor display advertisement repeated every month in a magazine to a major television campaign. Unfortunately there is a vast difference between simply buying time or space and advertising effectively. It is possible to have an eye-catching, award-winning campaign that fails entirely to achieve your desired results. It is also possible to have a highly successful, low budget promotion with copy you write yourself. Therefore, it is important to look closely at just what advertising can do and how you can get the kind of promotion you want.

Advertising is, first of all, an important medium for conveying information in our society. The success or even the mere survival of new products depends upon advertising to create an awareness of them and an interest in purchasing them.

Commercial messages provide us with both partisan and objective information about political candidates, major issues such as conservation, and charitable causes, such as the United Fund. We watch advertisements on television, hear them on the radio, or read them in newspapers and magazines to become aware of whatever is new. We gain more information from television commercials, for example, than we do from most programs. Granted that not all of it is of real value, it does make us think about people, products, and causes that might otherwise never enter our minds.

But advertising has an importance in our society in other ways. For example, much of our entertainment is possible only because advertising underwrites the cost. Television is free because sponsors are willing to pay for time to tell their stories. Most magazines cost far less to buy than they do to produce. The extra money for operating and profit comes from advertisers. And newspapers would be ultrathin weeklies at best, totally devoid of special features, if it were not for their being underwritten by advertisers.

Advertising is far more than just a sales tool. When a company sponsors a special television program, the audience relates the company with the subject of the program. Thus a company can improve its image in the public mind, perhaps gaining an aura of culture through paying for the televising of a symphony concert or aligning itself with the youth market by paying for a rock-and-roll show.

Advertising can be informational. When the oil companies began undergoing public attack for their extremely high profits, companies such as Exxon relied upon advertisements to acquaint the public with the real costs of oil. They told us about the expense of drilling and the number of times expensive efforts have ended in failure. The advertisements presented a side of the oil business the public knew nothing about and helped to reduce public hostility.

Sometimes an advertisement will announce the construction of a new plant. The advertisement will show a community the tremendous boost to the local economy that will be provided when hundreds of workers are used to build and run the business.

Utility companies use advertising to build goodwill by showing ways to keep bills to a minimum. They provide information about insulation, power requirements of various appliances, and similar areas of interest to the consumer. This is a public service in that it helps reduce consumption and builds goodwill for the company because it shows people how to save money.

Both management and labor use advertising to acquaint the public with the issues involved during contractual disputes. If the public will be inconvenienced by a strike, it is important that each side present its case.

A paid statement is one of the most efficient means of putting the information across.

Occasionally advertising is self-serving only on a secondary basis. A company might run warnings about how to avoid auto accidents during a holiday weekend, for example. The company's product is never mentioned, though there will be a small credit line with the organization's name.

The most effective advertising is that which shows the reader or viewer how he can gain by buying a product, supporting an organization, or voting for a political candidate. When it reflects the self-interest of the sponsor rather than the consumer, it is doomed to failure.

For example, camera companies make millions of dollars by showing would-be buyers that the equipment can help capture and retain the most precious moments in their lives. The truth is that the companies are more concerned with their profit charts than with some faceless person's memories. But how many cameras would they sell if the companies' advertising said, "Buy one of our cameras and help us have our tenth straight year of record-breaking profits?"

The initial planning of a promotional campaign is no different for paid advertising than it was for free advertising. However, instead of looking for an approach that would interest a particular magazine editor you must now directly consider the publication's readers.

Take the case of Elvira Worthington, heiress, international jet-setter, and the inventor of the Worthington Electric Belly Button Brush. This marvelous, battery-operated gadget utilized a tiny stream of soapy water together with a soft, vigorously moving miniature brush to clean and polish belly buttons. Unlike novelty items sold as a practical joke, Elvira's invention was well made, designed for heavy duty operation, and sold for $39.

Right from the start Elvira knew she was going to have problems. Belly button hygiene is not a subject of mass concern in the United States. Most people take their navels for granted, seldom worrying about dust and dirt that might accumulate in the tiny indentation. This attitude meant that very few people would be likely to take her product seriously. However, optimistic Elvira also felt it meant that she was entering a virgin market in which there was no competition.

Elvira's thinking was correct. She sold a dozen of her brushes to friends and a few more as a result of an appearance on some television talk shows. Unfortunately the hosts never took her seriously and treated the invention as a joke rather than a hygienic breakthrough. A few columnists also mentioned the item, but again they failed to take it seriously. Elvira knew that she had to start a paid promotion campaign or her product would turn into just another navel disaster.

The first step in Elvira's campaign was to decide who might buy an electric belly button brush. Everyone with a navel could use one, of course, but Elvira was practical enough to realize that it would take a strong motivating force for anyone to actually buy it. Most of the people in the United States would never pay $39 for her product. A shotgun campaign aimed at the people who have belly buttons would result in too few sales at too great a cost.

So who might have a vested interest in their navels? Belly dancers for one. The art of belly dancing has become increasingly popular in the United States in recent years, with thousands of women taking lessons. The dancers were extremely belly button conscious, even going so far as to include a navel jewel as part of their costumes. Right away she had her first clearly defined buying market.

The next step was to pick the right medium for her advertising. In this case it would have to be a special interest magazine such as *Belly Dancer's World*. It was the only publication that went exclusively to people interested in this art form, and thus it could be assumed that every reader was a potential buyer.

Knowing the market and knowing the medium was not enough. Elvira had to zero in on a specific use for her invention that would make it worth the price she was charging. She needed to find a motive for buying the brush that would be stronger than the desire to avoid spending so much money.

The answer came after Elvira visited a belly dance academy. One of the instructors was down on her hands and knees, searching through the thick pile carpet. She explained that she had lost her navel jewel and it was the fourth one that week. "Do you have any idea what those things cost?" she complained to Elvira.

Suddenly the Worthington advertising campaign became crystal clear. Navel jewels were attached to belly buttons with a mild adhesive known as spirit gum. If a navel proved somewhat dirty, the adhesive would have less of a surface against which to stick and the jewel might fall out during a vigorous dance movement. Although each jewel generally cost just a few dollars, losing several meant a considerable cash loss.

The advertisement Elvira worked out showed two belly dancers in full costume. One had an anguished look on her face as she stared at her navel. The caption read, "That's the third navel jewel I've lost in the last two weeks. Replacing them is costing me a fortune. John says I'm going to have to find a way to keep them attached or I'll have to give up belly dancing forever. Oh, Martha, what am I to do?"

The rest of the advertisement disclosed Martha's approach. "I haven't lost a navel jewel in months," she related in the copy. "Not since I started using a Worthington Electric Belly Button Brush to clean my navel before inserting the jewel. Everyone knows spirit gum can't stick to a dirty, lint-filled belly button. That's why your jewels keep falling out. With my electric brush I can dance anywhere, free from the fear of losing another jewel."

The advertisement was successful. Elvira had limited her appeal to a specialized audience that needed her product. Then she based her campaign on the self-interest of the potential buyer. The dancers were trying to save money and the brush, though $39, paid for itself when the women no longer had to constantly keep replacing their jewels.

There were other appeals she could have tried. She might have shown a bikini clad woman lying on the beach, complaining to a friend, "I thought I had won John until he caught sight of my dirty belly button. He said it turned him off and now he won't have anything to do with me. Oh, Harriet, what am I going to do? I mean, everybody has a dirty belly button, don't they?"

Such an advertisement might appeal to the audience of a woman's magazine. It would have been somewhat risky but perhaps worth a try after the brush began to sell well enough so that there was extra money for a little experimentation.

This example might seem a trifle exaggerated and perhaps it is. But when you think about product promotions you have seen, you will realize that either the product meets a genuine need or the advertisement creates the need in the consumer's mind. For example, for centuries no one minded the way clothing looked after washing. Then a laundry detergent was developed that had to offer something its competitors apparently did not. Suddenly a light went on in an ad man's brain and a new plague was released upon mankind—"ring around the collar." A man would get into an elevator and nuzzle up to the sexy secretary from his office, only to be put down by her whispered, "You have ring around the collar." The same thing happened when he was presented with a lei after arriving in Hawaii. Further humiliation greeted him at parties.

Through constant advertising the public was given the notion that one's social success was dependent upon the lack of collar rings after washing. Then, believing in the problem, consumers quickly began buying a laundry detergent whose major claim to fame was that it eliminated those rings. A market was born. Without the slogan, the product would have just been one of many.

There are three ways you can get your paid message before the public. You can use television, radio, or the print media. Television is the most dramatic of the three and most people feel it is essential for the sale of almost any product. The truth is quite the opposite.

There is no denying the power of television in our society. One study I read recently showed that in any given week, 95 percent of the American people will watch television to some degree. The programs they watch and the times their sets are turned on will vary, of course. But even with such variables, this is an extremely impressive figure.

But the fact that people are watching television does not mean that it is the most effective medium for your promotion. Take the case of cigarette advertising, for years a major source of revenue for the three networks. When cigarette advertising was banned from the air waves and limited to the print media, cigarette consumption actually rose! The success was even more dramatic when you consider the fact that all this happened at a time when respiratory ailments, cancer, and heart disease were positively linked with smoking.

Before we go any further I want to caution you about advertisements for both radio and television. While unpaid self-promotion through personal appearances is extremely important and can be quite valuable, preparing a paid commercial is something entirely different. Very few people have the training and/or ability to produce an effective television or radio commercial. Anyone can write salable advertising copy for the print media, and this book will provide a step-by-step guide as to how it is done. But radio and television are quite special. Therefore this book will limit its scope to showing the mechanics of such advertising.

Should you use these media you will probably want to seek professional assistance.

A second caution is to not let yourself be conned into appearing in your own television or radio commercials unless you really know what you are doing. Television advertising salespeople are notorious for encouraging sponsors to appear in their own advertising. Usually they suggest the appearance when the potential client is wavering over the expense of commercial air time.

"It's not just the cost of running the commercial that bothers me, it's having to pay for the camera crew and the actors," the business owner might say.

"What actors? People want sincerity. They want a business person to be their friend. Why, with your voice and looks there is no reason why you shouldn't deliver your own commercials. They'll be more effective than if you hired actors, and you eliminate the extra cost. As to the camera crew, if you come down to the station, we can handle all the filming for you for next to nothing. After all, we have to pay our camera crew regardless of how busy they are. The station's glad to do commercial filming for a client and we'll do it at cost," the advertising salesperson will say.

If the business owner still is hesitant, the smart advertising salesperson will enlist the aid of employees. "You think your boss would be more effective in a commercial than paid actors, don't you?" Naturally anyone who wants to keep his or her job is going to agree.

So the business owner goes down to the station, makes the commercial, and waits for the results. Maybe business picks up a bit and maybe it stays the same. But inevitably a few people are going to tell the owner that they saw him on television. Usually, if they are personal friends, they will say what a great job he did. Similar praise comes from those who want a discount on their purchase.

What no one is going to say is the truth—that the business person came across like a jackass. Yet if you think about it, when was the last time you saw a business person do an effective job of delivering his or her own commercial? Perhaps one or two have done a good job, providing they had some training and the writers knew what they were doing. But for the most part I suspect you will agree that the majority of such advertisements are rather pathetic.

Always remember that the people who sell commercial time earn their living when you agree to advertise on their station. They will say almost anything to get you to commit yourself. Thus it is important for you to remain objective about your background and abilities rather than let yourself be manipulated by false flattery.

Television commercials generally run 30 and 60 seconds on the networks, with local stations often selling 10 and 20 second slots as well. Usually these short commercials are not very effective, and the 30 second or 60 second spots are preferable.

Network television commercials reach the largest audience for the greatest expense. They are only practical under two conditions. The first is when the product is available nationwide and the market for it is so great that you want to reach the widest possible audience. Cosmetics, for example, generally fall into this category.

The second reason for buying network time is to build a company's national image. The Xerox Corporation, for example, often is the sole sponsor for programs lasting as long as two hours. The programs are specials and the advertising is geared towards improving the company image in the minds of the public. News programs, special symphony broadcasts, and "highbrow" dramatic presentations are other programs a company will sponsor when working to improve its public image.

Single sponsorship for image building is usually different from normal commercial air time. Generally the company is not trying to sell its products but rather to show what it is doing in areas the public knows nothing about. Sometimes commercials will mention the community services performed by executives on their own time. Or the firm's research division and the major improvements in health and public welfare it has made will be discussed. Or an oil company might explain how some of the employees are constantly looking for new and cheaper forms of fuel for use in the future.

Most likely neither the network spot nor the single sponsorship approach to commercials will be desirable for your promotion. The cost is usually prohibitive for all but the largest companies. Most firms and businesses need to reach a limited local audience. Often their potential market is limited to a radius of a few miles.

The cost for advertising locally will vary with the time of day, the number of spots, and the type of advertising. Keep in mind that television is a medium of fleeting images. When you advertise in a magazine you can buy space one time, sit back, and wait for the results before buying more space. The advertisement will be seen again and again with just the one purchase. It will be effective for days, weeks, months, or even years, depending upon the type of publication used. The only way television advertising can begin to have that type of impact is for a commercial to be repeated over and over again. The frequency of a commercial has as much if not more power than the quality of that advertisement. The best commercial ever made will not be remembered if it appears only once.

Television stations, aware of the limitations of the single commercial message, encourage the purchase of multiple spots with a frequency discount. Generally the rates are based on your message appearing five times or more during the course of a given week. The cost per spot decreases according to the number of spots purchased.

If your advertisements are scheduled at several times during the day, a package rate might be given. This is a price for the total schedule, which again is less than the per spot cost.

A surprising amount of advertising is sold at a discount rate with the understanding that if the station can sell the scheduled commercial time to someone willing to pay more money, the first commercial will not run. This is known as a preemptible rate and the advertiser pays only when and if the commercial is shown.

Preemptible commercials have cost variances of their own. Occasionally the advertiser wants a certain minimum notice—such as a week—before the commercial is preempted. The station charge is based on the understanding that the commercial will be scheduled for a set air time. Then the advertising department can sell that time slot to a higher bidder, up until one week before it is scheduled to be used by the first advertiser. After that the air time cannot be sold to anyone else.

The charge for a preemptible commercial with minimum notice time will be higher than the charge for a commercial that can be preempted right up to the moment of air time. However, it is less than for a regularly scheduled commercial.

The worst way to buy air time is by choosing what is known as a run of schedule clause. This means that your commercial will not be scheduled into any particular time slot. Whenever there is an opening during the broadcast day, the commercial can be inserted. Thus the commercial might be run at 6 A.M. one day, noon the next, and just before sign-off the night after that. Unless you are selling a product that can be used by people of all ages, all sexes, and all walks of life, buying run of schedule time is false economy.

Contrary to what you may think, not all air time is purchased. Quite a few stations will barter for air time, running commercials in exchange for material goods that can be used in a variety of ways.

Television quiz shows have prizes donated by companies in exchange for a plug about the product at the time when it is shown to the excited contestant. If you have ever watched one of these shows you have probably heard the announcer say something to the effect: "You have won a Carrie Nation Home Bar complete with 20 glasses, 10 bottles of imported wine, a serving counter, four stools, and one year's free use of Sonia, the Carrie Nation Company's buxom blonde barmaid. Total value is $500 plus $100 a night for Sonia's services. Carrie Nation Bar Sets are available in leading department stores across the country."

On a local level the merchandise often becomes a prize on a radio promotion contest. Radio stations, far more than local television stations, resort to gimmicks to boost their ratings. Contests provide a way of encouraging new listeners because clues are usually given only during certain programs.

When I was promotion director for a large radio station attempting to maintain its number one position, a barter was made with the owner of a local fur salon. In exchange for three "fun fur coats" retailing for $1,000 each, the store owner received $3,000 worth of air time. The coats were used as prizes for a contest. The air time was a combination of specific advertisements coupled with short mentions of the salon each time the contest was discussed. The station did not have to buy the prizes and the store owner came out well ahead of what he would have paid for comparable air time. Remember that he was given commercials equal to the coats' *retail* value. The actual cost of the coats to the store owner was less than half that figure.

If barter interests you it is worth asking about. However, many stations frown on such arrangements and others have a "cash only" policy. In general, it is local radio rather than local television where trades can most easily be made.

If you consider television, keep in mind that it is a *visual* medium. Pictures must tell your story. The narration is secondary. If a product lacks visual excitement on its own, the person writing the commercial must find ways to include visual impact in the allotted time segment. If visual impact cannot be generated, this medium should be abandoned.

Perhaps the best examples of strong visual use are commercials for many soft drinks, especially Coca Cola and Pepsi Cola. These advertisements use visual images that generate warmth, humor, love, and happiness. They seem to say that their soft drinks both enhance and generate good times. There is a minimum of narration, the short film segments providing all the message that is necessary.

Most television experts agree that there are optimum visual changes for every length of commercial. For example, a 10-second commercial should have no more than two changes in the visual. With 20 seconds you can go to a maximum of four images. A 30-second spot allows up to 6 visual changes and 60 seconds will enable you to make as many as 10 changes.

The ideal commercials are planned specifically for their running time. A 20-second commercial will be planned, written, and filmed. Then a 30-second commercial for the same product will be made. Each commercial is unique, the only common factor being the product promoted.

The ideal is seldom achieved, however. Usually a 60-second commercial is carefully planned and filmed. Then, when shorter commercials are desired, they are pieced together from the same film used for the 60-second spot. This is an economical measure that, unfortunately, is usually necessary.

Narration of a television commercial should be minimal. The maximum number of words to be used will be the same whether you are talking about television or radio—though, as you will see, the approach must be radically different. As a general rule you can use from 90 to 130 words for a 60-second spot. A 10-second spot gives you just 25 words. With 20 seconds you have 30 to 45 words to make your point. And with 30 seconds you have 45 to 65 words.

Anyone planning a commercial must be extremely time conscious. Too little material makes a commercial needlessly drawn out. Too much material, and your actors will either talk so rapidly that they are unintelligible or the message will be too long. Generally a commercial should be timed to be *slightly less* than a minute in the planning stage; the actual delivery invariably takes longer than was envisioned by the creator.

Television commercials are usually created with the use of a device known as a storyboard. First a script is prepared. A sheet of paper is divided in half vertically. On the left side will be the description of the visual to be shown. On the right is the dialogue or narration, if any, that will accompany the visual. The visual is always more important and should be planned first. Narration can enhance but is always secondary to the visual. Next a rough layout or storyboard is made. This can be done in a variety of ways. Some people tack cards to a bulletin board. Others take a large sheet of paper and block off sections. Whatever way is used, there are certain common factors.

The storyboard is divided into as many parts as there will be visual changes. Then a sketch of each visual change will be made. This can be a rough drawing using stick figures or a careful illustration prepared by a commercial artist. Beneath each drawing will be a second box containing a description. The word "visual" will be written, followed by an explanation of that particular scene. Below that, if necessary, the word 'audio' will be written, followed by whatever narration is to accompany that particular scene change.

Television commercials are either produced on photographic film or videotape or are done live. Live commercials are the least common and are primarily seen on television talk shows where the host makes the delivery. They tend to be limited in scope and seldom offer the dramatic excitement or visual effects possible with the other two approaches.

Color film is a common medium for commercials. The equipment is readily available, and anyone who knows how to make sound motion pictures can handle the technical end. Since any number of special effects are possible, these productions can be as elaborate as a major motion picture.

An advantage to film is that 16mm, still the standard in the business, can be used anywhere and shown on any station. Increasingly, stations have the facilities to handle the newer Super 8mm film as well. Such compatibility is not possible with the third medium—videotape.

Videotape is a relatively new concept in television broadcasting. It offers excellent color, clarity, and sound quality at a cost just slightly higher than for film. The big advantages are that it can be used indefinitely without deteriorating and that you can instantly replay the commercial. When time is a factor, videotape cannot be beaten.

The only problem with videotape is that different television stations may be equipped to handle different sizes of videotape. Unlike motion picture film there are no standards in the industry. Generally either one-inch-wide or two-inch-wide videotape is common for professional use by television stations. Tape as narrow as ¼-inch is used by home videotape equipment owners. Until there is standardization, which will probably occur in the not too distant future, it would be best to use videotape only when it will be shown on the same station that recorded the commercial for you. If you are going to be showing a commercial on a number of different stations, it would be wise to use motion picture film instead.

Videotape is far more durable than motion picture film. If you are going to run the commercial over and over again, perhaps 25 times or more, you might want to have the station receiving the film rerecord it on videotape. There will be no loss in clarity and the charge will be only slightly more than the cost for the raw videotape. When you are finished with the showing, the videotape can be erased and reused, and you still have the original reel of film for your files.

While both videotape and movie film can have a sound track recorded at the same time as the visual, this is not essential. You can have the sound track or any portion of it recorded separately. Thus you can have music or special effects produced in a recording studio, then combined with the narration.

The cost of a commercial can vary greatly. The cheapest commercials are generally the ones handled by the station on which you will be advertising. It has a staff capable of handling all aspects of the production and plenty of time in which to do it.

Keep in mind that there are several "hidden" fees when an agency does your work. The agency makes a commission on everything it does. If a separate production crew is hired, the crew charge is such that the production company makes a profit and the agency hiring it makes a profit. When time is purchased from a station, additional profits are made. Eliminating this expensive middleman saves you money. Unfortunately, there are circumstances in which it is a false economy.

Television stations make commercials as a sideline. The service is a way of ensuring that low budget advertisers can afford the use of their medium. It is also a means of keeping employees busy during off hours since idle time is expensive. Thus a station may not have people with creative skills as great as those earning their living working in advertising. A product that can be promoted only with a truly creative commercial may require the use of the relatively expensive independent agency.

There are many people involved in the production of a television commercial. The most important is the producer who, in some areas, may be the writer and art director as well. The producer handles all aspects of the commercial. He or she estimates costs, obtains bids from different film production crews if the commercial is independent of the station, and oversees all aspects of it until it goes on the air.

The writer creates the commercial, either originating the concept or translating your desires into visual terms. The art director will handle the visual planning.

A camera crew handles the physical filming of the commercial, though again there can be multiple roles for the people involved. Some camera operators are art directors as well. They do both the planning and execution of the visual aspects of the script. Thus there might really be only two people responsible for production. The producer may serve as writer and director of the actors while the camera operator also serves as art director.

The actors generally must be members of one of the main unions. These are the American Federation of Television and Radio Artists (AFTRA), the Screen Actors' Guild (SAG), and the American Federation of Musicians (AFM). Usually you will have to work with members of AFTRA and/or AFM.

Actors are paid in a variety of ways. They have fees for recording the commercial, of course, but there are additional fees paid according to the number of times the commercial is shown. These are known as residuals. The only nice thing that can be said about residuals from an advertiser's point of view is that they cost less than refilming the commercial.

There can be all kinds of rules imposed by the union when preparing commercials. For example, I once wrote and produced a radio commercial involving two actors using three different voices each. I congratulated myself on my brilliance in hiring actors capable of using three entirely different voices rather than making the client go to the expense of hiring six people. Then I had a chat with the union. It seems that each time actors change their voices, they earn the same fee as if another actor was doing the work. The purpose was to keep cheaters like myself from hiring the most talented people and forcing them to play a variety of roles for their money. My brilliant plan went awry; the commercial cost the same as if it had used six people.

*Advertising* 83

Before actual production the storyboard must be carefully reviewed by everyone involved, including the producer, the camera operator(s), writer, art director, and advertiser. Each panel is discussed in terms of cost, production technique, lighting, number of actors, and anything else that relates. It may be that the idea cannot be translated into film without going to greater expense than is warranted. In such a case it must be changed.

Music can be planned at this time. Will the sound track be taken from a recording on hand, appropriate royalties being paid, or will music be composed specifically for the commercial? If it must be composed, this is the time for such planning.

Next comes the bringing together of all elements. The location for the commercial is obtained. This might be a special studio, a shopping center, or just an area inside your business. Actors and actresses are hired, props gathered, musicians hired if necessary, rehearsals held, and the commercial filmed or taped. The reason for the rehearsals is to be certain that everyone knows what to do. Lighting must be checked and the production timed.

After the final taping or filming, the material is prepared for editing. This is done in a variety of ways depending upon the material used. What it enables you to do is to splice together different segments to get the strongest possible effect. If material must be cut, this is the time to do it. Finally, when the spot is perfectly timed and both the sound and images flawless, the commercial is ready to be run.

As I said earlier, there is so much involved with television production that it really does take someone totally familiar with the field to create an appropriate script. It also takes far more money than might be warranted.

If you do decide to advertise on television, check the rates for the different stations in your area. You will need to know what it costs for various types of announcements in the hours that have viewers who could use your product or business. In the case of someone seeking political office, you will want to be certain the programming reaches adults of voting age.

Next, learn production costs for the general concept you have in mind. Learn the cost for the station handling production as well as the charge from private ad agencies. In addition, have them show you other commercials they have done in the same general price range. Remember that the cheapest work is not necessarily the best buy. If the production crew is lacking in creativity and used to putting on rather meaningless trash, spending a little extra money for a better group is the only sensible way to go.

Finally, remember that images are fleeting. Repetition is essential to a television campaign's success. Be prepared to pay for multiple showings to ensure that all the other work is not in vain.

Radio is perhaps the most fascinating medium in which to advertise, though again it takes some degree of training to produce an effective commercial. Radio is a medium of the mind. It involves mental pictures. Through the use of verbal description, the listener uses his or her imagination to "see" all sorts of wondrous happenings.

For example, one advertiser wanted to prove how effective radio could be as a promotion medium. His commercial involved using words to get the listener to "see" the Great Lakes drained of water and filled with hot chocolate, massive gobs of whipped cream poured on top of the steaming liquid and, finally, a huge helicopter lowering a cherry weighing several tons onto the center of the cream. The entire make-believe operation took just 60 seconds and cost very little to make. The same commercial on television would have involved several thousand dollars to create realistic looking models.

Radio is also a personal medium. People want to be involved with a radio personality. The announcers and disc jockeys become friends to their regular listeners. With most stations you can actually contact the air personalities directly, sometimes during their programs.

Radio also has a more distinct audience than television. Each station prides itself on having a special format that appeals to a specific audience. It is more selective than television because of the greater competition. Thus the advertiser can zero in on a more specific market.

One of the big problems with radio is the lack of exclusiveness when running commercials. Arrangement can be made with television so that two commercials for rival products do not run close together. They might be separated by a program segment of 10 minutes or longer, but they will not be run back-to-back.

This is not the case with radio. Two rival companies may find their spots run close together due to the nature of radio and the frequency of commercials. This reduces the impact of each spot, though not seriously if the other airings of the message are not always close to those of the rival. Radio, like television, relies upon frequency of advertising to get its point across. If a spot is run 15 times and it appears with a competitor only once, the damage will be slight.

You can buy radio time either with a network or locally. Again the same considerations used when determining how to advertise on television apply here. Network advertising is only practical if your product or service has the broadest possible use.

Radio advertising relies almost exclusively on word imagery. The only exception is when a campaign is designed to familiarize the public with a company or product name. Under those circumstances a commercial might simply be a short, catchy jingle, perhaps lasting no more than 30 seconds, which is repeated over and over again.

The verbal imagery must relate to the product. This is essential. For example, suppose you are planning an advertisement to introduce the public to Wong Lee's Original Chinese Pizza Mix. Not only should the public hear the product name, it must be made to *desire* that product. When the commercial has been heard, the listener should actually want to go out and buy Wong Lee's Chinese Pizza.

But don't all commercials get you interested in the product? Not really.

A few years back a company manufacturing an upset stomach remedy developed the most talked-about commercials on the air. They were short, humorous stories, the funniest one being about a couple of newlyweds and the wife's first dinner. The public delighted in watching the spots and the dialogue was quoted by everyone. The only problem was that the spots were too clever. Everyone remembered the problems the actors endured but no one remembered the product that was supposed to ease their distress. Sales of the upset stomach remedy failed to increase noticeably. The campaign had to be dropped and an entirely new approach tried.

Keep in mind that a commercial is meant to sell someone or something. Every aspect of the commercial must be geared to that particular end. The commercial must be clever or interesting enough to get the listener's attention but that cleverness must not overshadow the product. You should not care whether or not someone remembers a commercial. You want to know if they remember the *product!* If they don't, the commercial is a failure.

Sometimes a radio commercial is designed solely to keep the advertiser's name before the public. A car dealer in Tucson, Arizona, Lee

Beaudry (Chrysler, Plymouth, Honda dealerships), has daily messages that range from public service to general information to outright plugs for the products he sells. He has the quality of voice and sense of timing that enable him to deliver the message himself, though, as we have seen, such an approach is usually to be avoided. The advertisements are so unusual and effective that I am going to quote several here to give you a better understanding of his approach.

### HUMOROUS MESSAGE

British novelist Anthony Burgess has written: Laugh and the world laughs with you; snore and you sleep alone. Snoring has caused quite a number of divorces, and was so disturbing in bomb shelters in Britain during World War Two that each shelter used to have a snore-warden to wake the errant sleepers or turn them over. Many found the snoring of neighbors more disturbing that the exploding bombs. On the other hand, a prominent but snoring British editor became so annoyed on one occasion at being constantly wakened in the shelter that he braved the bombs and spent the night in a bar. Many a weird invention has been offered to solve the problem, including a collar that delivers a light shock at the sound of a snore. The inventor says he can go snoreless for about three months after each training period. But the best and cheapest remedy is to avoid sleeping on one's back. A nifty way to do this is to strap a tennis ball across the back when retiring. So far a light punch or jab in the middle of the night gets the job done for me. Hope it continues to work, huh, Ulah?

Ulah is Lee Beaudry's wife. Mentioning her further personalizes the message. These spots run either by themselves or with a popular song during a three- or four-minute segment called "Time-out with Lee Beaudry." The time-out segments begin with a short, unvarying, pretaped lead-in. A woman's soft voice discusses how it's always nice to take time out and relax. She leads in to the Beaudry message (or nonmessage, as the case may be) and then into a popular song generally in what is known as the middle-of-the-road category. This is followed by a quick closing, again with the woman's voice. The dealer's name becomes extremely familiar but not in the harsh, hard sell manner common to this business. Here's another example of his spots.

### PUBLIC SERVICE SPOT

Once again it is time for the fantastic Sunshine Kiwanis barbecue at Randolph Park. For the third year in a row, a great meal with generous helpings for only two dollars. These Kiwanians, naturally, are not of Lions

*Advertising*   87

Club Caliber, though they're the nearest thing to that quality that Tucson offers. Once again this coming Sunday morning, dean of everybody at the U. of A., Bob Svob, will conduct his prebarbecue charm class for all the sunshine wives and teenagers to make sure they smile, make everybody happy, and serve good portions. For your choice of picnic or take-out, follow the signs or use the brand-new idea, a special shuttle-bus service. Park your car at Hi Corbett Field and hop on a jitney or muledrawn wagon or whatever else double-decker those resourceful Kiwanians can conjure up. Bob Palocasay, the chairman, will be displaying the new project, an Ark Mobile Unit. Treat your family to a great Sunshine Kiwanis meal of barbecue beef and all the trimmings this Sunday at Randolph Park. You couldn't find greater economy in a Plymouth Duster.

The comment about the Lions Club was made because Beaudry is a member of that group. Note that there is only one mention of a Beaudry product—the Plymouth Duster—made at the end.

Another public service message combined with humorous commentary:

Among the new arrivals in the aviary of our Arizona Sonora Desert Museum are several motmots—long-tailed, colorful Mexican birds hardly deserving the buffoonery their name has elicited there. Members should be advised that the museum staff includes several pundits whose callous concoctions have earned them places on the endangered species lists, and the motmots became natural targets of their mischief. For example, do two motmots equal four mots? Are all motmot eggs double-yolked? The motmots will nevertheless welcome your visit. Meanwhile, the museum has carried on or originated certain projects whose value may prove out of all proportion to their modest cost, including the establishment of a nature trail, the planning of an exhibit of the jojoba bush in cooperation with the University of Arizona Arid Lands Office, the design of a solar heating system, and a display for the Beaver River Pond. The degree of the museum's success in pursuing its objectives will depend on your continued devotion and support.

Finally, a commercial that really is a commercial:

Not only did *Motor Trend* magazine name the 75 Honda Civic the Economy Car of the Year, they also named Honda's president, Kiyoshi Kawashima, Man of The Year, essentially recognizing corporate courage on the part of Honda as symbolized by its head, a man who had the foresight and determination to begin and carry through Honda's successful attempt at building a low pollution engine using the stratified charge concept. Others had tried it and said it wouldn't work, and Honda, in ignoring this advice, risked its future on a gamble the rest of the industry refused to take; and he *won*. We've been handling the Honda since March of 1971, and we've been favorably impressed from the beginning. So have our customers. But this new Honda Civic is really something else. Come on in and handle a Honda yourself at Beaudry's: sedan or hatchback, 4-speed, five speed, or automatic, CVCC Engine or A-I-R, now America's lowest sticker priced car... and, soon to be available, a four door station wagon. Gosh, this news release got a shade commercial, didn't it?

The Beaudry commercials are of definite local interest. They get the dealer's name before the public and establish him as a friend. The delivery is such that you feel he is talking to you personally. They have helped make his dealership successful despite the fact that no claims are made for the prices he charges or other information specifically relating to the selling of cars. Only on radio can such an approach be effective.

There are the more common approaches, of course. There are interviews and faked interviews, designed either to build testimonials or make a point through humor. There are straight copy approaches with an announcer explaining the product.

Sometimes commercials are built around a popular song, current fad, Broadway show, or other happening that is quickly recognized by the public. A radio advertisement for stockings used the sound of a dancing chorus line in a take-off on all the revived Broadway musicals of yesterday, such as *No-No, Nannette*.

Celebrities are used for commercials because of the recognition factor or because the sponsor feels that the public will buy something a celebrity uses or to inject humor, such as a comedian's semi-ad-lib commercial message.

Radio commercials are frequently live. These are the ones delivered by an announcer or station personality. Sometimes they follow a set script. Other times the plug is ad-libbed by the reader using a sheet of product facts for background information.

Radio, unlike television, is a standardized medium in that a prerecorded tape that can be used by one station can be used by any station. The magnetic tape is ¼-inch in diameter, the same as is used for a home recorder. Thus, duplicates can easily be made and used on as many stations as desired.

Radio commercials can be prerecorded either in the radio station or in a separate recording studio. The private recording studio generally offers the most sophisticated equipment available and is capable of creating countless special effects with limited effort. It also charges the highest per-hour fee for its time and the staff seldom is able to do more than arrange for talent, musicians if desired, and the actual physical production. It is unlikely that anyone on the staff can also write a commercial.

Most larger radio stations can put together a commercial from start to finish. The creative ability may be minimal but they can handle the task. However, the most effective commercials are usually prepared by an experienced agency skilled in this task. Remember that because radio is such a time-tested medium and because so many of its commercials are competing for the audience's attention, radio has some of the best advertising writing of all the media. You want to be certain your commercial is of the highest quality so that the product name will be heard and remembered by your audience.

In the next chapter we will go into the specifics of writing an advertisement for the print media.

# 5

# Writing Newspaper and Magazine Advertising

The advertisement took a full page in newspapers and magazines around the country. It had a bright red border and a trick photograph showing a beautiful brunette's face attached to the body of a panther. The copy read:

"TABOO! For centuries man had feared that which can bring the greatest pleasure and sensual delight. If something could drive a person to ecstasy, he thought it had to be evil. He declared such enjoyments TABOO!

"Today we know better. We realize that it is not sinful to indulge ourselves in ways never before attempted. We have attained *enlightenment*. We are not afraid to seek total happiness.

"So let us give thanks for our advanced thinking. Let us shout our praise that what was once TABOO is now just $1.95 a quart at leading stores!"

The bottom of the advertisement bore almost illegible print reading "The Merchant Company, Decatur Falls, Minnesota."

The advertisement was written by Melville Blevins, the creative director of Langly, Langly, Langly and Rublehoffen. It won the International Advertisers' Golden Tongue Award and the Cornelia Cottonmouth Art Critics Award and was featured in the book *The 100 Best Advertisements Since the World Began*. Blevins was given a $10,000 raise and named Senior Vice President of his agency. Unfortunately, he also lost the Merchant Company account to another agency. He had forgotten to mention the fact that the product he was selling was motor oil.

The problem with most advertising copy being written today is that it is being produced for the wrong people. Too often the writer is attempting to impress his colleagues with his brilliant mind, his creative genius, and his advanced vocabulary. He forgets that he is being paid to sell a client's product. He spends so much time trying to win awards that he fails to adequately promote the merchandise. His campaigns win trophies instead of customers.

When you sit down to write an advertisement you must decide what your ultimate goal is going to be. Do you want people to stop and say, "My, what a clever advertisement someone has written!" or do you want them to say, "This sounds like an interesting product. I think I'll buy some to try it"? If you write to impress people with your cleverness, you may be left with an office filled with awards and not enough money to pay the rent. If you write to sell your product, you may not receive praise from the critics but you could well find yourself getting rich.

Good magazine and newspaper advertising is meant to sell a person, a product, or a business. The approaches to copywriting are basic. Many of them will be covered in this chapter. If you follow my suggestions you will be able to write salable copy without the assistance of so-called professionals who may or may not have your best interests at heart. You may never win any awards, but you will probably improve your profit picture.

As with television and radio campaigns, your first step is to analyze your product. You must decide your primary and secondary markets before you can begin writing copy.

Next list all the good points of your product. Put a star by those attributes that are most likely to impress your primary market. Remember that selling requires you to work with the self-interest of the potential buyer. If it is clear that your product will be of personal value to the reader, more often than not he or she is going to give it a try.

When you actually start writing copy, keep in mind that your message must be positive. If you are selling a convenience food item, do not say, "This product won't spoil for six months." The facts may be true but the approach is negative. You are telling the reader that the food is going to spoil if they do not eat it. This makes the item seem unappealing even though an objective reader will have to admit that all food spoils eventually.

Instead of the negative approach, be positive! Say, "You can store this product on your shelf for six full months!" Suddenly the product is appealing. It does not have to be used right away. It can be stored for use when it is desired. After all, six months is a long time. The facts point to the same conclusion—the food will go rancid if kept too long. But the positive copy approach makes the product sound appealing while the negative approach makes the buyer cautious.

Perhaps you are trying to sell a book that tells people how to prepare their income tax. The negative copywriter might say, "Never fear an audit again. This book tells you how to be certain you are paying Internal Revenue every cent you owe."

The positive copywriter would read the book before doing anything else. In the text there are 106 different special deductions that some of the readers may be able to take. Knowing this fact, the positive approach would read: "Now a book that tells you more than 100 ways to save money on your income tax!"

Which advertisement would get you to buy the book? The negative approach is asking you to spend the price of the book to learn how to pay even more money to the government. The positive approach is asking you to buy the book to save money on your income tax. Both advertisements are factual. But only the positive approach is going to sell the book.

The most significant part of an advertisement is the headline. This is what will catch the reader's eye. If it holds promise for him, he will read the rest of the copy. If it is uninteresting or confusing, he will turn the page without learning what you are trying to promote. Some advertising experts go so far as to say that the headline is the most important feature of any advertisement.

The first rule of headline writing is to go for the reader's self-interest. The tax book is of value if it helps the reader save money. An adult education course will be desirable if it helps the person advance in business. The headline should stress the most important benefit a person can receive from the product being offered.

Sometimes the headline reports a news event. Many oil companies are using the news approach to tell the public what it costs to drill for oil. Department stores also use this approach, perhaps discussing a special promotion or the opening of a new service department.

A good headline can also arouse curiosity. "Earn $20,000 a year without a college degree," or "Never wash dishes again!" are examples of curiosity-arousing headlines. They make a statement that involves the reader's self-interest without giving an explanation. The person who has never been to college is going to want to learn how he or she can earn $20,000 a year. Everyone who fixes a meal wants to know how to avoid washing dishes. Only enough information is given for the reader to want to find out what the advertisement has to say. If the headline told that the advertisement was about buying a dishwasher, many people would not read any further. But by simply arousing the reader's curiosity, the copywriter is assured that the total advertisement will receive more careful attention.

Finally, a good headline can provide information on a different way to do something. For example, a headline might read, "Now a new approach to gardening that cuts yard work chores in half!" or, "Now you can read all those books you've been hearing about but never had the time to enjoy!" The first headline might tell of a gardening tool that does a familiar chore in a new way. And the second headline might talk about a condensed-book club. In both cases the most important rule is followed—the reader's self-interest is served first.

Do not be "cute" with your headline. If the advertising copy does not relate to the headline, the reader will feel cheated.

For example, suppose you wrote a headline stating: "What do Jackie Onassis, Howard Hughes, Rin-Tin-Tin, Leonard Bernstein, and Mickey Mouse all have in common?" You certainly have aroused the reader's curiosity. He is going to have to go to the body of the advertisement to learn more. However, what happens if you were being merely cute? What happens if your next line is: "Not one of them has heard about Sloppy-Mop, the wonderful new way to clean and shine your kitchen floor. And why haven't they heard of it? Because we are introducing it for the first time anywhere . . . ."

If you are a typical magazine reader, you probably would not get past the second or third sentence. Sloppy-Mop may be the greatest cleaner ever brought on the market but few people are going to buy it with this approach to copywriting. The reader feels cheated. Even worse, he senses that the product cannot be very good if you had to trick him to read about it. Otherwise you would have been stressing its merits in the promotion right from the start.

Perhaps the most overworked example of poor advertising is the type of tiny space ad or classified advertisement that begins "SEX!" followed by the statement, in smaller type, "Now that we have your attention . . ." The writer is desperately searching for a gimmick to get you to read his advertisement. But the gimmick selected loses more readers than it gains.

Keep in mind that the reading public is interested in advertisements. The average person wants to keep aware of new items coming on the market. Advertising is consistently read in magazines and newspapers for as long as it seems relevant to the individual's life. Certainly a nonsmoker is going to ignore even the best cigarette promotions and a person who just bought a new color television is going to ignore ads for similar items. But anyone who sees a headline that seems to relate to his or her life is going to read further.

The classic example of a misdirected promotion occurred with the selling of the Dale Carnegie book, *How To Win Friends and Influence People*. The initial advertising involved a headline that read: 'How to Ruin Your Marriage—In The Quickest Possible Way."

If you were reading such a headline, what would you think the advertisement was about? Most people would say marital problems. If they were having problems with their spouses or if they feared they might, they would read further to learn what was being offered. However, if a person's marital relations are good or if someone is single, he or she is liable to stop reading after the headline.

The body of the advertisement discussed marital problems and the fact that the way we communicate with each other can cause happiness or difficulties in our lives. It then went on to promote the book which, in reality, was not about marriage but rather about interpersonal relationships.

What happened to the advertisement? It had to be dropped. People interested in interpersonal relationships did not bother reading the advertisement. And the people with marital difficulties read far enough to feel that they were being misled concerning the product, then went on to another page. It was only when the headline was changed to the book's title, *How To Win Friends and Influence People*, that it became a best-seller. With the new headline and a text discussing how success in life is determined by our ability to relate to others, the book became an instant best-seller. The title caught the attention of the very readers who were interested in buying the book. As a result, several million copies have been sold.

The first word of your headline can add to its drawing power. The public responds well to such words as *why, how, new, how to,* and *wanted,* among others. These all indicate the basic qualities of a good advertisement. They indicate that information will be provided that will introduce something, explain something, or otherwise be of special interest.

Another strong word is *free.* People want something for nothing, even if they are only writing for a free brochure offering details on a product they can buy. If you are offering a premium with your advertisement, stressing it in the headline will gain reader interest.

Headlines are helped by the use of special type face. By using bolder, larger type to emphasize key areas, you can draw the reader's eye to your offering.

For example, suppose you have the headline "Free bar of Aphrodite Beauty Soap when you buy 25 pounds of Scrubs-All Laundry Detergent." What you are selling is the laundry detergent. But the important part of the headline is the premium offering. Thus the headline can be strengthened with emphasis in the setting of the type. You might have "FREE BAR OF APHRODITE BEAUTY SOAP when you buy 25 pounds of Scrubs-All Laundry Detergent." Or you might make the bold words even fewer by saying "FREE bar of Aphrodite BEAUTY SOAP when you buy 25 pounds of Scrubs-All Laundry Detergent." In both cases the key words are emphasized—the fact that beauty soap is being given away.

The beauty soap offer is meant for a woman, but an approach could be developed to make the same premium available to men. This time the headline might read, "Free, for your wife, a bar of Aphrodite Beauty Soap when you buy a 25 pound box of Scrubs-All Laundry Detergent." The emphasis would not be on the beauty soap aspect of the promotion because most men would not be interested. However, they would like to do something for their wives that would make them seem more attentive and caring. Thus the emphasis might read: "FREE, FOR YOUR WIFE, a bar of Aphrodite Beauty Soap when you buy a 25 pound box of Scrubs-All Laundry Detergent."

Whether or not the masculine approach to advertising the laundry detergent would be successful is hard to tell. However, even if the typical male reader did not make such a purchase, the "FREE, FOR YOUR WIFE" emphasis might get him to point out the ad to his spouse so that she could take advantage of it.

Whenever you advertise a product, most retailers feel that you will have greater pulling power if you include an illustration of that product. This might be a photograph or an artist's rendering, though in most cases the photograph is preferable. People are sometimes skeptical of an artist's sketch, which might be idealized rather than completely accurate.

With newspaper advertising a drawing may be technically necessary, however. Few newspapers have the facilities to reproduce a photograph very effectively. If subtle tonal gradations are required to show your product, these may not reproduce from a photograph. Newspapers often do a better job working from an artist's rendering.

The type of photography you select will help determine whether or not your advertisement is read. The appeal must be strong and must relate to the product. Too many advertisements, as in the opening example, fail because the illustration is meant only to attract attention. It fails to relate to the product.

Sex appeal in photographs is as overused as is the word "sex" in headlines. A photograph of an attractive, bikini-clad girl holding a product does no better a selling job than a quality photograph of the product alone. In fact, such an appeal often does less well. In some cases women viewing such an advertisement feel that it is sexist and will boycott the product for that reason alone. At other times it is so inappropriate that it seems to indicate the product is not strong enough to stand on its own merits.

Photographs should not include too much detail. Remember that it is probably going to be reduced in size—usually to a small portion of the advertising space. If the photograph has too much in it, the small reproduction will reduce its potential impact.

There are exceptions, of course. A photograph of a crowded room tends to draw reader interest. The person viewing the scene tends to feel that he or she is part of the group. Likewise a photograph of an empty room has an appeal. But viewer interest declines when just two or three people are shown in the same room, probably because the reader feels like an outsider in an intimate scene.

Action photographs are also strong. Think how effective the cigarette advertisements showing cowhands and ranchers at work have been over the years. They are still getting results today, despite the acknowledged dangers of smoking. The action photograph gets attention and sells the advertiser's cigarettes to those readers who smoke.

Keep in mind that an advertising photograph is going to be viewed in the context of the magazine in which it appears. Our eyes have been scanning the text from left to right and we tend to study the photograph the same way. Thus a figure located on the left side of the page should be facing toward the right—into the body of the advertisement. A figure on the right-hand side of the page, facing right, seems to be leaving it. An otherwise excellent advertisement can be ruined by the improper positioning of people or by moving objects in the photograph.

When a person is shown in a photograph, a tight close-up is more effective than a full-length shot. The close-up gives the feeling of greater size and has more drawing power. The full figure pose tends to recede on the page.

Color is another factor in the success or failure of an advertising photograph. Warm colors such as red seem to leap forward while cool colors such as blue tend to recede into the background. Thus, a color photograph of a pretty girl sitting with some towels can be made more emphatic with color. If the girl is wearing red and the towels are cool in appearance, the eye will be drawn to the girl. If the girl is wearing blue and the towels are a warm color, she will appear to be in the background and the eye will be drawn to the towels. The careful use of such colors will enable you to give a three-dimensional effect to a two-dimensional color photograph, as well as highlighting the product.

If a person, horse, car, or other object is moving rapidly, there should be more space between the person and the edge of the picture toward which the subject is heading than behind the subject. A moving object whose head is flush against the edge of the advertisement looks awkward. The advertisement loses its impact.

It is also wise to have both horizontal and vertical photos of the same subject available for use. You can try both angles to see which will make the most effective advertising layout.

In deciding what to put in the body of your advertisement, remember that you are going to be limited by space. You will have to be selective.

The first essential is that the body of the advertisement relate to the headline. You must never mislead the reader or he will not trust your product.

Next you must provide your strongest points for the person who will be attracted to the headline. In the case of the soap, the advertisement meant for women will discuss the fine qualities of both the detergent and the free soap. The same product, when sold to men, will stress how appreciative their wives will be when they not only buy one of the best detergents on the market but also bring home a free gift of one of the finest beauty soaps available.

It is a help to refer back to the list of sales points you compiled before writing your headline. The most important point was emphasized in the headline so that can be crossed off. Mark the second strongest selling point *for the audience you are trying to reach* with a number 1. Then mark strong point number 2 and so on until you have marked every item on your list.

Always keep in mind that a strong point for one market is not necessarily a strong point for a different market. The free beauty soap is the motivating factor in the detergent advertisement aimed at women. The quality of the detergent is a close second.

The pleasure a woman will show when she gets the free gift from her husband is the selling point for men. The quality of both the free gift and the detergent are secondary.

Never give your reader a reason to skip over the advertisement. For example, suppose you are trying to promote a headache remedy. Your headline might be: "Feeling tired? Depressed? Plagued by aches and pains?" It is direct and to the point, and you have probably seen a similar approach dozens of times. More important is the fact that it also touches on the self-interest of many people.

But what happens when a well individual reads the advertisement? As soon as he glances at the headline he says to himself, "I feel great. This ad's not for me!" Then he turns the page, never having learned about the medication you are offering for sale. You have used a headline that gave at least a portion of your potential buying market a reason to not read your promotion.

How much better the sales could be with a headline reading: "New! For those times when you find yourself tired, depressed and plagued with aches and pains." The advertisement says the same thing as the first example, but this time it is speaking to everyone, no matter how they feel. More people are going to take the time to read all the copy.

Always be specific with your advertising. Too many copywriters spend their time trying to create a mood with their advertisements, ignoring the need for solid information.

Take a typical advertisement for a new car dealer. "Mammoth Motors is proud to present the greatest car America has ever seen—the Dinosaur 8!"

The ad continues: "The Dinosaur 8 is the car other manufacturers have only dreamed about. It has a cushion soft ride that transports you through time and space in luxury previously known only to royalty. You will fly past gas stations as your fuel conscious engine sips from your tank instead of guzzling greedily. This is the car you have been waiting for—exclusively at Mammoth Motors."

Rather than rushing to the auto dealer, the average person is going to have all sorts of questions raised in his or her mind. What exactly is a "cushion soft ride"? What sort of luxury features does the car have? How much gas does the car use? Some people may go to the dealer's showroom for the answers but many more are not going to bother. They will assume that a new car cannot be worth much if the dealer has to resort to meaningless generalities to sell it. Yet copywriters frequently make the mistake of thinking that such a sales pitch will motivate buyers.

How much better the ad would have been if it had been written with specific facts that would influence the buyer. "Now Mammoth Motors is proud to present the 40-miles-per-gallon luxury car—the Dinosaur 8!"

This better headline has several points in its favor. It uses the word *now*, which gets reader attention. It tells the reader that the new car is built for luxury and gas economy (the reader's self-interest), and it tells where it can be seen.

The advertisement might continue. "The Dinosaur 8 is a car other manufacturers wish they had created. It has a dual diagonal disc braking system for safe, sure stops even under emergency conditions. It's seats are thickly padded, richly upholstered, and designed by orthopedic surgeons for maximum comfort. The floor is carpeted with a luxuriously thick pile and the dashboard is covered with Moroccan leather. The leg and head room are as great as that found in a Rolls-Royce and the gas saving engine gets up to 40 miles per gallon on the highway and 28 in the city. It is the car for you—exclusively at Mammoth Motors."

Note the use of specific facts. You are not just told that the car is a luxury model. You are told exactly what luxury features it contains. Instead of stressing fuel economy in general, you are given actual mileage figures. The reader has enough information to know whether or not the car is right for his particular needs.

Some advertisements limit themselves to nothing but facts. For example, a printing calculator was offered on the pages of the *National Observer*. The headline read "A QUALITY PRINTER" with a subhead in smaller type reading: "15 Digits, Independent Memory, 3 Rounding Modes, Square Root." Below that was a photograph of the printer/calculator. Right from the start anyone reading this ad would know whether or not such a calculator would have value. If the person did not understand the technical information already given, the unit was obviously more elaborate than he or she could use. But if the features seemed interesting, the following copy would have been a clincher. It consisted of nothing but a list of features separated by dots known as *bullets* in the advertising field.

"Features for the Professional!" read the first line, followed by:

*15 Digit Capacity and Printout* • *Independent Memory System—Add, Subtract, Direct to Memory Bank* • *Prints Out a Separate Set of Accumulated Numbers from the Memory* • *Prints Out Accumulated Result from Memory, and Clears It at the Same Time* • *Retains a Constant Factor Automatically* • *Percentage Key* • *Square Root* • *Non-Add/Subtotal Key* • *3 Decimal Modes: Floating, Preset, or Automatic Cents* • *Entry for Straight Adding 3 Rounding Modes—Round Up, Round Off, Round Down* • *Signal Panel—Three Indicator Lamps Show When Unit is On, When Memory is in Use, or if an Error Has Occurred* • *Size 11"x4¼"x11". Wt: 7 lbs. 11 oz.*

The copy continues, giving some general information and including the clinchers for the advertisement. The unit is $100 less than retail and is available on a 14-day free trial basis.

Notice that no words are wasted. The advertiser has concentrated on filling the available advertising space with copy that is meaningful to the potential buyer. The headline grabs the reader's attention and gives enough information so the general nature of the product can be understood. The rest of the copy provides the details. There are no meaningless generalities.

Advertisements should be written in the present tense and should talk directly to the potential buyer. Never say, "People will enjoy the delicious cakes they can make with Typhoid Mary's Old-Fashioned Cake Mixes." Instead make it personal: "Your family will praise the tantalizing deserts you make with Typhoid Mary's Old-Fashioned Cake Mixes."

How much room will you have for the body of the advertisement? This will depend upon the size of type the printer uses. The type size is measured in "points." The greater the number of points, the larger the type and the fewer words per square inch. Have your printer show you the type sizes he can handle and then make your selection according to legibility, potential visual impact, and the space for the copy. It is always best to write copy for the space you have purchased instead of writing material, then seeking enough cash to pay for adequate space in which to run the ad.

As a general rule it is possible to know in advance the maximum number of words that can be fit into a one-square-inch space with different sizes of type. For example, 14 point type permits only 11 words in a square inch of space. As a general guide, you should observe the following:

 5 Point Type—69 words
 6 Point Type—47 words
 7 Point Type—38 words
 8 Point Type—32 words
 9 Point Type—28 words
10 Point Type—21 words
11 Point Type—17 words
12 Point Type—14 words
14 Point Type—11 words

Note that the number of words does not double when the point size is cut in half, as you might expect. It actually more than triples.

Knowing these figures, you can then guess the necessary space needed for different numbers of words set in different type sizes. For example, if you plan to use 8 point type and you have copy that should not run less than 640 words (a fairly large number, actually), you will need 20 square inches of space or an advertisement that is roughly 4" x 5". Additional space will have to be purchased for your illustration.

One of the more popular approaches to advertising in recent days has been the comparison advertisement, in which a competitor's product is mentioned by name. When Ford introduced its Granada line of cars, the vehicle's design was obviously imitative of the styling of both Mercedes Benz and Cadillac. The advertisements frequently compared the styling of the three vehicles, stressing the relatively low price of the Granada. One ad, for example, had a Cadillac parked next to the Granada with the Cadillac owner thinking the Ford was his car.

Comparison advertising can be effective providing that it is valid and that you are competing with an established product. When drug manufacturers realized that a large segment of the population could not take aspirin, research was done to find a substitute that would be equally effective. The result was acetaminophen, which was marketed under the brand name Tylenol. It was sold at a much higher price than aspirin, but despite this fact, sales climbed steadily over the years.

Bristol-Myers decided to compete with Tylenol, coming up with the product Datril. National advertising compared the two products, pointing up the fact that they are chemically identical. The only difference was the price.

Encouraged by the advertising comparisons, other firms began bottling acetaminophen under their own labels. Chain pharmacies such as Revco and Fed Mart, among several others, also came out with the product. They did not advertise on national television and in magazines as the major drug companies were doing, but their products benefited from the public awareness generated by the comparison promotions of Bristol-Myers.

Advertising comparisons are effective when your product benefits from the differences. Once again, facts must be stressed for the public to accept the information.

Politicians have been using this approach successfully for many years. The debates between candidates enables them to present their side of various issues.

The use of unwarranted superlatives can be deadly for your campaign. For example, calling a shoe clearance sale "The Clearance Sale of the Century" or saying "Our Prices Are the Lowest in Town" will often turn buyers away from your business.

The same is true for comparative statements that do not really compare anything. "Our laundry detergent gets your clothes whiter than white" or, "There is no finer pastry available" leave the reader cold.

Who says a sale is the "clearance sale of the century"? A store may discount some items but it is *not* going to have the "lowest prices in town" on all its stock. That's impossible. Competitors are going to offer loss leaders, for example, for prices that might be at cost or below in order to get people into the store. Anyone who would try to undersell everyone on all items would go bankrupt.

How can something be "whiter than white"? White is a specific color. Something is either white or it isn't. People know this and become quite skeptical of such claims.

The pastry claim is a matter of individual taste. A store might have a larger selection than its competitors. It might be the only store with a certain style of pastry. But whether or not it is the finest is a matter of individual opinion.

Regardless of how much space you can afford, keep your copy tightly written. If a word or sentence does not enhance the advertisement, throw it out. Restaurants know this. Many of them regularly boost their volume of business by advertising only the daily special or by running a portion of their menu, complete with prices. The reader has everything he really wants to know with such information. Additional statements concerning the quality of the food seldom have any value. After all, what restaurant is going to say that its fried chicken is soggy with grease or that the "Chef's Surprise" is heartburn?

The only time personal commentary can be helpful is when you use an endorsement approach in your copy. If you can come up with some genuine endorsements for your product from people who own it, eat it, support it or whatever, this is an added plus for you.

For example, a restaurant owner's statement about the quality of his food is meaningless to the reader. But if the advertisement mentions that a respected guide to good eating gives the restaurant a "4-star" rating, this is important to the public. Mentioning this endorsement will encourage people to eat there.

Extreme caution must be taken to be certain that these endorsements are genuine. For years athletes and actors have discussed the merits of coffee, razor blades, and countless other products. No one really knew if they used the items they recommended, but companies knew that the endorsements generated sales so they continued to seek such "names" for their ads.

Today this has changed. Celebrity endorsements still move merchandise but it is essential that the celebrities truly own or use the products they promote. A man may not promote a brand of beer, for example, if the strongest drink he ever takes is a glass of fruit punch "spiked" with ginger ale.

Theatrical promotional experts have refined endorsements to a fine art. They have learned to isolate the one favorable remark in an otherwise ghastly review to help their advertising. For example, suppose a reviewer said, "The curtain rose on *Night of The Watermelon,* though for the life of me I cannot figure out why. The actors were so unprepared that three of them obviously had bits of the script hidden in their shirt cuffs for quick reference. I have seen better performances in my daughter's third grade elementary school class plays. The author apparently could not decide whether he wanted to write a bad comedy or a bad drama, so he compromised by creating a bad play that fails miserably in both styles. The show's high spot was the acting of the lead, Jennifer Mansfield Monroe Welch, who flubbed 23 lines, talked like a hyena, and had body odor evident to this critic sitting in the third row of the theater. You will understand how bad this play is when I tell you that the performances of all the other actors were worse!"

That devastating review suddenly becomes high praise when the play's promoter quotes it in the newspaper advertisement. He will use: "The show's high spot was the acting of the lead, Jennifer Mansfield Monroe Welch . . ." said Sammy Silvertongue of the *Evening Standard.* The fact that Silvertongue really hated both the lead and the rest of the cast will be overlooked.

In normal practice such an approach is going to cause more trouble than benefits. Most likely the critic would sue the promoter for the out-of-context quote, which implies an endorsement of a play he publicly denounced. However, it does show that endorsements in ads can have an effect on the reader.

Whenever you have completed an advertisement it is important that it be carefully reviewed and tested. Start with just the copy. Put it aside for an hour, a day, or a week, depending upon how pressed for time you happen to be. Then try to go over it objectively.

Reviewing your own work is probably the most difficult aspect of writing an advertisement. By the time you have finished working on it you have a tendency to either love it or hate it. If you love it, you can see no wrong. You overlook problem areas that could seriously reduce the effectiveness of the copy. If you hate it you can see nothing of value. You want to toss out everything and start fresh, when in reality, few if any changes may be necessary.

It is essential that you try to be as objective as possible. Approach your work with the attitude, "How can I make this better?" Throw out unnecessary words and phrases. If a bit of additional description will enhance the copy, do not be afraid to add the extra words. Your goal is to make the advertisement promote yourself, your product, or your business. You must be certain you have written it in a way that will keep the reader's interest through to the end of the advertisement.

When you are satisfied with what you have written, get other opinions from people you feel will be objective. This means avoiding asking those employees whose jobs you control. It might mean asking your spouse, someone else's secretary, or even strangers. Many advertising copywriters take an advertisement to a shopping center and ask passersby for their comments. This is as good a check as any and probably one of the more objective checks you can make.

When you ask others to evaluate your ad, try to obtain specific comments if possible. A little later in this chapter we will explore ways of testing your advertisement for more accurate criticism. However, when you are new to writing promotional material, it is worth the trouble to obtain other opinions of your initial efforts.

Next, refer to your original list of selling points. Go over who your potential customer is and what points will have the strongest influence on this person. Then return to the advertisement you wrote and see whether it reflects your goals.

Does the headline grab the person's attention, involve self-interest, and encourage your potential customer to read further? It doesn't matter how many other people enjoy your advertising. The important question is whether or not it will appeal to the potential buyer of the product or user of the service.

A political promotion is an excellent area to show some of the problems that can arise. If a politician is from a poverty stricken farming community that is desperate for any congressional action that will increase the profits from the food raised there, his constituents are not going to be interested in his views on the recognition of China. They want to know how the politician stands on the issues that are of greatest importance to them. They may have strong feelings about communism, the role of China in international affairs, and other topics of the day. But their immediate concern is limited to the farm products situation. The politician's campaign literature will be successful if it addresses itself to that area of interest. But if the literature stresses other topics that are of concern to a totally different constituency, he or she is likely to be ignored by the local people whose support is needed.

Even when you are certain that you have reached the audience you are after, study the writing for weak points. Look again for meaningless superlatives and copy that is devoid of facts. You must learn to be a harsh critic.

When you have completed the advertising copy, it is time to worry about the visual layout. Ideally, either you or someone on your staff will have the basic art training necessary to accomplish this chore. If not, newspaper and magazine advertising departments have staff artists to assist you with the layout. Many times they can do the sketches you need for illustration. However, it is usually best to supply the newspaper or magazine artists with all elements of the ad—copy and artwork—and let them arrange it in an effective manner.

There are three sources for artwork. The most expensive is through a commercial art studio. Commercial artists have both knowledge and experience in planning advertising for magazine or newspaper reproduction. Even the least talented among them can probably do an adequate job for you.

Talk to several commercial artists if possible, getting cost estimates and viewing samples of similar assignments they have handled for other clients. When you find one whose prices and quality best fit your needs, go ahead with the work. However, be sure you have a written work order or some other paper that specifies not only the work to be done but also the completion date. Timing is always critical and you want to be certain the work will be ready when you need it, not at a time that might be more convenient for the artist.

A second source for skilled art talent is a local art school, if there is one where you live. Senior students often have as much training and talent as full-time commercial artists, though not the experience. A check of a student's portfolio will show you whether or not he or she has the skills to do what you want.

A third approach to obtaining art is through the use of what are known as "clip books." A clip book is a book containing varied drawings that you can cut out and attach to your advertisement without paying special fees. Sometimes these are produced by art studios. Sometimes they are sold on a limited-use basis. Other times anyone can use them without restriction. Many art supply stores stock clip books, and the cost is always far less than for custom work.

The only disadvantage to clip art is that it is highly unlikely that you will find drawings relating directly to your product. Usually clip art is used to enhance an advertisement that would otherwise be visually dull. It is not meant to take the place of a carefully drawn product rendering.

Your copy supplies an important visual element of the advertisement. The size of type and the style you select will help to catch the reader's eye. Bold type is used for emphasis. Stylized type, such as script, also catches the eye. However, be careful that the stylized type you select is not difficult to read.

If your sentences and paragraphs are short, the reader's eye tends to move quickly down the ad. Some advertisers prefer to vary paragraph length so that an occasional long paragraph breaks up the pattern of several short paragraphs.

Experiment with different types of illustrations. Use one that is square, another that is long and narrow, another that is oval, and so forth. Manipulate them on a piece of paper cut to the size of the advertising space to see which results in the most interesting effect.

As I mentioned earlier, the actual layout work should be done by someone with skill in this field. Visual impact is a strong selling factor. Many books will teach the novice to produce an adequate layout. But an adequate layout seldom—if ever—achieves the sales effects of a professionally done advertisement. This book can teach you how to write effective copy, but you should leave layout to the experts.

When you have finally assembled all elements of an advertisement, it is time to do some testing. Testing requires the use of two or more slightly varied advertisements. The tests can be run prior to an advertising campaign (also see the following chapter on direct mail promotions) or in the publications where you plan to buy space. Many completed advertisements are tested in shopping centers to get a preliminary response prior to buying space. This is fine if you are going to be dealing with a local publication. But if the advertising campaign is going to be national in scope, shopping center testing is usually too limited to be of much value. It will not reach a broad enough cross section of your potential market to produce meaningful results.

The ideal way to test magazine advertisement is with what is known as split run printing. In essence, split runs are handled by publishers equipped with printing equipment that can produce two copies of the same page at the same time. The pages are identically laid out. The editorial material takes up the same room in the same spots on both pages and the same advertising space is also retained. However, advertisers have the option of running two different advertisements in the space they buy—one ad on one page and one on the other. When the magazines are bound for shipping, they are split half and half so that every newsstand will have as many copies of the issue containing one ad as it has copies containing the other.

But exactly how do you test an advertisement? What elements are changed?

An advertising test is valid only when you keep your variables to a minimum. Ideally only one element of the ad will be altered for the split run test. For example, suppose you are trying to sell a 50-piece set of dinnerware. One advertisement will describe the various dishes, give a price and ordering instructions. The second advertisement will be identical except that there will be a coupon attached, which can be turned in at the time of purchase for a free set of carving knives. This particular test is meant to determine whether or not the premium increases sales enough to warrant its continued use. If the additional sales are not great enough to offset the cost of the premium, the carving knife offer will be dropped.

Other tests may involve the use of different headlines, different prices, or other such variables. It is important that there be some way for the customer to call the particular advertisement to your attention so you know which offer was seen. This can be done with coupons, or, if you are working locally, by giving two different telephone numbers to call for ordering. The people answering each phone tally the number of calls received, and you compare the two to see which advertisement gets the greater response.

There is also an approach known as keying the advertisement. This is an established technique of mail-order sellers and will be discussed in the next chapter.

You can run several tests with the same advertisement provided you vary only one aspect per test. Thus you can try premium offers versus straight sales. Then, if the premium is more effective, you can vary the premium to see what sort of offer brings the best response. You can vary the headline, then vary an element in the body of the advertisement to see if that has an effect.

One type of test that is occasionally tried is never valid. This is a test that utilizes two different magazines in the same field rather than a split run in one of the publications. If a seller of photographic film wanted to run a test, he might place one version of the same advertisement in *Popular Photography* magazine and the other in *Modern Photography*. But these publications do not necessarily reach the same type of audience. The difference in their circulations is a variable in itself, thus invalidating the test. The only valid comparison that could be made would be to take exactly the same advertisement and run it in the two different magazines to see which one draws a better response. You must vary only one element of the advertisement when it is printed on a split run.

As you gain some experience in preparing newspaper and magazine advertisements you might try to keep a file of clippings for stimulating ideas. Every time you see an advertisement that particularly arrests your attention and truly sells the product, clip it. Then, when you are seeking inspiration, study each advertisement to see what approach the writer used when preparing it. This can lead to finding ways to improve the response to your own promotions.

# 6

# Direct Mail and Mail-Order Advertisements

Of all the possible methods for promotion, none has quite the love/hate relationship with both advertisers and the public as direct mail. Many people refer to direct mail advertising as "junk mail" and claim they throw it away unopened. In reality, direct mail is not only one of the best methods for reaching a carefully selected segment of the public, it is also extremely popular with the people receiving it.

Take the case of Harcourt Bigwig, executive vice-president of Frammis and Moyniham Manufacturing Company. Bigwig started in the mail room; through perseverance, hard work, and the seduction of Cindy Lou Frammis, the boss's daughter, he rose steadily to the top. He still works a 48-hour week and values what little time he has for relaxation. He constantly tells people that he is so busy he just throws direct mail advertising away unopened.

What Bigwig does not say is that he is an avid record collector who looks forward to the monthly catalog of record offerings sent to him by the Music Appreciation Society of which he is a member. He also delights in the information that comes in the form of a bulletin from the book club to which he belongs. And there are the catalogs sent by the electronics stores where he shops on a regular basis. He often drops everything to study them from cover to cover.

Bigwig's wife, an avid gardener, also has no time for direct mail advertising. She is too busy reading the numerous seed catalogs she receives every year from which she purchases the many exotic flowers that adorn the family estate. She also is an avid reader of the church bulletin that provides information about special projects she supports financially. Then there are the monthly mailings of the postage stamp company that sends her approvals for adding to her large collection. And the monthly bulletin from the Mystery Book Club to which she belongs.

The point of all this is that direct mail advertising is important to almost everyone. The problem is that most people do not recognize it when they receive it. They have the idea that only advertisements that fail to interest them fit the "junk mail" category. They do not realize that they regularly take advantage of direct mail offers.

Many direct mail advertisers use terminology that helps to further public misconceptions. For example, book clubs never send "advertisements" for new books the members can buy at a discount. They send *bulletins* or *newsletters* or *magazines*. Since the club's selections are valued by the members and purchases are frequent, the average person does not equate the book lists with direct selling.

For you, the person with something to promote, direct mail is the best method for reaching a selected segment of the population. For example, suppose you are trying to promote a new book on photography. If you use magazine advertising you will most likely select the various amateur and professional photography magazines. You know that the readers are all interested in photography and that many will be potential book buyers. Of course, a great many of the people who see your advertisement will lack either the money or the interest for your book. Some will feel that the magazine tells them everything they want to know so the purchase of a book would be a waste of money.

When you go with a direct mail campaign, you will send literature on your photography book to a specialized mailing list tailored to include only those people who are your prime customers. You might use a list of names of members of photography book clubs since such people are known to be in the habit of buying books.

Of course there is always a chance that photography book club members will include some poor risks since some may feel that they spend all they can afford on club selections. They have no interest in buying photography books from some other source. Thus you may refine your market even more by mailing promotional material only to those people who regularly purchase books from publishers and distributors selling independently of book clubs.

Direct mail selling allows you to target your appeal in the most selective manner possible. Take the case of a political candidate. If a politician places an advertisement in a newspaper, he or she will have to limit the text to rather innocuous generalities. Votes are needed from all segments of the community and what is important to one group is not important to another. If the candidate comes out strongly for one issue and not another, votes will be lost. Thus, it is best to say little that is concrete when the message will be read by a great number of people with divergent backgrounds. Unfortunately such vagueness is also resented by many voters.

With direct mail campaign literature, a candidate can address a specific audience with ideas related to their area of interest. For example, a congressional candidate might send literature taking a strong stand on integrated education and the busing issue to inner-city parents. A statement about the drug problem might go to suburban families. Both groups will want to hear about the economy but blue-collar workers may be more concerned about obtaining jobs than people on the executive level.

Another advantage of direct mail promotion is that it is noncompetitive. When you advertise in a newspaper or magazine, that message is one of hundreds that the reader will see. Unless there is something that is eye-catching, such as your illustration or a strong headline, the average reader may pass over it. If the reader is in a hurry when reading the publication, he or she may skip over whole sections that do not contain material of immediate interest. When your advertisement is located in such a section, it will not be seen at all.

An advertisement sent in a letter receives no competition. When the envelope is opened the reader devotes his full attention to the contents. While the presentation still must hold the reader's interest, there are no distractions from other promotions. The reader can sit down and study the material as closely as he wishes. The full impact of the message is felt by the reader. There is no confusion such as results when competitors are making claims and counterclaims. The advertisement is in its most effective form.

There are other advantages, too. Direct mail advertising can be cheaper than buying space advertising in terms of the cost per order. It can allow a manufacturer to bypass the wholesaler and retailer, thus either increasing profits per sale or increasing sales by being able to charge less than retailers offering the same item.

Direct mail advertising can be personalized. You can use various techniques, to be discussed in this chapter, that can make the recipient of your promotion material feel specially selected.

Direct mail advertising gives you room to tell your story to the best advantage. When you buy magazine space you are going to be limited as to how much you can say. A good direct mail promotion piece can run several pages in length and still be effective. You have the opportunity to present your product or program in full.

You can experiment with the unusual for direct mail promotions. You might send a potential customer a phonograph record he can play to hear your story, for example. Or you might try special cardboard pop-up figures as a gimmick in your mailing piece. Whatever you think will be effective can probably be handled by direct mail.

Direct mail marketing also keeps time problems to a minimum. Magazine advertising requires you to plan all your sales around the publication's lead time. Often this means that you must have your advertisement in their offices no later than three months before it will actually appear. There can be no last minute changes to alter prices that have suddenly risen.

You are also at a disadvantage if you have a timely item you are trying to offer in a magazine. If the item has only a short-term potential, waiting three months for the advertisement to appear could destroy your chances for making heavy sales.

When your message is carried through the mails, it can be changed almost to the moment when the material is to be taken to the post office. News of a timely product can be in the public's hands a week after you decide to offer it if you really want to move quickly. You constantly adjust your campaign to changing circumstances instead of being a victim of circumstances, as can happen with conventional advertising.

You have total control over testing your advertisements when you use the mail. Instead of worrying about whether or not a publication is equipped for split run printing, you can test small segments of your mailing lists.

Your success with display and classified advertising is determined, in part, by the specific newspapers and magazines in which you decide to buy space. In the case of direct mail advertising, the mailing list is the major factor. Having access to the right list will do almost as much to make or break your campaign as the way in which your advertisement is presented.

Where do you find lists? There are numerous sources. Perhaps the best single guide available is the regularly updated catalog called "Direct Mail List Rates and Data" available from Direct Mail List Rates & Data, 5201 Old Orchard Road, Skokie, Illinois, 60076. Some libraries subscribe to this publication. If yours does not, contact the publisher directly for information about current subscription costs. The catalog includes more than 25,000 mailing lists indexed according to type.

Lists are either rented or sold. As a general rule, a list that you buy outright is likely to be less current than a list you rent. Companies usually make more money offering their list on either a one-time or limited territory basis.

Suppose, for example, that you have just developed a left-handed widget. If a list is available on a per use basis, you must pay a fee each time you send a promotion to the names on it. Even though you may be planning to send two or three different promotional mailings for the same product to the same people, each follow-up mailing requires the payment of a rental fee. The only time you get around this is when you make a sale, receive a contribution, or otherwise get the desired response. At that time you can legally and ethically make your own mailing list comprised of the names of the people responding. This then becomes a personal customer list, which is quite different from the larger list you rented when first trying to reach people. For future campaigns offering similar products you can either use your personally created list or combine it with one that you rent.

When a list is rented according to territory, you are given permission to reach people within a certain area. For example, suppose an Ohio list broker had names and addresses of certain types of people arranged according to city. He might charge a fee to rent all the names in metropolitan Cleveland. Another fee would have to be paid for the names of people in Cincinnati. More money might get you Dayton residents or those from Columbus. This can be very helpful when a product is localized. It is also of value for political use and fund-raising efforts.

A list that is sold might be offered on an exclusive or nonexclusive basis. An exclusive list would be the most expensive. It is offered one time and whoever buys it obtains all rights. There is a complete transfer of ownership.

A list that is sold on a nonexclusive basis is retained by the person originally offering it. Once you pay the purchase price, you have the right to contact the names on the list for as many times as you choose. However, other businesses will be buying the same list and using it for promoting items that may or may not be considered competition for you.

The quality of any list depends upon what it is and how it is maintained. Take a list of names of subscribers to a special interest magazine, for example. The best list contains the names and addresses of current subscribers. The addresses are likely to all be current—an extremely important detail when you consider that statistically one out of every four Americans will move in any given year. (One out of every three business executives will change jobs and/or homes annually.) Also the names include people who retain an interest in the sport, hobby, or whatever is the subject of the magazine. They are likely to be spending money on a regular basis.

Magazines will also have lesser value lists of past subscribers. Perhaps the subscriber died and the family just let the subscription expire rather than notifying the publication to cancel it. Perhaps the subscriber lost interest in the publication or no longer has the income to make purchases in the field. Whatever the reason for letting it lapse, past subscribers are often poor targets for a direct mail campaign. Even worse is the fact that little or no effort will be made to keep the addresses current on such lists.

Of mixed value are lists of magazine subscribers that include everyone who has ever had a subscription. If a magazine does not weed past subscribers from the lists it sells, there is a good chance that a large proportion of the names for which you are paying will no longer be prospects for your promotion. This is a waste of money.

The best lists include people you know are interested specifically in the product line you are offering. For example, suppose you set up a booth at a trade show or convention. You have your product line on display and a register for passersby to sign when they stop at your booth. In theory only those people who are interested in what you are showing will bother to put down their names. This register then becomes at least one of the lists you use when making direct mail sales appeals since it has a large number of interested parties.

The same is true with a list compiled from telephone inquiries. Salesmen in stores often make lists based on people who have called for information or to request a demonstration. Political parties obtain records of voter registrations as well as campaign contributors and others who have expressed an interest in the organization.

Before using any list you should know the standards for putting down names, how it is maintained, and all costs involved with its use. Some list owners insist upon doing all the mailing for you—at additional cost to you. You supply the literature to be mailed and the list owner sees that envelopes are addressed, stamped, and mailed according to your time schedule. Some go so far as to handle the printing. Ideally you will also be able to learn how successful people in fields similar to your own have been when using the same list.

It is often difficult for the average person to learn all these variables when attempting to determine which lists to rent or buy. The solution is to work through what is known as a list broker. A broker acts as a middle person between the list owner and the list buyer. The broker helps to link buyers with the appropriate owners, taking a commission for his or her efforts. The commission is paid by the list owner and is included in the cost of the list. The renter pays the same price whether or not a broker is used. This means that the list owner takes a slight loss with brokered transactions. However, the broker gains the list owners far more business than they might be able to obtain on their own. This increased volume more than offsets the expense of the commission.

A broker's job goes beyond linking list owners and renters. A good broker will handle all the screening that you would need to do yourself to properly evaluate a list being offered. The broker will know how current a list happens to be, how well it is updated and what past response has been for other users of the list. The broker can assist the renter in testing segments of the list and represents the renter by overseeing any work done on the renter's behalf. Thus if the list owner insists that all mailing be handled by his firm, the broker will make certain the work is completed on time and to the renter's satisfaction.

Where can you find more information on brokers? Perhaps the best approach is to use the Direct Mail List Rates & Data already discussed or you can go through the Direct Mail and Marketing Association, 6 East 43rd St., New York, New York 10017. This latter organization can offer guidance. It is also an excellent association to join should you decide that direct mail marketing will be a regular part of your company's business methods.

If you decide to work with a broker it is essential that you provide as much information as possible. The broker should understand your aims and objectives for using direct mail. You will need to explain what you hope to achieve and how you want to conduct the campaign. Be certain the broker knows your mailing schedule, priorities, and how current the lists must be.

Many people feel that list renters are naive. "What's to stop someone from making a copy of a rental list and then using it for all future mailings?" someone might ask. Nothing, in theory. However, list renters are neither naive nor trusting. They assume that some of their renters are going to be dishonest and they protect themselves through a practice known as "salting" or "seeding" a list.

Basically a seeded list contains one or more phony names that offer no clue to the fact that they are not legitimate. Each time a list is rented it is seeded in a slightly different manner, with the renter retaining a record of who rented it and how it was seeded. If the phony person receives a solicitation other than the one for which the list was originally rented, the renter will be prosecuted for violation of contract.

How is a list seeded? Suppose the renter creates the name Fanny Hildebrand of 597 Lickety Lane in Dry-As-A-Bone, Nevada. The name Fanny Hildebrand is fictitious. The address is that of the list renter's brother-in-law who gets a small commission for forwarding all mail received in that name.

The first time the list is rented it will go out as described. The second time the name might be changed to Fannie Hildebrand. The third time it might be Fannie Hilderbrand. The fourth time the address might be changed to Licketty Lane, and so forth. The change is never so great that it is obvious, nor is it ever done in a way that will prevent delivery of the material. Thus any name on a list could be seeded and the renter cannot safely use a copy of the list without paying for the right.

When you are planning a political campaign or a localized promotion, there are several types of lists that can be quite valuable. Clubs, churches, and fraternal organizations often sell the names and addresses of their members. These lists are invariably kept up-to-date as the organization has much to gain by keeping in regular touch with those who belong. Their survival depends upon the voluntary contributions of the members so they like to be certain they always know where everyone can be reached.

High schools often sell or rent the names and addresses of senior class members. Local merchants offering jewelry, photographic services, and numerous other items take advantage of such lists.

When you start compiling your own lists, probably based on direct mail sales, queries to your firm, purchases in retail outlets, and so on, it is going to be important for you to keep it up-to-date. Experts in the field say a minimum of 10 percent of the budget you develop for direct mail campaigns should be spent keeping the list current.

One inexpensive approach is to mark mailing envelopes with the words "Address Correction Requested." If someone has moved and left a forwarding address with the post office, this will be given to you for a nominal fee, providing the statement is on the envelope.

Larger companies computerize their mailing lists. This is especially helpful if you are using several lists that may have names appearing on more than one list. For example, suppose you are trying to promote an around-the-world cruise. You are going to need to reach fairly high-income people who enjoy traveling by boat.

The first list you select might be comprised of subscribers to expensive travel magazines. These people probably have more money than average and their subscription indicates they are interested in seeing places outside their home communities.

Another list would be comprised of the holders of travel and entertainment credit cards such as American Express, Carte Blanche, and Diner's Club. The requirements for receiving these cards are greater than for bank credit cards and the holders are paying an annual fee for the privilege.

A third list would include subscribers to yachting magazines. A fourth might include subscribers to magazines such as *Physician's Management* and *Medical Economics*. Both publications reach high-income professionals and both relate to spending money.

The problem arises when a person on one list is also on others. For example, a doctor might own a travel and entertainment credit card and subscribe to a yachting magazine. The doctor could receive three separate mailings—all identical.

Duplicate mailings are frequently nothing more than a waste of money for the advertiser. They do not effect the potential buyer's decision in any way. In fact the cost of avoiding duplication may be greater than the amount of money spent when duplication is allowed.

There are times when the duplication problem is serious, however. Occasionally you are going to be interested in producing a prestige mailing piece that appears to be totally personal. An AutoTyper (discussed shortly) may be used to give the appearance of an individually typed letter even though thousands of these letters are being mailed around the country. When a "class" mailer with the illusion of individual attention is desired, duplicate mailings will ruin the sale. The apparently personal appeal is the real selling point and duplicate mailings destroy this image.

Should you need to use a computer to avoid duplicates, it is important that you try to second guess the machine's programming. A computer is a complex tool that is often misused. The computer operator programs the machine so it eliminates all but one of the John Does who live at 111 Maple Place in Seattle. Unfortunately this does not eliminate the name J. Doe at 111 Maple Place or Dr. John Doe or John Doe, M.D. or Dr. J. Doe, etc. If you tell the computer to retain only one John Doe, that's what it will do. But it will also retain all the variations of the name that might appear on mailing lists. I frequently receive direct mail packages sent to as many as four different spellings of my name and I am certain that you have probably had similar experiences.

When programming the computer to eliminate duplication, have the programmer account for variables other than just the name. Let it eliminate all Does but one for any given address, for example. Thus the machine might keep John Doe, J. Doe, Dr. John Doe, and J. Doe, M.D. during its first sweep of the lists, then eliminate three of the names when it also checks the address. This is not 100% foolproof but it results in the lowest possible duplication, and that means a greater number of potential orders.

Computer mailings can be made more effective by taking advantage of the many advances in computer technology. One of the more popular uses among direct mail advertisers is computer personalization. The

## Direct Mail and Mail-Order Advertisements 121

computer inserts the name of the individual to whom the mailing is going somewhere in the body of the letter. An address and other personal information might also be worked in. Sometimes the type is the same for everything. Other times there is a noticeable difference. But either way the mailing seems more personal. Catalog advertisers such as Spencer Gifts regularly personalize their covering letters. Sometimes promotional contests are run in which the person can receive a check for a large sum of money if he wins. An oversize check facsimile is included with the mailing and the "check" is made out to the person receiving the circular.

Computer letters fall into two categories. One is the fill-in variety just mentioned. The other has the computer write what appears to be an original letter, typed by a secretary, specifically for the person receiving it. The use of an AutoTyper is generally required but the results are magnificent to behold.

An Autotyped letter starts with a form that can be used as a standard for everyone on the mailing list. It might introduce a product, make an offer, or ask for money. If there are parts where you want to make mention of the person's name, his or her job, or other personal information, these areas of the letter are left blank. The computer will fill them in each time a new letter is written.

The body of the Autotyped letter has to be carefully planned. It must be reasonably casual, within the bounds of normal business. It must not seem a promotion piece and must never use the same type of phrasing found in normal direct mail advertising campaigns.

In some cases you are going to have to vary the copy according to the individual who is to be reached. This might mean the addition of one or more paragraphs that will differ from letter to letter. To accomplish such a task the Autotyper can be programmed to stop at the appropriate point. Then a secretary can type the personal insert and let the Autotyper continue the letter.

Autotypers utilize conventional typewriters for producing the letters. One or more typewriters are hooked to the Autotyper, which then operates them at high speed, exactly duplicating the master letter.

The original letter can be edited until it is flawless so that every Autotyped duplicate will be perfect. However, you may wish to add to the illusion of a personal letter by either leaving one or more minor mistakes in the text or by setting the machine so the keys strike with the same intensity as a human typist might use. Thus some of the punctuation marks will poke through the paper just as they do on a personally typed letter.

If a paragraph or name has to be added, there is never any indication that this was done because the secretary uses the same typewriter that the Autotyper controls. It is placed on manual control during the time necessary for the addition.

The personalization of the Autotyped letter must be carried all the way through to the final signature. If the mailing is small you will probably sign your name. If it is large you might want to take advantage of a signing machine that utilizes a fountain pen to write your signature in a way that appears to be personal. Such automatic pens are regularly used by Capitol Hill politicians among others.

When should an Autotyped letter be used? When it is felt that the results cannot be achieved through a less expensive method. There are few approaches you can use that are any costlier so this is definitely not a standard tool of mail-order advertising.

Fund-raising campaigns often benefit from Autotyped appeals. The individual receiving such a letter feels as though a personal appeal is being made. Many recipients mail checks to causes that they normally would not think about. Typical of their reasons is the following comment: "I normally don't give to most charities. They send out some form letter and never take the time to ask me in person. But your organization took the time to treat me as an important individual. You wrote me a personal letter asking me for my contribution and I appreciate the trouble you went to. Enclosed is my check for . . . ."

Political campaigns are the same way. Potentially large contributors can be sent Autotyped letters to insure a more generous donation. Naturally the cost is too great to use it for an entire mailing list but it is effective for attracting larger sums of money.

It is wise to be extremely selective in the use of Autotyped letters when soliciting for charity. The letters are expensive and the public thinks they cost even more than they do because they seem to have been personally written. This implies that a large percentage of collected revenues is being channeled back into the fund-raising efforts. Many people resent such needless waste. They want their contribution to be used primarily for the good work of the organization and not for overhead.

One way to avoid resentment is to make it clear in the letter that the special appeal is only going to a handful of potential contributors. You will not use a personal letter for the bulk of your solicitations and the person receiving the Autotyped mailing must be aware of this fact.

Advertisers generally find that Autotyped letters pay for themselves only with fairly expensive products. An encyclopedia costing several hundred dollars, for example, might warrant an Autotyped letter, especially if the subject matter is of extremely limited interest. When someone is being asked to pay a lot of money for a product, he wants the seller to take a little time to get his money. If the potential buyer feels that the seller is only interested in making a "buck," he is going to be reluctant to take advantage of the offer. The Autotyped letter adds that essential personal touch.

Remember that when you sell by direct mail you are not offering a product. If the customer was in a store, he or she could go up to a sale item, feel it, touch it, smell it, and examine it very closely. When the customer is at home, looking at a direct mail circular, the product does not exist.

One advertising expert has likened this problem to selling the "sizzle" and not the steak. What you are doing is selling the concept of a product, a business, or a person—not the real thing. You must create an image in the person's mind—an image strong enough to make him want to commit himself to sending in money or casting a vote in your favor. This means that special care must be taken when preparing the direct mail advertising piece.

Direct mail campaigns are very much like those conducted through newspapers and magazines. You must outline your objectives, analyze what you are promoting, and list the important aspects for the people you are trying to reach.

Once again you will have a headline that must involve the reader's self-interest. It should stress the strongest aspect of what you are promoting and use attention getting words such as were discussed in the previous chapter. The reader must feel that there will be a benefit to him that will make him want to read further.

Your opening paragraph should elaborate on the main points brought out in the headline. In the case of a letter format, the opening paragraph will use the same features as the headline.

Let the reader know exactly what he is going to get by responding to your mailing piece. If it is a product, give the details of what it does, why it is better than competitors (if it is), the price, and all other details. Stress its unusual aspects.

In the case of a charity you will want to explain what the organization does to deserve support. If the money will be used to start some new project, this must be discussed in depth.

If you are a political candidate you must discuss your intentions as an officeholder. Discuss the issues that seem relevant to the people on the list you are using. You will be sending different brochures to different groups, sometimes stressing the same points but usually making a slightly different appeal. Just be certain that you never make opposite statements in your literature. Many people will acquire everything you mail and they will study it closely. Be honest and open but limit what you say to those appeals that are strongest for the people in the group you are contacting.

Use endorsements and proofs for what you claim. If a product was compared to similar items by a testing laboratory and the results put it in the most favorable light, by all means tell about it. If you produce a car that Ralph Nader is willing to buy, this should be stressed in the text.

Valid endorsements are equally valuable. Just be certain that the person doing the endorsing will be familiar to the readers and will be in a field that relates to the product. If the person is an expert but unknown to the general public, provide a small biography. For example, if you are selling a protein substitute that has been highly rated by Dr. Salvatore Fleenel of the Fleenel Institute of Protein Research, the average person will not know who you are talking about. The public may be unaware of his role as the world's leading expert on nonmeat protein. Thus your endorsement might read: " 'This protein substitute contains everything you will find in meat with none of the dangers of cholesterol and for a cost far lower than even the cheapest cuts,' says Dr. Salvatore Fleenel, Director, The Fleenel Institute of Protein Research and winner of the 1976 Golden Soybean Award." The public may still not know who the man is, but the explanation gives them a reason to respect his endorsement.

In the case of a charity drive, important and respected citizens in the community should be approached for endorsements. The mayor, congressional representatives, corporation heads, and others should be quoted as backing the cause.

The same is true with a political campaign. Use quotes from politicians and civic leaders respected in the party. However, do not use the endorsement of someone whose career may be coming to an end for one reason or another. A well-known senator's backing can backfire if that senator is facing a primary challenger who appears capable of unseating him, for example. It means that either respect for the senator has declined or that there is strong feeling that new ideas are needed. To slightly abuse a well-known quotation, never hitch your wagon to a fading star.

Photographs of the men and women whose endorsements are quoted adds to the impact of what they say. Just having a person's name or initials does not inspire the confidence that seeing his or her picture can bring. It makes the endorsement seem honest and real.

Always try to give the person receiving your mailing piece a reason to act promptly. Remember that with a magazine advertisement, if a person sets it aside he or she is liable to return to it later on. Newspapers generally have a life of 24 hours. Magazines have a life of from one week to several months. Not only will the original reader return to them but so will others who chance upon the publication.

A direct mail piece may have a life of only a few minutes. It may only be read by the person to whom it is addressed. If that person does not have reason to act promptly, it may get tossed in the wastebasket before any action can be taken at all.

Perhaps you can offer a discount for mailing early. This might be 10 percent off if mailed within 30 days or some other bonus. Perhaps there will be a free gift included for the first 1,000 people responding. Whatever the premium, it should make the reader act the same day the letter arrives if at all possible.

Keep in mind the time necessary for your mailer to arrive, however. Do not make the time limit for the offer so short that a delay in the mail delivery will invalidate it. Some people will buy only because of the special incentive, regardless of what the product might be. Take away the extra incentive and you eliminate the reason they had for buying.

Finally, rephrase the important benefits of the product, business, charity, or other cause you are promoting. Be certain there is no doubt in the reader's mind about the merits of your offer.

Then provide the means for a reply. This can be done in a variety of ways.

If you want the person to send a check, you should enclose a self-addressed envelope. In general, the envelope should be stamped or be a business reply envelope that requires no additional postage. The latter is the best way to handle return mailing. You pay only for the envelopes mailed to you. The business reply permit is available from the post office and is well worth obtaining. Without it you are forced to spend money for postage that will be used only in part. This is far more expensive than paying for the business reply mail actually sent to you.

If the reader is just to express interest in a product, perhaps to receive in-depth literature or to get a free trial offer, a postcard may suffice. Again the business reply stamp is a wise investment.

In reality you may not need the business reply permit or postage in any form. The envelope or card may be enough. However, this can only be determined through testing the identical mailing piece with half your sampling receiving a business reply envelope or card and the other half receiving an envelope on which they have to attach postage. The public may be willing to spend the money to get the product. However, until you can make the test, assume that you will get more replies if the reader does not need to get postage than if he or she must go to that extra bother and expense.

Costs are reduced when you use a window envelope for your mailing. The address on the letter or the return address on the enclosed mailing card or envelope will be visible through the window so only one printing of the customer's name is necessary.

Bear in mind that the return postcard or coupon ordering form may become separated from the rest of the mailing piece. The basic offer, the bonus for prompt action, all costs, and instructions on what to send should be repeated on the coupon. That way the person can take advantage of your offer regardless of how much of the mailing piece is retained.

The least expensive type of direct mail promotion is printed on a self mailer. This contains the customer's name and address, the letter or promotion information, and a postage paid order card all in one. The customer merely opens it, reads your message, tears off the reply card and returns it to you. Unfortunately, while this is inexpensive, it may not get the response that a multipiece mailing will get.

Advertisers using direct mail have found that sending several different pieces of literature brings a greater response than just sending one single item. This is true even with catalog houses that mail catalogs containing from a dozen to perhaps hundreds of different items. The advertisers have found that if their catalogs are sent along with one or two separate mailing pieces they can get more orders than with the catalog alone.

The reason for this is the way the public reacts to multiple pieces of literature sent in one package. Some people will read everything. However, many people will throw away most of what they have found, just glancing at one or two items when several are sent. If they receive only a single circular, it is readily discarded.

A good example of this type of marketing is done by the various book clubs. Once a month they send catalogs of books to the club members. The majority of the members read the catalog from cover to cover, perhaps placing an order for one or more books. A few of the members occasionally feel they lack the time to read the catalog. They discard it, knowing that the featured selections will be available as alternates in the next catalog.

In an effort to catch the people who feel they are too busy to read the catalog, the book clubs also include two or more circulars advertising books not included in the catalog. These special offers are invariably read regardless of whether or not the person ordering has taken the time to read the catalog. Thus, sales are made to people who would otherwise have been missed that month.

There are limitations to the multipiece mailing approach, of course. The main one is cost. The more you have printed, the greater your expenses. Charitable organizations and others on a tight budget often find that they do better with an attractive self mailer sent to a fairly sizable number of people than they do sending several pieces of literature to a limited list.

One point that must be mentioned here is the cost for mailing. Postal rates are rising and may go higher. First-class mail has become a luxury for advertisers and should be avoided when possible.

There are only two times when First-class postage should be used. One is when your offering is so timely that a delay of a few days will adversely affect your sales. This situation rarely occurs but, when it does, first class is vital.

The second time is when you are mailing Autotyped letters or making a similar personal appeal. The image of the mailing is all important and the use of third class hurts your chances of making a sale or receiving a donation. For the bulk of your mailings, though, first class must be considered taboo.

The paper stock you use is important. It must be heavy enough to travel well through the mail but not so heavy that it reduces the number of pages you can send for the one-ounce rate. A good way to test different paper stocks to see how they travel is to mail yourself letters, each containing a different type of paper. Use the lightest weight you can find that looks attractive and holds up in the mail. The only exception is the personal appeal where a fairly heavy, quality bond stock will make the best impression.

No matter how well your direct mail promotion material is written, it will be of no value unless it is read. Thus many advertisers let their envelopes serve as a lead-in. They put copy on the envelope to serve as what is known as a "teaser."

Some teasers are individualized. They might read: "For all parents who are worried about their children's health..." Or the teaser might say, "Important Information for the Customers of Daphne's Discount Department Store." Or even, "Good News for the T. P. Detwiler Family," an approach possible with computerized name writing.

Other teasers encourage action. "Special Limited Time Opportunity," "Last Chance to Renew at Our Old Rates," "Air Mail Reply Envelope Enclosed," and similar teasers encourage the recipient to open the envelope and respond.

Teasers can be news announcements. "At Long Last! Good News For Heart Patients! Here's News of an Exciting Product You've Been Waiting for!"

The profit motive can be a strong factor. "$5 Bonus Offer Enclosed," or "This Letter Can Save You $25," or "Here's Information on a Safe Way to Double Your Money" are all examples of profit teasers.

The teaser can be a question—"What Did Howard Hughes Tell Bernard Baruch to Help Him Triple His Money?" Or it can arouse curiosity—"You Have a Rendezvous with Jackie Onassis on Saturday May 12."

The teaser can promise seasonal help—"At last, the perfect Mother's Day gift." Or it can arouse sympathy—"This naked, starving orphan has just one chance at life—through you!"

There are other appeals as well. "The Mayor, the City Council and 25

Prominent Business Leaders Have a Plan to Make Our City Grow—But They Need Your Help" invokes civic pride. "As She Passed the Darkened Doorway, a Hand Grabbed Her Arm and Pulled Her Towards the Inky Blackness. She Started To Scream...." creates suspense and arouses curiosity. Or perhaps the appeal is to the special interest of the reader—"Now 26 of the nation's top golfers can help you play like a pro!"

A good teaser is like a good headline. It encourages the reader to continue into the advertisement where he or she will be induced to buy your product or support your cause.

The teaser must always relate to the specific promotion and the first part of the copy should elaborate on it. If you like, the teaser might be repeated as the headline inside the envelope.

Teasers have such an impact on the person reading them that they must be strong. If you cannot think of a teaser that will grab the reader's interest, do not use one. Leave your company's return address on the envelope and nothing more. Tests have indicated that using no envelope message is almost as much of an inducement to open the letter as a strong message. A weak teaser can get the entire envelope discarded unopened.

Expensive, "class" mailings should not have a teaser on the envelope. Personal letters do not have teasers, and you are trying to give a personal image to your Autotyped and similar correspondence.

Many direct mail campaigns involve the sending of two or three different circulars concerning the same product. The circulars are sent in stages, each one strengthening the appeal of the previous one. This is frequently done when offering very expensive items.

When you plan to make multiple mailings to an individual, do not use an envelope of the same design for each different circular sent. This approach works against you. The cost savings in not printing new envelopes with different teasers is offset by the number of follow-ups that get thrown away because the recipient thinks he has already read the mailing piece inside. Each envelope must be different or the person receiving it will think it is a duplicate of a previous mailing.

Direct mail copy should be scrutinized as closely as your space advertisements. Be certain the information is clear, concise, relates to the self-interest of the person who will be receiving it, and has an incentive that relates to the product offered. A good incentive for an encyclopedia sales brochure would be a free bookstand. An inappropriate offer would be a box of assorted Florida fruits. The former relates to the item offered so a person interested in the books would also be interested in the bookcase. The fruit would not relate to the books in any way and might not hold an appeal for the person reading the brochure.

There are numerous ways to use direct mail sales appeals beyond the obvious ones. For example, direct mail sales literature can be included with every order or bill sent to customers. If someone buys one of your products, include literature on other items you offer when packaging the product purchased. The buyer will see the offer at the same time he or she gets his order. The buyer is relaxed, has faith in the ability of your firm to deliver, and is most vulnerable for being induced to make an additional purchase.

This "piggy-back" approach can be used when mailing follow-up literature. If someone requests information on a product you are advertising include one or more brochures for other items when you send the material requested. Often someone will decide against the product originally under consideration but will buy something else from your line.

Direct mail can build interest in your organization. The chapter on nonprofit promotion details the use of newsletters for promoting your cause and raising funds.

Direct mail advertising is a way of keeping contact with customers who have come into your store. Each time someone makes a purchase in your place of business, take the person's name and address. Then use this list for mailing special offers to these established customers. The customer is told that the direct mail offering is your way of saying "Thank You" for that customer's business. In reality it is your way of increasing that customer's business.

Direct mail offers to inactive customers of your retail business can return them to your store. Once again, the list you have established for yourself is invaluable.

Department store owners find that direct mail advertising is effective when they have limited interest sales. Instead of using newspaper advertising for products that will appeal to only one segment of their customers, they use direct mail appeals to single out their best prospects. The cost is reduced for reaching those people most likely to buy.

Sometimes your direct mail offering can be used to increase consumption of your product. If you produce a food item, for example, you might use direct mail to send advertising brochures filled with recipes that require the use of your food product. The recipes should cover a wide range of tastes so everyone finds something that is appealing. Such a direct mail promotion increases product awareness, product demand, and, of course, product consumption.

Many department and specialty stores use direct mail to announce after-hours sales for selected customers. These help build traffic and make the recipients feel that they are part of an elite group.

Direct mail advertising can even be used to build your present mailing list. Numerous companies offering product catalogs include a business reply card with room for three or more names and addresses. The card is marked, "Do you have a friend who might enjoy receiving our catalog? Give us the person's name and address and we will send a free copy." You are then able to reach a broader market than you could find through more conventional means.

**Mail Order**

Mail order is the child of direct mail and space advertising. It is the offering of products through the mail, primarily with the use of newspaper and magazine promotions. The customer makes purchases direct from the mail-order dealer instead of having to go to a store for the product being promoted.

The business aspects of mail order would fill a book and there are several available on the subject. The promotional aspects of mail order follow the same concepts as for other space advertising. The only difference is in "keying" the advertisement, something that needs to be covered in this chapter.

If you are advertising a product in one magazine, everyone who sends you an order is going to be requesting the same item. It does not matter if they ask for the product by name or just send their money. You will know what they are requesting.

But suppose you begin offering different items, either in several magazines or during different months' issues of a single magazine. Or suppose you decide to test your offer by offering the product in a split run—half the offers being for the product, the other half being for the same product at the same price but with a bonus included. If someone sends you a check with a note reading, "Please send me the items you have offered," how are you going to know what the person is ordering?

The answer is to code or key your advertisements. They are marked with an identifying number so you always know who is responding to which advertisement.

The code must include several items of information. You will need to know the name of the magazine, the date of the issue, the product, and, if there has been a split run test, which offer was seen. The easiest way to do this is with a combination of initials and numbers.

For example, suppose your advertisement was in *Better Homes and Gardens* for October, 1976. The first part of your code might be BHG1076 so that you have the magazine and the date it appeared. Depending upon where you advertise you might be able to use different initials. Some advertisers who limit the publications in which they advertise make a list of the magazines and put a letter of the alphabet next to it. Thus, *Better Homes and Gardens* might be "A," with *Newsweek* designated "B," *Seventeen* marked "C," and so forth. With this approach the code is reduced to A1076.

Next make a list of your products and number them consecutively. The number of the product being advertised is then added to your key code. Thus, if you are offering your eighth product, your code might read A10768.

Split run notations are easy. All you have to do is note that one is designated A and the other B. The new code might be A10768A, which tells you that the ad was in the October, 1976, edition of *Better Homes and Gardens*. The offer was for a left-handed widget (your 8th product on the list) and you gave a 10 percent discount (split run offer A).

Admittedly if someone is going to be reluctant to put down your product's name, there is nothing to convince them they should mark down the code. That is why the key is carefully hidden as part of the address.

Usually the key becomes a department. The company address might then read: Baxter Grimace Corporation, Dept. A10768A, 33 Commercial Parkway, Blimmel, Alabama, 00707. Other advertisers use Suite A10768A or something similar. All that is necessary is for you to try and convince the buyer that if the code is not included with the address, the order will never reach your company.

### Free Publicity

When you begin advertising a product line it is possible to get free mention in trade journals whether or not you advertise. Follow the same procedures you would with general interest magazines. Analyze the subscribers and decide what aspects of your product would be beneficial to them. Then write a letter to the editor describing the reasons the magazine's subscribers would want to know about your product. Include illustrations suitable for reproduction, of course.

The emphasis will vary from magazine to magazine with the same product. For example, suppose you are offering security devices for the home. When you contact a builder's magazine, you may want to stress the low cost of installation and the increased sales value in a home buyer's mind when he or she sees the security devices.

A magazine for law enforcement officers might stress the effectiveness of the devices and their availability. Many police departments conduct crime prevention programs that include discussing home security products. They will be interested in mentioning yours if they feel it is of value.

In some cases you may be asked to submit a sample for testing. This is to be expected but make it clear that you are limiting the time when the editor may have it. Ask for its return in 30 days, 60 days, or even 90 days if it seems more appropriate. You may have to bill the publication for the price of the item if it is not returned in the alloted time. Fortunately few editorial staffs ever try to retain items sent for testing when it is made clear at the start that their return is expected.

Trade journal mention can be followed with a paid advertising campaign that will be all the more effective because the product is already familiar to the reader. Some companies prefer to go the direct mail route, mentioning the write-up in the trade journal as a selling point. As was pointed out earlier, whenever you have a magazine mention, the reader looks upon it as a product endorsement regardless of the intention of the publication. Thus reminding them of the write-up, perhaps even including a copy, will be extremely beneficial.

# 7

# Nonprofit and Charitable Organization Promotion

It always seems that no one needs promoting more than those who can least afford it. Churches, hospitals, social welfare agencies, and numerous others are dependent upon promotion for the raising of funds yet usually have the least money to organize a campaign. This chapter will show you how to become better known and mount successful fund-raising programs even when you have almost nothing to spend.

One of the major problems with many nonprofit organizations is that they try to operate by committee. In an effort to make everyone feel that they have a part, they take the attitude that "if one person can do a job well, three people can do it better." Unfortunately when it comes to promotion it is essential that one person be given a free hand at coordinating a program. Others will have to be involved, of course. But no campaign will be effective so long as everything is subject to constant review or group decisions.

The essential first step when planning a promotion is to know the organization you wish to publicize. By this I mean what it is, what it does, how it does it, and what its history has been. You must also know the plans for the future. Too often the person planning a campaign is ignorant of many aspects of the organization he or she represents. This ignorance comes through during questioning by the news media and the public, reflecting unfavorably on the project at hand. Many is the time that a potential contributor decides against giving a donation because "those people over there don't know what they're doing. I'd be afraid my money would be wasted."

A second essential is to have one or more people who can act as speakers for television, radio, and group appearances. This may be the person who is coordinating all publicity or it may be someone else in the organization. Large groups might have several people they can send out.

The speakers selected must be able to articulate well and be relaxed in pressure situations. They must also have the same intimate knowledge of the organization that the publicity coordinator has.

Always be selective when deciding who should act as a spokesperson. The "logical" person is not always the best. Many church members assume the minister should speak for them, for example. But the minister may not be the best person. He or she is trained to give sermons and will be fairly relaxed in front of a group. But the minister may not have experience communicating in ways that will gain money, new members, or support for special projects. In addition, some people resent a minister's asking for funds that are, indirectly, of personal benefit. A lay spokesperson dispels this cynicism. He or she has nothing to gain but the satisfaction of helping a worthy cause. The lay person's enthusiasm becomes infectious and results in greater success.

Many times the organization president is selected to speak for the group. But the president may be a business person, capable of acting as an executive and not as a spokesperson. The president may not even be very familiar with all the organization's projects since his position is often that of administrator.

The best publicity is free publicity, so far as the budget is concerned. Fortunately the news media will delight in offering a degree of time or space to your organization. The reason is that they all must meet certain public service requirements. In the case of radio and television this is a matter of law. In the case of newspapers and magazines it is a matter of individual policy that is fairly consistent all across the country.

Admittedly the public service work of many radio and television stations is laughable. Public service programs are often buried at odd times during the broadcast day. They are not considered important in terms of audience and advertising revenue since they seldom attract either. The Federal Communication Commission does not designate when such material must be used, just that it be used. Thus you have a guaranteed outlet but not always when you might like to have it. It's possible to work around this problem, though, as will be shown later in this chapter.

The first step towards promoting your organization is to prepare the ingredients for a press kit. You will want to set down on paper all the details of your organization that might prove of value to the news media.

One important story you have to tell is the history of your organization. When was it founded, by whom, and for what purpose? Describe its growth and, if it is a branch of a national group such as the Red Cross or the various Scouting groups, its history in your immediate area. Never assume knowledge on the part of members of the press. Most people are ignorant of the background of even the most familiar charitable organizations.

If your promotional efforts are on behalf of a group of several different programs, such as the United Way, then you should give a history of the combined drive and a brief background of some of the more important member agencies. Do not worry about telling everything. Cover the areas that seem of greatest interest to your community.

For example, suppose you are involved with promoting the United Way. In my community the United Way represents more than 100 different agencies both local and national in scope. To try and write a history of each one would be an unnecessarily demanding task. It is doubtful that any of the news media would be interested. All the press would like to know about is a cross section of the organizations. Thus there might be a history of a low-income clinic serving the area, a children's home, the Red Cross, and a few others. The agencies discussed should serve a broad segment of the city including the very young, the very old, the disabled, the ethnic community, and others. The groups should be selected with an eye toward including enough to interest every potential contributor. The broader the cross section, the greater the appeal. Usually this means from eight to a dozen, though the exact number you select will depend upon the community in which you are working.

There must also be a list of all agencies, their directors, and the name or names of people who can be contacted for in-depth information on any member. Sometimes this will be the director, sometimes it will be a public relations person working for the agency, and sometimes it will be the person handling promotion for the several organizations conducting a united campaign.

Next you are going to need to prepare material on what the organization is doing today. People want to know what benefits the community is receiving and, in the case of fund-raising drives, how the money is currently being spent. If there are plans for the expansion of services, new construction, or a special research project, these should be revealed in detail.

An excellent example of the type of history and current information material that should be used was prepared by Martha Murphy of Tucson General Hospital. She was responsible for helping to raise a million dollars for expansion of the hospital's facilities. Martha's first problem was in explaining not only the hospital but its medical philosophy to the community. Tucson General is an Osteopathic Hospital. Osteopathy is an area of medicine that is little known to the average person. Either the public is at a loss to know what the name implies or they relate it to chiropractic care, which is radically different and often held in low esteem by osteopaths and M.D.'s alike.

The problem was handled by starting with a brochure that detailed the concept of osteopathic medicine and its development during the last century. It discussed the number of osteopathic physicians in the nation, the hospitals where they work, and the training they receive.

Next a pamphlet was prepared detailing the history and needs of Tucson General Hospital. Again there was some history of osteopathy included, for there is a chance that the person reading the material would receive just one of the pamphlets and not both. This second pamphlet answered such questions as "What is the capital program?" "Who will benefit?" "Who will be asked to give?" "Will there be corporate and foundation support?" "Will all funds given remain in Tucson?" and "Why should I support your hospital?" There were 25 questions and answers in all.

Finally, there should be material on the principles involved, if they are important. For example, suppose a local Cancer Society was trying to raise money for an area researcher who was trying to develop a new approach to the treatment of leukemia. The public is going to want to know not only about the Cancer Society but also the background of the researcher. The average person will not be able to understand the technical aspects of leukemia research, but everyone can understand that the doctor has 12 years of training; was formerly involved with successful, award-winning research in the field; and is considered one of the world's leading experts. Remember that in a case such as this the public must have faith in the person doing the work because there is no other incentive. A hospital expansion program has the potential of helping everyone since it will service the community. But a research program is intangible. There may or may not be community benefit. Giving money is a gamble, and potential donors want to have some incentive for taking the risk. Thus the background of the principles becomes imperative.

Always try to personalize your organization by providing stories about the individuals who work there or the people you serve. Saying that a relief organization helped three million people worldwide the previous year means nothing. The number is too large. The average person reads it, says "that's nice," and goes about his business.

The wise promotion will personalize the organization's work. Instead of just stressing numbers it will stress one person or one family that has been helped. The person's plight will be discussed in detail. His background and problems will be covered. Then the apparent hopelessness will be mentioned. The reader will see him at his lowest point, not knowing where to turn or what to do. Then he is shown becoming involved with the organization. Assistance is provided and the person's life is made better. He can go forth with hope. Perhaps all the problems will be solved, perhaps not. But the person will have a chance for the future, which once seemed overwhelmingly bleak.

The public can relate to such a story. It can see how the past contributions were put to use to aid real people. The vast numbers assisted may be impressive, but it is the case study of a single individual that grabs our hearts and forces us to open our wallets.

Relief agencies operating around the world are keenly aware of this fact. Many have literature featuring a small, ragged, undernourished child. The pamphlets tell of the child's home life, the lack of food, the family's bare subsistence living. It gives you the impression that your money is going to be working for the good of a real person whose needs are obvious. Your contribution is not going to the agency or to faceless, nameless masses around the world. It is going to help a real person—a child like the one about whom you read. The appeal is irresistible to many Americans.

Sometimes there are human interest stories of a specialized nature. For example, an organization working to help the handicapped might have a successful, highly skilled worker who is also handicapped. Such a story shows not only the good work of the agency but also the eventual results of successful rehabilitation. A self-sufficient handicapped person is teaching other handicapped people how to cope with their disabilities. Such stories provide a double incentive for giving money.

Human interest stories always have value because they are eagerly sought by newspapers and the broadcast media. Often a newspaper will be reluctant to provide much coverage of an organization in general. However, it will run extensive feature stories on the people involved when they feel the stories are of community interest. By preparing such material in advance of your promotion efforts, you are insuring coverage that might otherwise be inadequate for your needs.

Perhaps the biggest concern of nonprofit and charitable organizations is fund raising. Any time donations are needed to sustain services, fund raising must be a priority concern. Annual fund-raising drives need to be planned throughout the year if they are to be increasingly successful. Remember that with rising inflation, it is essential that each year's campaign bring in considerably more money than the previous one or services may have to be curtailed. Let us therefore look at successful, low cost approaches to fund raising.

The first question that arises is why someone wants to give money in the first place. Perhaps it can be argued that there are as many reasons for giving as there are people making donations. However, experts in the field feel that there are a few basic motivations.

One reason for contributing to a charitable organization, surprisingly enough, is the desire for power. A person can make himself feel important by giving money to one group and withholding it from another. In fact, some experts on fund raising feel that the best approach to raising money emphasizes the greatness of the donor and not the needs of the people to be benefited. Although this may be subject to challenge, it is important to make the donors feel important after they have contributed, as will be discussed shortly.

Another reason for giving money to a group is to feel a sense of importance within the group. After all, if someone is going to go to the trouble of helping an organization survive, the reasoning goes, then he certainly should have control over its activities. The money equals importance in the donor's mind.

The contributor seeking importance is the type of person who will call staff personnel with comments and criticisms on an annoyingly frequent basis. Such a person attends all public meetings and often challenges every statement made by the staff. The person usually tells himself that he is motivated by civic pride. The truth is that ego satisfaction is the all-important factor.

How you decide to raise funds is also important in the psychology of giving. Some people fail to give when confronted by someone collecting for a charitable organization because they have no idea how much to give. Others make a contribution that is so small as to be almost meaningless. They want to do something but become flustered and unsure. Such people are often reachable only with direct mail.

Then there are those who equate giving with parental love. They are most likely to contribute when the person collecting seems like a father or mother figure.

Some people feel that making a contribution is a sign of weakness. They feel it is wrong to be moved by the sentimental appeal of a fellow human being in trouble. It is a little like the attitude that prevents many men from showing emotions in public.

Obviously you are not going to be able to motivate all the people all the time. However you can plan your campaign strategy so you reach the greatest number of people possible.

Perhaps the easiest problem to overcome is that of the person who does not know what to give. You can set guidelines for such people, encouraging their contribution by telling them what their money is going to buy.

Many successful campaigns detail what $1, $5, $10, $25, or more will buy. The campaign might say, "One dollar will buy enough grain to help feed a family of four for a day. Five dollars will buy the tools needed for a family to start farming the land that they own. Ten dollars will buy books and supplies needed to send a child to school for a year. Fifteen dollars will bring medical assistance to a small village ravaged by disease . . . ." The quotes are strictly examples and do not represent a particular fund-raising campaign. But the approach is typical of highly successful drives. The potential donor not only has suggestions covering a wide range of contributions, but he also has a clear understanding of how that money will be used. The organization has personalized the contribution and enabled the donor to say to himself, "I'm helping a family start a new life farming their land."

Some fund-raising campaigns use the "fair share" approach. A chart is prepared showing different income levels and what each level can theoretically afford to donate. Thus a person need only check his income to learn what his "fair share" contribution should be.

I have to assume that the fair share approach is successful because it has been used for several years by fund drives such as some of the United Way campaigns. However, I have heard a great deal of resentment from many contributors who feel that they are being unfairly pressured. Many refuse to donate or limit their donations. Others are embarrassed because they feel that the organization is going to know how much they earn—often a sensitive area to people.

If you feel the fair share approach is for your group, by all means use it. However, it will probably be more successful if coupled with a chart showing what the different amounts of money will buy. Showing such a breakdown makes people understand where their money is going so they are more willing to participate.

One way to increase contributors is to honor the people who give money. This might be done by circulating a news bulletin with the names of the donors. The dollar amounts need not be given, though if you are trying to increase your number of large contributors—$100 or more—it can help to list those who gave that figure. No dollar figure is mentioned for those giving less money, but the fact that a list of larger investors exists often motivates a donor to give a little extra.

Some organizations have found that producing a list is a good way to obtain reluctant contributions from members. Churches, for example, have found that when they publish a list of contributors, they can use this list as a motivating factor. Usually the church sends a tentative list of names of donors to a member who has not offered any money. The list is accompanied by a note saying something to the effect, "It's not too late to add your name to our list of contributors to the church's fund drive. Your donation will help support our day care center, our inner-city missionary program, our Sunday School, and the special teen center. Won't you send a contribution today? Then we'll be able to add your name to our list before sending it to the printer."

Church members are embarrassed by such an appeal because they do not want their friends to know that they have not made a contribution. It is a strong motivating factor when a campaign is aimed at an organization's membership list, though it is quite effective for obtaining community contributions of all sorts.

Many organizations have volunteer workers organizing business offices. They play up the team spirit and encourage reluctant givers to be part of the group. They try to get the office staff to "get on the bandwagon" by contributing like everyone else. The list of names is a tremendous asset here because it means that others can check on who gave and who did not. If a person wants to belong, he is going to make a contribution.

Giving recognition to the donors should not end with the close of the campaign drive. One of the common complaints against charitable organizations is: "They only want my money. The only time I hear from them is when they have their hands out. I'd be willing to give them more if they just paid some attention to me. But I guess the only thing they care about is how many dollars they can get from me next time."

The best way to avoid this problem is to produce a newsletter that is issued periodically during the course of the year. The newsletter is meant for the general public but especially for past contributors.

It tells what the organization is doing and outlines its plans for the future. It spotlights individuals on the staff and those receiving assistance. It gives the contributor a sense of belonging and the feeling that someone cares about him as a person. Why else would they take the trouble to keep him informed when such information was never requested? The contributor might not even bother to read the newsletters, but you can be certain that he will willingly give money when the next fund-raising drive is held.

Invite the contributors to participate in the organization to some degree. For example, one newsletter each year might include a question such as: "How can we better meet your needs?" or "How can we better serve the community?" or "What programs would you like to see us initiate?" The answers can be compiled and mentioned in the next newsletter. Many will be impossible to implement because of cost, lack of need, or because it is not within the scope of the organization. But some will be quite valuable and these should be discussed in detail. When one or more ideas are adopted, the people who suggested them will get further recognition.

It is always a wise idea to develop a donor profile. Contact donors with a questionnaire that asks such things as: age, sex, marital status, number of times they have contributed to the organization, how long they have known about the organization, how they first learned of it, why they support it, number of children, size of community, family income, religious affiliation, other organizations they support, and club memberships. The questionnaire must be completely anonymous, a fact stressed at the beginning, before the question and answer spaces. An envelope should be enclosed, preferably with postal permit and a notation reading, "Your stamp placed here means additional money that can be spent helping others," or a similar comment.

Naturally not everyone who donates is going to respond to your questionnaire. However it does help you to establish additional information on which you can base further appeals. The more your promotional literature relates to the potential donor's self-interests, the greater his contributions are likely to be.

When planning a campaign, the use of volunteers is going to be essential. Unfortunately it is true that "you get what you pay for" when it comes to campaign workers. Volunteers who are not "paid" are likely to be poor workers of limited value. Fortunately the pay that motivates a volunteer is not monetary.

Plans should be made in advance to reward volunteers for their efforts on your organization's behalf. Inexpensive certificates can be printed for each volunteer to receive following the campaign. This might be done at a "thank you" dinner or, if the budget will not permit the serving of a full meal, during a special honors meeting followed by coffee and cake, or similar refreshments. The head of the organization should hand the certificate to each volunteer as the person's name is read.

In the case of fund raising, special awards might be provided for the most successful volunteers. These might be in the form of small trophies or special plaques. The special awards might even be displayed in your organization's office during the campaign as a constant incentive for the volunteers. There is seldom money enough to generate the enthusiasm that is produced when someone has a chance for a trophy and special recognition. The feeling of importance and accomplishment buys more work than any salary, and the cost to the organization is minimal.

Rewards of this type should be planned for all volunteers, regardless of their position in the community. Even company executives succumb to the ego satisfaction that a certificate or a plaque can bring.

One of your best promotion vehicles can be the people already involved with the organization. Most nonprofit and charitable groups have boards of directors that include prominent men and women from the community. These are usually business and civic leaders who may be involved with a half dozen other worthwhile groups at the same time. Despite this fact, they can be extremely valuable when promoting your cause and attempting to raise money.

Never assume that because someone is on your board of directors he or she knows very much about the organization. Such people frequently know nothing of the organization's history; they often have only a superficial knowledge of current involvements and little or no information about future plans. Their activity is often more of an ego boost than the result of personal belief in the cause.

Despite the fact that your board of directors may be somewhat ignorant, it contains influential people who can motivate others to give to your campaign. Therefore, it is a wise first step to provide the background they are lacking. This can be done in several ways.

One approach is to prepare a press kit for the members of the board. This serves the double purpose of giving them needed facts and showing them the ongoing community relations program you are conducting.

A second approach is to prepare information specifically for the board. This might be done with a multipage bulletin, perhaps titled: "Did you know?" and containing various facts about the organization. Or you might use a question and answer format. Whichever method you choose, you must be certain that they have enough information to be able to speak intelligently to others.

The information provided the board will be different from the information provided your speakers' bureau. The board will be talking to employees and friends for the most part. If your board members are also going to be meeting with civic organizations, then they must be thoroughly prepared for such speeches. They must have comprehensive information.

It is always wise to rely upon your board of directors for names of people to act as volunteers. They can recruit the heads of area businesses and industries in most cases, people who would not otherwise become involved. Such volunteers may be of limited use in your campaign, but they will at least obtain contributions from the people who work for them. After all, when the boss is a fund raiser for an organization, what employee is going to risk the wrath that will come if a contribution is not made?

When your fund-raising campaign is going to be largely direct mail, the business leader volunteers are invaluable because they can supply names and addresses of their employees. If the firm is large enough to warrant a special printing of your brochures, you might start it with a picture of the firm's executive and a quote from him or her endorsing your campaign. This has a similar psychological effect as the boss asking who will be willing to contribute.

In the case of smaller businesses the cost of printing the photograph and quote may be prohibitive. However, the smaller business is liable to have employees in more direct contact with their employer so he or she will get the message across.

Many times you can enlist volunteer support from community groups. Fraternal organizations, women's clubs, and similar groups often "adopt" a charity. If the group has a known special interest, such as the Lions Club work on behalf of the blind, then you should see if there is a way to appeal to this area of concern. This is where your initial study of your organization comes in handy. You can often find a particular project that is not really typical of your organization but has enough appeal to interest the group.

For example, suppose you are involved with the Scouting movement. If there is a special program for handicapped Scouts, groups interested in such youths may lend wholehearted support even though their interest in Scouting, as such, is extremely limited. A group of agencies such as the United Way has the easiest time enlisting the aid of widely divergent groups because their efforts affect so many different people. However, any group can usually find enough different areas to emphasize in order to gain help from special interest clubs.

Direct mail fund-raising campaigns can be handled in a variety of ways. The best approach is to utilize many of the techniques of direct mail and space advertising. For example, the use of multiple mailing pieces should be considered. One information sheet or brochure will discuss the organization seeking money. This will be illustrated if possible, with black-and-white prints preferable to color. You never want to prepare such an elaborate pamphlet that your promotion costs equal or exceed the pledges you receive. All costs must be minimal.

Another information sheet discusses the costs for maintaining the organization and perhaps the plans for the future. A third sheet will include a pledge form and a discussion of what different size donations will accomplish for the organization.

Direct mail can be used for the entire fund-raising effort. The mailing package includes a postage paid envelope with a notation that money will be saved if the donor supplies a stamp. Perhaps the effort will be a "one-shot" or there may be two or three different mailings to those who fail to respond in a reasonable time to the first request.

A second approach is to use direct mail as well as a community campaign that involves volunteers knocking on doors and speaking before various groups. The lists used might include previous donors or both past donors and selected citizens chosen for their group affiliation, business affiliation, or other connection. Sometimes the direct mail approach is used only after volunteers have canvassed the community. The volunteers keep a record of who was not at home when they called and these people are contacted by direct mail. This saves a volunteer's time and patience while keeping your direct mail costs to a minimum.

Sometimes direct mail is used to prepare the community for a volunteer contact campaign. This is a questionable approach for the reasons cited at the beginning. When you ask for money in person, there are many people who will hesitate to give despite the fact that they might be willing to mail a donation.

If you decide to let direct mail act as a lead-in for a personal contact campaign, it is wise to treat the mailing almost like a solicitation for funds. In addition to providing the information about your organization, you supply details of what various contributions will mean for the people you serve. Thus they have advance guidelines for planning what to give when someone comes to collect.

Some organizations have found that people are happier when the size of their contribution is not known to the person coming door to door. In theory you will have volunteers canvassing their own neighborhood. They will be asking for money from people who might be embarrassed by the solicitation. They might refuse to contribute, claiming they gave at work or by mail rather than letting the volunteer know the size of the donation they would otherwise have made.

To avoid such problems, you might include an envelope with the initial mailing. This envelope will be addressed to your charity but will not contain postage. The person will be told that the envelope can be used for making a pledge in complete privacy. The envelope can be stamped and mailed in or saved for the volunteer. Receipts, if desired, will be issued from the organization headquarters. The volunteer receiving the sealed envelope will act only as a courier. He or she will not know how much money is being donated.

Direct mail solicitation can also be used as a supplement to a personal contact campaign. Previous donors can be contacted and encouraged to increase the size of their donations. Or perhaps special appeals can be made between traditional campaign drives. This is an excellent way to help sponsor a new project for which there has been no budget prepared.

Once you have had at least one campaign fund drive, it is a good idea to include a list of previous donors with your direct mail campaign, though *not* the amount they gave. The list might be headed, "We'd like to add your name to our distinguished list of contributors." In some cases an additional reward might be offered. For example, in the case of a religious group there might be a special honor roll of contributors of $100 or more. These people not only have their names on the list but also will have their names inscribed in the front of a prayer book. In theory, giving is its own reward. In practice, providing special recognition increases the pledges.

There are many ways to upgrade donations. One approach is to sell something well above cost and then give a bonus to each buyer/contributor. For example, a popular local artist might prepare a number of prints for a charitable organization. The prints are either donated or given at extremely low cost. These are then sold for a set minimum figure, such as $50, $100, or more, with the bulk of the money going to the organization. Obviously, to be successful, the cost of the item to your charity must be no more than a dollar or two.

Each buyer of the print takes a tax deduction for the purchase. The buyer is also sent a bonus such as a small calendar or, in the case of a religious organization, a drawing of the new church or synagogue. The bonus item costs a few pennies at most, but its extra appeal is often irresistible.

When you use direct mail as your primary fund-raising approach, be prepared to follow up your initial mailing. There are all sorts of reasons someone does not respond to an initial contact. Sometimes the reason is almost childish—the person wants to be certain you care enough to try and woo him. Other times the letter gets mislaid, then forgotten. The person meant to donate and will if reminded of the fund drive. However, if only one appeal is made, the incident is liable to be forgotten.

Seasonal appeals might have their follow-up after the holiday. The annual Christmas Seal campaign is an excellent example of how this can be done. The initial appeal is made between Thanksgiving and Christmas, theoretically the prime giving period. However, those who are unresponsive receive another direct mail contact in January. This time the letter stresses how easy it is to overlook sending a contribution during the hustle and bustle of the holiday season. Then a second attempt to get a donation is made, often quite successfully.

If you are making contact with a high quality mailing list, you may want to use personalized letters. Such a list might be the compilation of the members of the organization seeking to raise funds, for example. Or it might be made exclusively of previous contributors.

The personal letters are frequently Autotyped and no enclosures are added, not even a mailing envelope. The amounts and number of past contributions might be mentioned, as some experts feel this is a strong motivating factor. Mentioning the benefits that will be reaped should the dollar amount be increased can also gain a favorable response.

One of the most controversial areas of direct mail fund-raising is the inclusion of gifts in the initial appeal. Such gifts range from stamps and seals to handmade items or inexpensive novelties.

The average person is becoming increasingly concerned about the money spent for fund raising by charitable and nonprofit organizations. With costs rising for everyone, a contributor is concerned that the bulk of the money donated will be used to help the cause, not to pay for an expensive fund-raising campaign. As a result there is often great hostility to unwanted, unordered gifts that come with direct mail solicitations.

I am on the mailing list for several missionary schools, for example. Once or twice a year these schools mail me small handcraft items ranging from a tiny doll to a tiny weather indicator. The idea behind the gifts is to make me feel either generous enough or obligated enough to mail a contribution. I am to "pay" for the gift, in effect, a concept I abhor. Although I must admit to feeling a bit of guilt, I always toss such appeals into the trash. Even though I may want to contribute to the causes involved, I am afraid that all my money is going to be used meeting the cost of the gifts and that very little will ever benefit the organization. More important is the fact that there are many others who feel as I do.

Stamps and seals, such as the Easter and Christmas seals, enjoy great popularity. First, they are extremely cheap. Their production cost is about the same as for other forms of printed literature, so they do not seem like a waste of money.

Secondly, stamps and seals are meant to be used on correspondence mailed during the time when the fund-raising drive is being conducted. This means that the recipient is acting as another fund raiser, calling attention to the organization with every letter that is mailed. The public rightfully feels that when they use such seals, they are acting as promoters of a cause in which they believe.

Another value to such stamps and seals is that they offer a minimum contribution amount to the recipient. If someone does not want to contribute much money, he or she usually counts the number of seals, assigns an arbitrary value of perhaps one cent to five cents a seal, and mails that figure as a contribution. Such a person is unlikely to give any other way, making the inclusion of stamps or seals well worth their minimal cost. Naturally you will also include a list of suggested contributions and the benefits they will buy, as discussed earlier.

If you do decide to send stamps, seals or other items in your initial mailing request, do not ask to have the items returned if the recipient does not wish to make a donation. First, you have no legal basis for such an action. No one need return unsolicited merchandise according to the law. Second, such requests are a nuisance for those who feel compelled to comply. They resent the organization and the trouble it caused them, turning so hostile that it is unlikely the organization will ever receive a contribution.

Direct mail campaigns and any literature prepared for handout purposes for the press and the public should always be illustrated. Too many organizations feel this is an area where they should try and save money. They hand a Polaroid camera to an ambitious but unknowledgeable volunteer or staff member, then expect the person to produce high quality photographs. Very seldom does such an approach prove successful.

Photographs are an essential aspect of your campaign. They graphically tell your organization's story in ways that words can never match. For example, suppose your work with minority groups is a major campaign appeal. You can discuss the number of Indians or Puerto Ricans or blacks or other groups you have helped and people may or may not believe it. But when you can show a picture of your staff actually involved with minorities, it makes your appeal irresistible.

Or suppose your group works with the handicapped. You can tell your success stories and they might be quite moving. But a far stronger motivation is achieved when you can show a picture of a handicapped youngster grinning proudly as he takes his first few unsupported steps.

The only way to be certain of obtaining quality photographs is to use professional photographers. This is expensive but it must be done. Fortunately there are two ways to reduce your costs.

The first approach is to talk with various professionals, look at their portfolios and decide which ones seem most able to pictorially tell your organization's story. Then determine your budget for the project. Decide how much you can afford to pay for the photographer's time and skills. Perhaps this will be $100, perhaps $500, perhaps somewhere in between.

Next, analyze your organization and the people you are trying to reach. What aspects of your group's work would most impress the potential contributors? When you can decide this question, you will know what needs to be emphasized and the photographer can decide how much time it will take.

Finally, sit down with each photographer and explain both your budget and the work to be covered. Ask what you can expect for your money. Sometimes the photographer will go so far as to work by the hour, turning over the negatives to you so you can have the prints made. This is not a professional's normal practice and many are rightfully against it. The profit from the sale of prints is much too important. However, some photographers make an exception when charity is involved. Others will quote you a figure for both their time and print charges. If you can work out a satisfactory arrangement, by all means do so. Hiring a professional is always the best method.

The alternative to hiring a professional is the hiring of an advanced amateur who has not yet started to try and earn a living in the field. Many communities have universities and art schools offering photography courses. Senior students are frequently every bit as skilled as area professionals. If you go through the school's placement office or administration office, you can usually get some referrals.

Senior students must present themselves just as a professional would be required to do. Proof of competence must be shown through the use of a portfolio of prints. If the student can handle the job, you can probably hire him or her for a small hourly fee plus all expenses. This can save you a small fortune without sacrificing quality.

Sometimes a photographer will be interested in your cause and willing to donate time and talent. Such a photographer might do the work for normal rates, then bill you only for print costs. The rest of the bill is donated as a contribution.

It is a wise idea to check with your local Internal Revenue Service office to see if professionals can donate their hourly rate to your organization and deduct it from their tax returns. If they can, information to that effect should be disseminated. You might have a sign made for your headquarters that reads "Professional Services Donated to Our Organization Are Tax Deductible." However, do not push such an approach. Make certain the professionals with whom you deal are aware of this fact but do not make such donations a requirement for hiring. Many professionals cannot afford to make such a donation, especially with business profits frequently lower than in past years. A photographer or anyone else who feels he must donate his time if he is to work with you will quite likely refuse to work with your organization.

Always have the photographer take as many photographs as possible in the time available. These should cover all aspects of your organization's work or as many facets as possible. The pictures will not be made into prints but stored in the form of "contact sheets"—a sheet of photographic paper on which the negatives have been laid and printed so they yield "same size" pictures. These tiny frames can be studied with a magnifying glass. Pictures that do not relate to immediate needs can be found at a later time, then enlarged as need. The cost is limited to the film printing charges since that one hourly fee served multiple purposes.

For example, I once photographed a fund-raising party for a nonprofit organization. I was hired to take pictures of the guests, all of whom had made sizable contributions to the organization. The photos were to be run in a newsletter as a way of giving the people recognition. I was asked to work three hours and provide a dozen 8″ x 10″ prints for a fee agreed upon in advance. However, instead of just taking the 12 photographs needed for the immediate future, I was asked to photograph everything possible during the time I was scheduled to be there. I took candid party shots; separate, fairly formal portraits of everyone present; and even photographs of the new building in which the affair was being held. I took almost 200 photographs in all, under the direction of the person who had hired me. These photographs were filed in the form of contact sheets, 36 frames to every 8" x 10" contact. Only 12 of the pictures were actually printed at the time.

During the next two years more than 100 of the photographs I had taken were ordered at various times from the contacts. Some of these were formal studies I had made. Such prints were mounted and used for special displays and/or promotions. Everyone in attendance was fairly wealthy and prominent in the community. The organization knew that using their pictures from time to time in newsletters and displays would insure and perhaps increase donations to the cause the following year.

The advantage to the follow-up orders was that the organization was only charged the price for making each print. Had I not taken so many photographs the night of the party, I would have had to be brought in to take the necessary pictures on special orders. This would have meant additional hourly charges that the organization could not afford. By taking advantage of my time and utilizing me to the fullest with the first assignment, a major expense was saved.

What types of photographs are effective? Anything with human interest that explains your work. Suppose you are promoting a hospital that has just added a new wing. Showing a photograph of the building may indicate where the money was spent, but showing a patient being treated in the wing will involve the donor's self-interest. After all, the donor or a loved one could need emergency treatment some day, and the photograph of the patient shows that by making a contribution that treatment will always be available in the community.

Use photographs that are taken in close. If the picture is going to be printed fairly small, do not try to show masses of people or vast expanses of space. Both will disappear in the tiny image. The strongest effect comes from tight photographs showing one or two people at the most. A picture showing a crippled child moving slowly towards a therapist during treatment has far more impact than a picture showing all the crippled children an organization has helped in the past year.

Normally photographs will not be taken in color. The cost is prohibitive for most budgets and the impact of black-and-white can be just as great. However, if there is some reason for taking color photographs, have the photographer use color negative film. This can be made into slides, color prints, or black-and-white prints. With the negatives on file, you will always have a choice as to the type of material you can use for any given occasion.

There is one condition under which you might consider having the photographer use color negative film exclusively. If the speaker's bureau has people who like to give audiovisual presentations, the photographer can prepare color slides from the negatives. Then the work that is shown in black-and-white in the brochures can be used in color to illustrate talks to the community. You get additional mileage for minimal expense.

The brochure's copy must be clear and appealing. You must be careful to state the problem with which the organization is involved. This might be providing health care to the poor, aiding missionaries overseas, fighting a disease such as cancer, or any number of other areas.

Next discuss what is being done to solve the problem. Talk about the research, outreach programs, crisis centers, or whatever fits your particular organization.

This is followed by information on what needs to be done in the field and what your organization is planning to do. This might mean a continuation or expansion of existing services. Or it might mean something far more ambitious—perhaps a building program or an all-out research effort against a disease.

Why will your organization be able to accomplish its stated objectives? No matter how famous your group, people may still know very little about what you do, who is on your staff, and what you have accomplished in the past. Explain your community involvement and the success you have achieved in the past.

Finally get to the financial aspects of the campaign. Explain what it will cost to accomplish your goals. Then tell what individual contributions will mean toward reaching this goal. Give different dollar amounts and explain what they will buy. A person may feel that if he can only afford $5 it is such a tiny part of a multimillion dollar research program that he might as well not send anything. If you can show him that the $5 can buy a specific, needed laboratory item, for example, his contribution will suddenly have tangible value. He will be proud to donate the $5 rather than feeling it is a waste of effort.

Tell the person exactly how to send the money to you. Is there a pledge to be mailed in a donor envelope? Is there a card to be checked asking a volunteer to stop by? Is there a space for marking monthly contributions for which the person will be billed? Can credit cards be used to meet the obligation? Such card use can increase a donation greatly, so be certain to include this information if it is relevant. You always want to make contributing to your cause as simple as possible to ensure the greatest number of donors.

The mail must continue to be used even after the donor has made a contribution. First a letter of thanks must be sent. This should be simple but sincere, perhaps signed by the head of the organization.

Next, the donor's name and address should go on a list used for distributing regular newsletters throughout the year. The person must be made to feel a part of your organization regardless of the size of the contribution. The person who feels he or she belongs is going to be more generous in the future.

The second fund-raising campaign is a critical one. If your efforts have been successful, you will receive another contribution. You might use your normal mailing pieces for new potential contributors and for those you hope will repeat. Or you might send your former contributors a personalized mailing mentioning their previous pledges and discussing the rising expenses due to inflation and/or expanded programs. Encourage the person to give more, perhaps by explaining again what increased dollar amounts will mean. If the person gave $10 last year, you might say something like: "If you give just $5 more than last year, you will have paid for a week's camping experience for an inner-city youngster." Just be certain you never give the potential donor the impression that the previous gift was inadequate or ridiculously low. Conveying such an attitude will cause him to disregard further fund-raising efforts.

When you work to upgrade a donor, be certain your suggested increase is realistic. It is one thing to ask a $25 donor to give $35. The difference in the amount is not overwhelming. Even if the donor feels $35 is too much, he might be willing to send $30. It is quite another matter to ask that $25 donor to send $100. The request will be so high that the person will most likely send nothing.

Be wary of making suggested donations such as, "Please send just $5 to help our cause." Unlike a chart listing different size donations and what they mean to the organization, the suggested donation limits the contribution in the mind of the potential donor. If you say to send $5, the person will send that amount. The fact that the person might be quite happy to send $10 or more is irrelevant. If you ask for a specific figure, few people are going to think to upgrade it to anything higher. It is usually best either to give no set dollar amount or a list of what specific dollar amounts will accomplish to help the person make up his mind.

Testing methods for direct mail sales are equally valid for direct mail fund raising. You want to create the most effective promotion piece you can without going to great expense or giving the appearance that you went to great expense. Vary the layout. Vary the way you make the appeal. Vary the use of photographs. If you feel that testing through actual use will be too costly or impractical, put together alternative approaches and show them to your staff, volunteers, or even people in shopping centers.

Some nonprofit organizations use a letter writing approach to solicitation. Sometimes the letter is sent to selected community leaders. Sometimes the letter goes to a list of thousands of names. However it is done, there are several points to follow in order to ensure its success.

First be certain that the letter is exactly that—a letter. Write in a personal style that is quite different from the way you would word a brochure. A letter must be warm and sincere. It must convey an attitude of two people talking together even when it is mass produced.

The letter's length should be dictated by the subject matter. Use clear, concise sentences and reasonably short paragraphs, although the letter itself can run on for several pages. Take as much space as you need to tell your organization's story. If you can do it on a single page, fine. But if it takes several pages of type, that's all right, too.

Be careful not to try to impress people with your vocabulary or with numerous "in" terms for your organization. Write so the average person can understand what you are saying. A medical organization can discuss a disease without relying upon highly technical terminology, for example.

If you use letters to keep in touch with contributors between campaigns always make the letters tell something new. One excellent approach is to discuss a particular person who benefited by the organization since the last letter. Human interest stories have tremendous appeal.

When you want the person to make a contribution or become involved in some way, make this position clear. However, do not ask the person to do something every time you write. Convey the impression that the person is a valued friend you wish to keep informed. Otherwise your appeals for money will be ignored.

Experiment with sending financial appeals at different times of the year. Supposedly there are seasons when people are more likely to donate money. One expert thinks that November and January are among the best months, for example, though whether or not there is any proof of this is subject to question. All that is certain is that everyone who solicits funds by direct mail finds that there are good and bad periods. By experimenting with the timing of your appeal you will find times that are best for your group.

Perhaps the best promoters of any nonprofit or charitable organization are the staff members who are usually overlooked. Too many promotions take staff members for granted. It is assumed that a staff member will be enthusiastic about the organizatoin, but you can never assume anything about your staff. If you do not make an effort to bolster the ego of employees, as you do for volunteers, they will be neither effective workers nor of value in gaining new funds.

Try to involve the staff members in the fund-raising campaign. Discuss what you are trying to do and why. Often staff members get so involved with just one or two aspects of an organization that they have no broad concept of what the campaign is all about. By explaining the group to staffers as you might to those outside the organization, you will promote better understanding and more of a team spirit.

Ask staff members for suggestions as to who should be added to mailing lists and how to better reach the public. Encourage them to suggest new approaches to fund raising and ask them if there are things that should be dropped. Often staff members are aware of problems in community relations but do not bother mentioning them until they are asked.

Assign each staff member, and each volunteer for that matter, a specific task for the fund-raising campaign. People are more enthusiastic when they must face a known task instead of just having to fill in here and there with whatever has to be done. A specific job can be a challenge they enjoy meeting.

In addition to the newsletter periodically sent to contributors, prepare a simple information sheet for the staff. This can be one page without illustrations or it might be as many as four pages with a few black-and-white illustrations to give it more interest. The information sheet will discuss the organization's activities, suggestions that have been made for improving or adding programs, and the names of staff members making the proposals. Try to use the names of as many staff members as possible, discussing briefly what they are doing. Be certain that everyone receives a mention at least once during the course of putting out two or three newsletters. Personal mention is a job bonus that cannot be matched by extra pay. It can greatly strengthen morale and improve your organization's productivity.

When you are ready to begin dealing with the news media, it is important that you have a comprehensive plan in mind. You must have specific goals as well as an idea of how you wish to achieve them.

For example, suppose your job is to promote the United Way campaign. Your ultimate goal is to gain cash contributions, but in order to do this you must acquaint the public with the work of the various agencies involved.

Start by analyzing the different member groups and which segment of the public might be interested in helping them. Crisis centers, VD clinics, and similar health programs primarily serve young adults. Although parents may be interested in such programs, people in their teens and early twenties are your prime target. Thus radio stations and television programs that are meant for this group will also be interested in hearing about your agency's work in this field.

Programs specifically for the aged have an appeal for the elderly but also for middle-aged people. Adults in their forties and fifties are likely to have parents in need of nursing services, extended care health facilities, and similar programs. Radio and television programs that reach this audience will be good targets for discussing the agencies that relate to these areas.

Youth programs such as the Scouting movement are of interest to parents and religious groups. Sunday programming on most radio and many television stations may have room for the mention of these areas of community service.

Next find out the different radio and television stations that have live programming. In some communities only the news is locally produced for television. All other programs originate from the networks or are purchased in syndication.

In other communities there are one or more original television programs, often of the variety or interview type. Such shows are in constant need of new faces and welcome hearing from all segments of the community.

If your community has stations that have no local television programs, you may be able to work through the news director. Is your organization involved with work that would be of community interest? If not, is there some aspect of the work, or even an individual employee, volunteer or service user whose story would be of general interest? In one hospital near my home, for example, a volunteer in the rehabilitation department is a former gymnast, now confined to a wheelchair due to illness. However, she not only helps others in the hospital, she teaches gymnastics from her home. This girl's dramatic story is excellent material for a short news feature on any station, including one that would not otherwise mention the hospital or its work. Such a story, if brought to the news director's attention during a fund-raising campaign, will result in excellent free promotion that personalizes the hospital and makes contributing money to it seem desirable.

Whenever you contact a news director keep in mind that whatever you mention will have to be news. Most stations are not going to just mention that you are trying to raise money. Nor will your fund raising be of general interest. It is only when there is a potential story in your activities or your staff that you are going to have a chance to get on the air.

A station that has one or more live programs is often a little more flexible. If your organization is important, there is a good chance that a representative will be asked to appear to talk with the host. Again a fairly broad area of interest to the community is important, but you will not need to come up with so dramatic an approach as for news. For example, the United Way campaign promotion director might be asked to appear and discuss the various member agencies and what they do. This same person would only get on a news show if he or she could discuss one aspect of the campaign that is of vital community importance or of general human interest. News shows would not just talk about the fact that the campaign is going on and what the members do. That would not be considered "news."

Radio stations are far more flexible than television stations. Most radio programming is "live." Only a limited number of stations are automated to the point where almost all air time is pretaped. The rest utilize on-air personalities to provide news, commentary, and whatever programming other than musical segments the station happens to offer. Since radio stations generally operate on either a sunrise to sunset or 24-hour basis, seven days a week, this leaves a lot of air time to fill up. Thus the stations are always anxious to work with community organizations attempting to publicize themselves.

The radio station contact for a nonprofit or charitable organization is the program director. This is the person responsible for what goes on the air. The program director can either assign an on-air personality to work with your group or can refer you to the person at the station who is charged with developing public service programs.

In general, radio stations will offer to interview an organization representative. This will either be done during a regularly scheduled broadcast, usually in the "housewife" segment between morning and afternoon drive times, or during periods when public service programs are specifically used. Usually this latter time is a slow period on Saturday or Sunday when religious programs are also broadcast. Remember that radio stations must do community service programs but they have great flexibility about when they put them on. Most stations prefer to bury them during slow periods when advertising revenue is always low.

Occasionally your organization will be allowed to prepare its own program. You will be given from five to thirty minutes, including commercial breaks, to present your message.

If you are allowed to present your own program, you must plan what you do with extreme care. Unless one or more people on your staff has training in radio, your show could be a disaster. Ask the station if there is a staff person who could assist you. Often a producer or one of the on-air personalities will be provided. If that fails, see if you can locate either an instructor in broadcasting from a nearby college or an on-air personality from a different station who will be willing to help you. Hire someone to assist only as a last resort. But always use professional assistance.

With short programs of just a few minutes you are best off staying with just one small area of your organization's work. An interview approach is usually best. There is a moderator and at least one other person. Perhaps this will be the director of the operation or agency affiliate you are discussing. Or you might have an interview with one or two people who were assisted. An interview with a couple who had successfully received family counseling from a nonprofit organization would have dramatic appeal, for example.

Longer programs can present a cross section of information. In the case of a multiagency appeal such as the United Way, several different member agencies might have satisfied clients tell their stories.

Every program should stress the community service aspects of the organization. Information should be provided to let the public know how they can take advantage of what is being discussed. The mention of the campaign drive should be a secondary aspect of the program. The program must remain informational, not a plea for funds. You want to fully acquaint the public with your organization so when a direct mail and/or personal solicitation campaign is begun, the public will be familiar with what you are doing.

It is a good idea to try to have year-round contact with various radio stations serving your area. You will want to use the radio programs to provide an update of what you are doing just as you use your newsletter to keep in contact with contributors. If you can arrange to appear on a program once a month or even more frequently, each time talking about something different, it will make your next campaign that much easier. You might even use different staff members to add variety to the appearances. Just be certain you only select people who are familiar with the topic to be discussed and who are capable of speaking clearly and in an interesting manner.

Before appearing on a radio program, prepare notes on the topics you would like to discuss. You might even prepare a list of possible questions for the person who will be conducting the interview. Use the press kit you prepared to refresh your memory concerning the general history of the organization as well. It would be wise to carry a list of donation sizes and what they can purchase in case you are asked about giving.

Arrive at the station early. Take a drink before going on the air. If your throat has a tendency to get dry, you might want to bring a Thermos with coffee or water unless the station can provide something to drink during the program. Sucking on a mint helps, but avoid chewing gum.

If you do a regular program, have a tape recording made of each segment. These can be used to convince other stations to let you appear; or, if you are part of a national organization, other chapters can utilize the material in their areas.

Should you write a script for a short program, do not time it too closely. Be prepared to cut your remarks short or to spread them out to fill additional time. Always be familiar with far more material than you think you can use so you do not have to fill remaining air time with meaningless talk.

Newspapers can be used in a variety of ways, depending upon your specific organization. Most newspapers have specialists on their staffs. One person handles religious organization news, for example. Another might handle subjects relating to science. In larger cities there may be a specialist on housing and urban renewal or on labor relations. This person may have several other assignments as well. However, all matters relating to the person's specialty are assigned to that reporter automatically.

If your agency or organization falls into a specific category such as health care, call the newspaper during a slow period and find out who normally handles news relating to your field. If it does not relate to a specific reporter's assignment, your best approach is to work through the city editor who will assign someone to work with you.

Newspapers desire several types of articles. They want specific information about fund-raising efforts that will receive limited space inside the paper. Sometimes the information will be part of a calendar of events affecting your community. Other times it will be a small news item buried wherever there is room.

The newspaper will desire news stories about your organization. This may include such topics as a new construction project, a research grant received by the staff, or anything else that fits into the news category.

Finally, the newspaper will want feature stories. These are generally personality pieces such as the one about the crippled hospital volunteer who teaches gymnastics.

Earlier in the book I discussed working with newspapers and the preparation of news releases. The information is identical for the nonprofit organization. News releases will be used for such items as the dates of a fund-raising campaign and general information about grants and similar events that fall into the news category. You may also hold a press conference for such announcements as discussed earlier.

In the case of feature stories you will want to make personal contact with the appropriate writer or editor. Your first step in obtaining a feature story is to find feature material. Often your staff and volunteers can help you. If the story is something with which they are personally involved, internal relations will be greatly improved by letting the person talk with the reporter.

The ideal feature story is about a person helped in some way by your organization. You are trying to gain support so it is always beneficial to show the results of the work you do.

Next in value is a feature on a staff person or volunteer who brings unusual talent or circumstances to the job. An organization aiding the handicapped might have a young teacher who is also handicapped, perhaps originally trained at the school and now taking an active role helping others. Or perhaps a staff member is a talented magician who uses his magic to help reach emotionally disturbed children.

Finally there are the feature stories that get your organization's name in the paper but do not promote its work. The story might be on the wood-carving skills of one of the teachers, for example. Or a teacher who is a prize-winning pastry chef in his spare time. The talents are seldom if ever used in relation to the person's job so the organization mention will be secondary.

A newspaper reporter is going to want to write the feature story but you can assist in gathering information. Prepare a fact sheet that gives the name of the person under discussion, the person's job, and full background information. Include family members, activities in the community, and an overall profile. Put down the full name, address, and telephone number of every person who can provide additional information. Naturally include your name and telephone number as well. Such background sheets make a reporter's life less difficult and make the reporter interested in receiving other story ideas from you in the future.

Feature stories must be exclusives to the media in which they are offered. If there are two or more newspapers in your area, only one should be given the information for a feature story. You can give the same feature to the paper's rival only after you are informed by the first that nothing is going to be done with it. Naturally you should alternate between two papers when passing out feature ideas to assure continued coverage from both publications.

You might wish to cross media, however. You can offer a feature to the newspaper and the same feature to a television station, for example. If the story if visual, such as the one about the therapist who uses magic, there might be a one- or two-minute spot for it on the evening news.

Always remember the limitations of the news media. Newspapers and magazines can use almost any story. Television wants features with visual appeal and radio needs features that can be told entirely with sound.

Your media appearances are often aided by making a newspaper, radio and/or television executive one of the chairpersons for your fund-raising drive. When you have one or more members of the news media taking an active role in the campaign, you can bet that coverage will be extensive.

Some newspapers will be receptive to your running a daily article on the work of an important agency having a fund-raising drive during the period when money is being collected. In the case of the United Way, each day's story might discuss a different member agency. The article might be a short history or, preferably, a short feature story about a person or family helped by that member agency.

One of the most effective human interest campaigns is put on annually by the *New York Times*. Each day during the Christmas season the newspaper writes about one of the city's 100 neediest families, telling the family background, troubles, and needs. These articles invariably bring a tremendous outpouring of money, goods, and services from the readers. It would be impossible to achieve the same reaction if the promotion were limited to a bland announcement of a fund-raising drive to help poor families.

When it comes to receiving publicity in magazines, you must approach them as you would when trying to get free mention of a product. If your program has an importance to their readers, you are quite likely to get a write-up. However, remember magazine lead times. If there are local or national magazines that could be beneficial to your organization, be certain to contact them far enough in advance—as much as three to four months for monthlies—so that the story will appear during the period of the campaign.

It is essential that you develop a media list that you regularly update. The list will give the names and addresses of the different segments of the news media that can be beneficial to your organization. It will include the names and telephone numbers of the prime people at the stations or papers as well. You will note program directors, editors, publishers, feature writers, columnists, and others. After a while, as you get to know the people with whom you have to work, you should make notations as to their likes and dislikes in copy style and types of features. Many writers prefer to specialize. If they are not interested in the area you need to promote, they won't bother using your story even if the paper's editor would be receptive. (This is assuming you contacted the reporter directly and did not go through the editor. A reporter who refuses an editor's assignment will likely become unemployed.) Under such circumstances it is best to give the story to the person most likely to use it.

Nonprofit and charitable organizations, more than businesses, need the goodwill of the members of the news media who write about them. A business can afford to advertise regularly, countering any adverse information that may appear. A nonprofit group cannot afford to spend that kind of money.

One approach to keeping the news media happy is to have periodic background days when the press is invited to have simple refreshments and an update on what the organization is doing. Food served will include coffee and tea and cookies and/or cake, preferably prepared by volunteers. Expense must be minimal.

Press kits should be available during the background days. These will give the organization's history, its executives, and names and numbers to contact, as described earlier. There will also be a special release detailing the information being imparted at the meeting. Be certain that this kit is mailed or delivered to anyone on your media list who was unable to attend.

The telephone can be an effective means for promoting your organization but great care must be used when planning for telephone solicitation. First, be certain you can use volunteers who will work from home. The cost for installing a bank of telephones is prohibitive.

Be certain that the number of names each volunteer must call is limited. You do not want to overwhelm anyone with work, or you may find that the people call no one. Keep the size workable, such as 10 names a day.

Have an in-depth briefing for everyone who will be calling. It is a good idea to have a role playing demonstration with toy telephones in which you play the part of the person being called. Let some of the volunteers try to get your contribution and analyze the approaches used. How a caller handles himself will determine whether or not a contribution is made. Role playing helps everyone spot problem areas before they affect the success of the campaign.

Be certain the volunteers have a list of points to cover when making their calls, but keep the lists abbreviated enough so that no one can just read off what is on the paper. A list might include points such as: 1) Make mention of building program. 2) Make mention of research grant. The person knows what to talk about but how it is discussed is left to the caller's own style. There is nothing worse than having to listen to someone read a prepared speech. It is annoying and may make your potential donor somewhat hostile.

## Special Nonprofit Organization Promotion Problems

### The Religious Group

A religious organization has two types of promotions possible at any given moment. One is the promotion of the church or synagogue to the membership. At a time when there is a decline in religious activity, it is important to be able to communicate effectively with the members in order to keep them active and happy.

The other is the promotion of the church or synagogue to the general public. It is important for the community at large to understand what religious groups are doing and how their activities might affect the lives of nonmembers. Sometimes this is just to promote good relations between the church and the community. Other times it is to try and bring people to worship who might otherwise not attend services anywhere.

Church members are best reached through direct mail. The bulletin or newsletter, mailed on a regular basis, is essential. In it you should provide not only church news but information of interest to members of the congregation. Try to include members' names and stress that anyone who has information of interest to other members should contact whoever is in charge of the bulletin. Getting one's name mentioned is as important in the bulletin as it is with volunteers for a charitable group.

Try to learn which members of your religious group have special skills. There may be advanced amateur or professional photographers who will donate some of their time and skill to church needs. All work is done at cost, providing you with a way to liven the bulletin.

Most religious group news is handled by reporters specifically assigned to this area. Most newspapers have a section for religious news, generally either on Saturday or Sunday, and radio stations usually devote a segment of their Sunday programming to religion. Learn who handles these areas and direct your promotions to them.

What types of promotional material will interest the general public? Releases can cover news of unusual people connected with the church. Is there a lay leader who is an ex-convict? Is there a Sunday School teacher who uses puppetry to teach about the Bible? Does the religious leader have an unusual hobby or did he or she have an unusual job prior to entering the clergy? Is the clergyman doing double duty as a police counselor, parole officer, or some other "civilian" job? Anything that is unusual and interesting will probably warrant feature coverage.

Normal church and synagogue news is not of particular interest but stay alert to anniversaries of the religious organization's building or existence in the community and to other items of historical or community interest. Fund-raising drives for special projects that can be used by everyone, regardless of affiliation, are also of interest. A community day care center or drug abuse center, for example, will be given space to help the promotion.

Whenever there are special honors bestowed upon members of the congregation, a release concerning them should go to the religion editors. If the individuals honored are well-known for their normal activities, such as the head of a corporation becoming president of the congregation, a release might be sent to the business page editor or one of the columnists.

Having members mentioned in the local papers does little for building membership. However, it does help to retain members who are vain enough to delight in the write-ups.

You might want to talk with the religious page editor or the managing editor about producing a multiarticle feature entitled "Know Your Religions." This would be a project of your religious organization and the many different groups in your area. A representative of each segment of religious thought would write a brief history of the group and its beliefs. The articles would be designed to acquaint the public with the diverse groups in even small communities. It would be best to have the article signed by your clergyman.

Try to have special celebrations open to the general public. In past years many Episcopal churches celebrated folk masses and rock masses as special events designed to increase youth participation. Such events are of interest to the community at large and should be open to the public. A press release about them, sent well in advance, should get you publicity and perhaps even a photographer to cover the event as a news story.

The lead time for getting material to a newspaper's religion editor varies. However, the religion pages are generally planned well in advance. Usually you must be at least a week ahead in your publicity and some papers want releases sent 10 days to two weeks before they will actually appear.

Keep abreast of the periodicals relating to your church or synagogue affiliation. News of interest to others of your faith, though not to the public at large, should be sent to these publications. Feature items can also be used here, so do not overlook this avenue for group promotion.

*The Crisis Situation*

Any organization dependent upon voluntary contributions for money cannot stand too much adverse criticism. Unfortunately crises do occur and a promotion department caught unprepared is going to have months or years of carefully nurtured community relations go down the drain.

Perhaps the crisis will be a campus upheaval such as were so common in the 1960s. Or perhaps two factions of a religious group will clash over the hiring of a clergyman or the Sunday School curriculum. There may even be picketing or other visible forms of protest.

Sometimes the crisis does not reflect upon the group at all. Sometimes the crisis is one to which the organization must respond. For example, an earthquake occurs and the Red Cross must send relief workers, food, clothing, and other items to help the people caught in the destruction. In order for the group to function effectively, donations are needed from the public at large. There is no time to plan a special campaign. The money and supplies are needed immediately.

The best way to handle a crisis is with advanced planning. Sit down with the staff of your organization and discuss the types of problems that can arise. If the crisis is something that can happen to your group, such as student riots, you will need one course of action. If the crisis is something for which you will need public funds, you will take a slightly different course of action.

When your organization is faced with a problem that affects it directly, it is essential that you be willing to discuss it openly and honestly. You will only arouse hostility from members of the press if you try to play down an incident or, worse, not admit that it exists.

As soon as a crisis occurs, call a press conference in a location that is most convenient for everyone. Usually this will be at the site of the news event, but it might be in a nearby hotel or other location. Have an important representative of your organization, preferably the president, explain what is happening in detail. Be completely honest and, if there are areas that you do not want published, explain what they are and why silence would be appreciated. Most reporters are extremely cooperative so long as they understand your reasons.

Next allow the reporters to question you. Answer questions to the best of your knowledge. If there is something you cannot answer for the moment, either because you do not yet have the answer or because the issue is too sensitive to discuss, promise you will answer it at a later time. Make a note of what the question is and get word of the answer to all members of the press as soon as possible. Once reporters know you will eventually provide all answers, they will be extremely cooperative.

Do not look upon the press as your enemy. Reporters are just doing their job—reporting the news. Certainly the crisis you face is liable to be embarrassing. But it will soon be over and the public will have other events to occupy its mind. If you have been open and fair with the reporters, future stories will be favorable enough to let the crisis be buried and forgotten. However, if you approach the press with a chip on your shoulder, the reporters may be somewhat hostile in print. Or worse, they might ignore your group altogether. Such a reaction may not seem fair, but it is only human.

Provide regular updates to the press as the crisis runs its course. Try to arrange for reporters to meet with the principals involved in the trouble. The greater your cooperation, the more sympathetic the response will be.

If your organization assists others during periods of crisis, your problem will be to acquaint the public with what has happened and how it can help. Once again press conferences must be called and all details provided. Be certain to tell the scope of the problem, what your agency's role will be, and exactly what money and/or supplies will be needed.

Prior to the crisis you must talk with area banks and the owner of buildings with storage areas you might be able to use. Find officials who will agree to cooperate with you. For example, locate a bank executive who is willing to let his institution serve as the clearinghouse for financial contributions. Obtain an address where the public can be told to mail checks and be certain to get the names of officials who are to be contacted when the crisis occurs. You will need to alert the bank immediately, day or night, so you can tell the reporters where people should send their contributions. Your headquarters can also serve as a collection point, but a bank has the double advantage of security and branches around town where people can conveniently drop off a donation.

Schools, warehouses, and other buildings often have areas they will donate for the temporary storage of clothing, food, and other items during an emergency collection drive. Again you will need to know these places in advance. Have addresses you can give out and telephone numbers of people to call when the crisis strikes. You will want the public to be able to go to the collection points first thing in the morning. Some buildings might normally be closed so you want to be certain you have the names of people to notify of the impending collection.

Many times the news media will want to go to the disaster scene for coverage. In some cases they will desire to ride with relief workers. Plans should be made for assisting the press in reaching the area and in helping them when they arrive. Reporters and photographers may be somewhat of a nuisance to relief workers, but their coverage is going to give the public the best possible understanding of what is happening. It is better to plan on helping them than to risk losing even a portion of that much needed coverage.

When several people must be contacted at the same time, names should be divided among the staff members who will be on call. Each person is given a limited number of people to locate. In this way information can be given to everyone at about the same time. This enables the news media to tell the public what is happening at about the same time.

Once again try to get reporters in contact with principals involved with the crisis. In the case of a disaster, the workers probably will not be able to talk to reporters until basic rescue work has been completed. However, as soon as they can be spared for a few moments it is a good idea to allow reporters a short question period.

The period immediately following a crisis is a good time for the organization that provided relief to seek additional funds. The work of the organization is fresh in the public's mind. The news media has provided information and publicity you could not begin to buy.

The appeal for funds can be handled in several ways. The least satisfactory method may be through the use of volunteer collectors, primarily because of the time necessary to organize them. Unless you have a group of people on whom you can rely at the moment, you will be far better off selecting a different approach.

Perhaps the best method when time is a factor is to combine a direct mail campaign with additional newspaper publicity. Try to obtain disaster photographs from the news media and print them together with a small brochure describing the relief work just accomplished and the fact that existing resources were greatly depleted and that money is needed. Discuss what the various contributions will mean and include an envelope for mailing a donation.

At the same time that the direct mail campaign is being conducted, contact the local news media. Explain the situation in a press release, again accompanied by photographs, and say that you are seeking contributions from the general public. Provide an address where people can send their donations and a telephone number the public can call for further information. At such times the cooperation of the news media is usually extensive and you will get far more publicity than during the regular, annual period of fund raising.

# 8

# The Window Display

Seymour Sugarloaf wanted to attract more customers to his store, Seymour's Funky Fashions, located in the Lucky Pot-O-Gold Shopping Center. He hired a local rock group, The Electric Steam Engine, and had them play their music in the window of his store. More than 2,000 young people flocked to the shopping center for the free concert. They filled the mall area in front of his store, gyrating their bodies in time to the music. For hours they blocked aisles, disrupted area businesses, and caused mass confusion. Unfortunately, when the promotion was over, only three people had bothered to come inside the store.

Wanda Wishbone wanted to attract more people to her candy store, Wanda's Sweet Shoppe. She decided to combine the making of candy and the new sexual freedom by having a naked model decorate various sugar concoctions in the display window. Within 10 minutes 500 people had gathered to watch, 15 cars had smashed into each other, and the police riot squad arrived. Only quick thinking on the part of the model saved her from being arrested for indecent exposure. As she heard the approaching sirens she leaped into a vat of chocolate, completely encasing her body in a thin candy shell. When the crowds cleared away Wanda was presented a bill for $25,000 in damages. No one had come inside to make a purchase.

These slightly exaggerated examples relate the problems that can arise with the use of window displays as promotion vehicles. Too often the store owners are so concerned with attracting attention that they create a display that draws comments rather than customers.

Window displays, for many store owners, are an important merchandising tool. Unfortunately this is a highly competitive type of promotion in major shopping areas because it is estimated that a strolling shopper passes five such display windows every minute. There must be a reason for a shopper to want to pause at any particular window. More important, once the person has stopped by the window, there must be an incentive to go inside.

Display window decorating, like television and radio advertising, is an art that must be learned. There are professional window decorators trained in all aspects of display. They are experts in creating effective visual impact and their knowledge should be utilized whenever possible. Department stores keep such people on their staffs. Smaller stores generally have to hire firms specializing in display productions in order to develop the most effective means of using windows.

It would be beyond the scope of this book to try and provide all the information needed for you to create a truly professional display. However, this chapter will cover various fairly simple ideas that are effective and easy to produce with limited knowledge.

There are several basic rules for the preparation of window displays. The most important is: Design a display around the space you have available. Do not try to take a display concept and then adapt it to your space limitations. It will probably be either too cramped and crowded or it will have to be spread so thin the impact will be lost.

Keep the display simple. If you clutter the window with too much merchandise, nothing will get noticed. Remember that your window will have to attract passersby who might be 50 or 60 feet from your store. Unless merchandise has space around it and is readily visible from afar, people may not bother to come over.

Be certain your window display shows only what is in stock. If you show a dress, for example, you must have an ample supply of the dress in a variety of sizes. If your customer cannot buy the displayed item, he or she will feel misled, become angry, and probably will leave without making a purchase. The exception to the stock rule is when you have just two or three of an item left and you are anxious to be rid of it. Many businesses put the remaining stock in the window with a sign reading "Just These Three Left," along with the special discount price. Each time one is sold, it is taken from the window and the number on the sign is corrected.

Window displays generally have a set theme. They might be built around a particular line of fashion, for example. Or perhaps the display will show various models of one product such as pocket calculators. A drugstore might display sickroom supplies and a new bookstore might highlight the current selections on the best-seller list.

There are actually two types of window displays. The most common is commercial in nature. It presents products for sale. The purpose is to gain customers for the store and to boost revenue.

The second type of display is meant to enhance the store's image. It is what is known as an institutional display. For example, the store might have photographs of the different United Way member agencies and a sign asking for contributions. Or the display might promote the work of a local drug abuse treatment center. It might even highlight a local symphony orchestra or resident theatrical company. The display is meant to show community concern on the part of the business in order to enhance its reputation.

Window displays should be planned as carefully as a magazine advertisement. There must be a goal in mind and an image conveyed to the viewer.

For example, television spy shows were extremely popular a few years back. One large department store decided to promote its trench coats—symbols of adventure in the minds of many people. The store personnel created a window display that showed a man and woman, spies for opposite sides, both dressed in trench coats. The display window was designed to look like an office. The woman mannequin was sitting on a chair by the desk, her hands and feet tied and her mouth gagged as she stared helplessly at the male mannequin kneeling by the safe, turning the dial.

The spy display was not selling trench coats to the average customer, it was selling adventure. That was the theme of the window and the trench coat represented the means to the end. It proved extremely successful in bringing customers into the store to buy the coats.

Shoe stores seldom offer shoes. They offer comfort or style.

A store owner must carefully plan the elements of a display window regardless of who actually arranges the display. The product line to be promoted must be carefully considered. Sometimes the items chosen are part of a current fad, such as shell necklaces. Other times they represent the new line of a particular designer whose work is carried. Still other times slow-moving merchandise is shown and discounted.

Once the items are selected, the sales staff must be made aware of what is going into the window. Nothing is worse than for a customer to come inside, ask to see an item similar to one on display, and have the salesperson not know what is meant.

If the display merchandise is going to be discounted, be certain a list of the items and the sale price is near every cash register if the stock has not been premarked with the sale price. Customers become irate when they go to purchase a special sale item and the clerk writes up a bill for full retail.

There are probably as many opinions of what motivates customers as there are store owners. A Cleveland shoe store manager, for example, believes in filling the window with an example of every style of shoe the store has in stock. Anyone coming inside has been presold by the window and it is just a matter of producing the right size for the customer's foot. His store consistently does a high volume of business as a result.

A commercial photographer believes in showing all the services offered by the studio. The window includes examples of portraits, wedding photos, architectural and industrial photography, and even a special display showing the restoration of old, badly damaged family photos. The person passing by the window immediately sees the range of the photographer's skills.

A store selling glamour and figure-correcting clothing for women displays both slinky outfits for parties, lounging, and intimate moments as well as padded bras and similar nature "assisters." Women passing by know that the store is the place to go when they want to accentuate or add to what they've got.

A display window can use a gimmick to get people into the store. At Easter a huge jar might be filled with jelly beans. A sign invites the public inside to register their guess of how many beans are in the container. Theoretically, once inside the store, people will also look at the merchandise offered for sale.

Animated displays are quite popular, though the type of animation will determine the public response. Perhaps the most familiar is the animated Christmas display produced by many department stores. Figures dance and move about, sometimes showing various gift items available inside and other times just typifying the joy of Christmas. Often music is played through a loud speaker for people to enjoy as they look at the displays.

A second type of animation invites public participation. This is more elaborate and its effectiveness is dependent upon what controls the public really has.

For example, some displays are nothing more than darkened windows with several lights controlled by one or more buttons on the outside. When someone pushes the buttons, lights illuminate the display in sequence. Sometimes a tape recorded message is heard as well. Such displays hold little interest and people move on quickly.

Far more effective animated displays have the audience control a variety of activities. One popular display tried by a department store selling precision instruments was a weather gauge. By pushing different buttons, various instruments went into operation measuring temperature, wind velocity, and related conditions. The dials returned to zero when the buttons were released so that each person could feel in full control of what was happening.

A hobby store had an elaborate HO train layout, complete with operating equipment, all controlled by buttons on the outside of the window. Depending upon the button pushed, one or more trains were activated, as were crossing gates, special lights, and a variety of other mechanical devices. The public was fascinated by the display and many people came in to buy.

Window displays are meant to bring people inside, entertain them (Christmas windows), or provide information. The display is successful only when the goal you set is achieved.

One of the best ways to dramatize a product in a window is to surround it in black. This is frequently done for jewelry but is effective with almost anything.

To accomplish the black display, seal off the window area. This can easily be done by dropping a black cloth from floor to ceiling. All black paint and materials used should be matte finish rather than glossy. Black velvet is extremely effective and you can use a matte black paint as well. Display stands should be covered in black. Black thread and black wire can be used to suspend objects from the ceiling. The thread, stands, and other holders, when covered with black, tend to recede and blend into the black of the background.

Next, light the objects with bright spotlights, high intensity bulbs, or other forms of pinpoint illumination. An unusually dramatic effect can be achieved with the use of ultraviolet light. However, this will alter the colors of the objects being displayed. Be certain to study the objects under such a light before using it. There is a chance that the alteration in coloring will be grotesque rather than dramatic.

Every display must call attention to the objects shown, not the way they are presented. People must not be able to say, "Oh, look how cleverly the stand has been covered with black so the jewelry seems to be standing in midair." Instead they should be saying, "Isn't that watch magnificent? Let's go inside and see what it costs."

You can reduce the chance of someone studying the construction of an all black display by using tinted glass and arranging it so the viewer is a slight distance away. Too much light striking the display will reveal some of the methods used. Keeping people slightly away will add to the illusion of depth.

Signs and posters are to be avoided or kept to a minimum. Large paintings or immense photographic blowups, including grainy photos, can make excellent backgrounds, however. They are excellent eye-catchers across the room.

Audiovisual tools can be used to enhance your display. Slide projectors using circular trays can be set to endlessly repeat a showing of up to 80 different slides. The images are projected through a screen from the rear. Material for such a screen can be ordered through almost any large photographic equipment store.

The public is fascinated by constantly changing photographs. The slides might show a designer's complete fashion line, for example, when otherwise only one or two outfits would be able to be shown in the window space. Or the slides might show exotic settings designed to enhance the product displayed in front of the screen.

Motion pictures can be presented in a similar way. Several audiovisual equipment manufacturers now offer special television-size players in which you insert a Super 8 film cartridge and continuously play the film contained on it. Your display can be effective with little more than the projection screen visible to passersby who can watch the animated sales message.

Sound can be transmitted through a separate speaker suspended above the window or door of your business. Be certain the sound is kept low enough so that it doesn't interfere with a competitor's display or the "canned" music piped through most shopping centers. You are not trying to impress people with the loudness of your message. You are trying to get them inside to buy merchandise.

Film and slides are especially helpful for stores selling high-priced items that are best kept in vaults. Rare, valuable coins, heirloom jewelry, and similar items can be photographed and shown in full color on the screen.

Commercial photographers can easily handle the photography involved. Often, when film is to be used, the same firm that produces the television commercials also uses some of the footage for a cartridge film to be run in the window. The film is reduced from the 16mm normally used for commercials to the Super 8mm normally used for viewing units. This is done by a motion picture processing lab and is inexpensive. By having the footage taken at the same time that a commercial is being filmed, you reduce the hourly fees you must pay and keep costs to a minimum.

At this writing a variety of manufacturers are selling video disc players. These are similar to the records used on phonographs, except they send both a picture and sound through an attached television set. Some companies, mostly in larger cities, are encouraging the use of this equipment for window displays. They are dramatic but they must not be utilized at the moment.

The current state of video discs is somewhat like the state of home videotape recorders discussed earlier. The units are not standardized. Each manufacturer has a unique approach that is not compatible with other units. Therefore, you could spend a thousand dollars or more for an elaborate piece of equipment that becomes obsolete and unusable in a year or two. Super 8 film has been around for several years and will continue to be for many more. You are wisest to stay with a projection system using this type of film.

Sometimes rear projection can add to a special effect. For example, suppose your window has a nostalgic theme. The projector might run slides or films of old-time street scenes, silent movies, or something else that is appropriate. Often your local historical society has old still photographs that you can rephotograph for making into slides. These will then be projected on the screen.

Stay conscious of the lettering size when you decide to use signs with your displays. Different sized letters must be used to attract passersby who are walking at different distances from your window. For example, if you want to catch the person who is as far away as 60 feet, the letters must be at least two inches high. On the other hand, someone standing eight feet from the sign can read ¼-inch letters. Any good sign painter can help you prepare a sign that will be most easily seen in the area where it is displayed.

The width of letters is also important. Generally they must be at least ¼-inch wide to be visible at 60 feet. Regardless of the lettering size used, the words must be spaced so that each line of lettering is separated from the next by a distance at least 1½ times the height of the individual letters.

Lighting can also be important. Most windows are illuminated by overhead lights that provide an even effect. You can create a silhouette effect by lighting the background quite intensely and not lighting the object being silhouetted.

A spotlight can create a flat lighting effect when striking a display object head on. If the spot is angled to the side, a shadow can be cast. Sidelighting can bring out the texture in linens and blankets or the facets of a gemstone. If you want to sidelight without worrying about shadow, let a second light illuminate the wall where the shadow would normally fall. Such a fill light will not detract from the texturing possible with the sidespot but will reduce or eliminate the shadow. Of course, if your background is black to begin with, the shadow will disappear by itself.

Experiment regularly with light. It can create a mood and enhance the objects displayed. You can also buy colored filters to place over the lights, further adding to the creative potential.

Some stores like to have live demonstrations going on in their display windows. This definitely has impact but it must be carefully planned. A demonstration must be fast paced. If someone is showing how to use various pans for cooking, no one is going to want to stand around for five minutes while one of the ingredients is being mixed. The person giving the demonstration should have several different stages of the ingredients so that the entire meal can be prepared quickly. The demonstrator only needs to say what would normally be done next. This keeps the pace rapid enough to retain the interest of the public.

Every live demonstration should be timed for repeating every 10 minutes. If it runs much longer people will lose interest. Some demonstrations call for a question and answer period. Once again the 10 minute rule should be retained so that the demonstration, questions, and answers are all handled in the allotted time.

Every window display should be photographed and full details of the promotion recorded. The written information, picture, and a record of how much merchandise was moved will all become a permanent file. Then, when you have made several window displays, you can compare the various designs and their results (be sure to include the date so you can allow for seasonal shopping variations).

If you use professional window designers, record the name of the individual who designed each display. You may find that one designer's ideas consistently get better results than others.

Stay alert to the displays others are using. Roughly sketch or photograph anything that has unusual appeal or seems to be drawing an abnormally large response. You may want to imitate the technique at a later date.

Use mannequins freely if your display lends itself to their use. It humanizes the window and has a greater appeal for the public than when merchandise is shown alone. Flowers, dried leaves, and other "natural" items also have strong appeal.

Many times manufacturers can supply display ideas for you to use. They research the best ways to display their products and may offer retailer assistance in this area. It is worth contacting the company to find out.

Be careful about materials used for display. Fire retardant fabric and paper are preferable. They are a "must" when floodlights will be used close enough to generate fairly high heat.

Wiring to the window should be checked. You should not run an extension cord across the showroom floor to the window to power lights or mechanical devices. Instead run the cord along the wall where no one can trip over it. Most hardware stores sell holders for keeping the cord flush with the wall. If the display area will require extension cords on a regular basis, investigate the cost of having it specially wired to eliminate this problem.

You must be security conscious when planning window displays. Everyone knows about the use of special glass and/or sensing tape alarm systems to protect you from someone smashing through to get the merchandise. However, if the window is not sealed in back, there is a chance that someone could step inside the store, grab an item on display, and rush back out. I once witnessed just such a theft in a camera store. The thief's haul retailed for more than $500. Even a drop cloth over the back would have discouraged such an action.

Ideally the window will be sealed in back with a locked door for access. If you regularly display small, easily taken items, it may be worth the cost of having a carpenter seal off the back for you.

A variation of the window display is the exhibit taken to conventions and special exhibitions. This is used to promote your company or your product and should not be designed by amateurs. Professional display manufacturers should be consulted for the proper approach. However, there are a few points you should know so you can offer a degree of guidance to the firm you hire.

First have a display designed to utilize the entire space of the booth area that you will be renting. Most booths are available in multiples of 10-foot widths. Thus a display should be designed to completely fill a 10-foot-wide space or 20-foot-wide space if you want a double area. If the display is going to fall short of this, you must fill the area in some other planned manner such as with chairs or a table containing literature.

Displays should be made with lightweight materials to facilitate shipping. A display need not be heavy to be sturdy. The more it weighs, the greater your transportation costs.

Displays should be so designed that they can be taken down quickly and stored in one or two containers. Sometimes the units are put together in panels, hinged at the back. This can be a tremendous help when preparing for transportation.

The mechanics of running the display should be kept simple. You might use rear projection techniques or sophisticated lighting equipment. However, the people operating it should be able to put a plug in an outlet and throw a switch or two to get everything working. You do not want to have to send an electronics expert along to every exhibition.

A display must be self-sustaining and have its own illumination. Too many times a company relies on the lighting in an exhibition hall only to find that the booth's location is in harsh shadows.

Keep the display simple and let it follow a basic theme. This is the same advice as for a window display.

Be sure the display is not cluttered. People should be able to move about freely while studying the exhibit.

Your company and product name should be highly visible. You've gone to a lot of trouble to plan the display. Be certain people are aware who you are.

Finally, make the display colorful. If you use black-and-white photographs, surround them with color. Let the display draw the eye and be fun to look at.

# 9

# Shopping Center Promotions

If you are involved with a shopping center, either as an owner or a business person located in one, promotion should be uppermost in your mind. Too often shopping center managers feel that the public will come to the center simply because of its location. Store owners agree with this theory and also assume that their businesses will benefit with a minimum of advertising because people visiting the mall will pass by their shops and come inside. But not enough business is generated for these reasons to make the center—or any single business—as successful as it could be.

In our extremely mobile society, people like the convenience of a nearby shopping center, but they are also willing to get into their cars and drive a few miles to a different mall if they feel there is reason to do so. Generally their motivation is not loyalty to specific stores in any one mall but rather the special promotions being held there.

A customer usually goes to an isolated store to buy the food, clothing, appliances, or other products offered. The store's selection, quality, price, and related factors are known. People enter the store because they are seriously considering making a purchase.

Shopping malls are quite a different matter. Our society has turned a trip to a shopping mall into a social event. The elderly go to spend a no-cost afternoon of "people watching." They can sit on the benches provided for their comfort and talk with friends, contemplate the passing of the years, or just watch the shoppers.

Teenagers go to shopping malls to see their friends and have an inexpensive date. They can stop by a restaurant for a sandwich, perhaps take in a movie, and do some window shopping. Many teens spend every Saturday in shopping malls.

Parents like to take their children to shopping malls when there is a way to keep them entertained while they get their shopping done. If the family goes to an isolated clothing or food store, for example, the children quickly become bored and are quite a nuisance. The parents cannot take as much time shopping as they would like, so they often make fewer purchases. In a shopping center, the parents can go to one store while the children are looking at toys or taking in a mall promotion feature such as a petting zoo. Everyone relaxes, takes their time—and spends more money!

But how do you get people into your mall? There are two ways. The first is through special events meant to attract the public. These include such relatively expensive, but guaranteed crowd pleasers as small traveling fairs set up on part of the parking lot, a petting zoo, puppet shows, or even a hand-carved, animated circus. Local booking agents can help line up groups that regularly appear in shopping malls around the United States.

Other approaches include turning a section of your mall over to groups that will pay all costs for being there. For example, you might let the local professional photographers' association have display space for showing their member's photographs. Likewise local amateur photographic groups might be invited to display their work.

Other hobby groups might also appear. Stamp and coin collectors can have a display or you might let dealers set up a combination sales area and coin show. Gem collectors, wood-carvers, jewelry makers, and others might also appear at their own expense. If tables and chairs must be set up, this can either be done by the group or by the mall. In the latter case a fee to cover the costs should be charged.

Every special event must be heavily promoted with newspaper, radio and/or television advertising. This should be started a week in advance and run through the time the activity is being held.

Events that allow mall visitors to participate in some way can also draw a crowd. For example, if a group of artists or art galleries has a display, it is a good idea to also have one or more sketch artists present. These people will make drawings of the shoppers for a nominal fee. The public enjoys having this done as well as watching the artists at work.

Live demonstrations of all sorts can be popular. You might have a wood-carver or glassblower demonstrating their arts at the same time that finished work is for sale.

The cost for promotion can be absorbed by the mall or shared with the people involved in whatever activity is going on. Always have the mall involved, at least in part, with the advertising rather than trusting the members of the attraction to handle everything. You want to be certain that you reach the maximum number of people possible so that you can completely fill the mall. If you trust someone else to make all the arrangements, there may be less advertising than you would like.

Some promotions can be used to improve the image of the mall, and, hence, the stores therein. For example, you might let charitable organizations set up displays. During the United Way campaign, member agencies could be invited to show how they serve the public. Or the Red Cross might have an exhibit including regularly held demonstrations of emergency resuscitation techniques.

Lions Clubs often will arrange for a trailer to come to the mall with medical personnel to offer free glaucoma tests. Free or low-cost blood pressure and blood sugar tests are also of interest to the public. The local county medical society can be of assistance with these.

Musical groups have a definite appeal to the public as well. One Cleveland mall increases the number of shoppers on its slowest night—Monday evening—by having small groups of professional musicians perform. Each week a different type of music is featured such as jazz, rock, or "easy listening." Sometimes there is a singer. Other times just the musical group. They are hired through the local American Federation of Musicians chapter and are delighted for the work on what is a slow day so far as club work and other normal activities.

Shopping malls can build goodwill in other ways, of course. Like individual businesses, a mall can sponsor a Little League team, Scout troops, and other worthwhile activities. The mall can have a drive to send children from low-income families to summer camp.

Mall stores should attempt to coordinate sales with each other whenever possible. A full page advertisement can be taken in a newspaper with the page divided into even segments, the total of which is equal to the number of different shops. Each store lists one or more items that will be on special. Shoppers who might not be lured to the mall for a sale in any given store are attracted when they realize that merchandise will be reduced to some degree in *every* store.

Stores can have promotions for each other. For example, a jeweler and photographer might work together. The jeweler might have a sample wedding album on hand as well as a discount coupon for portrait work while the photographer might have a discount coupon for one of the jeweler's services. Or perhaps a discounted meal at a restaurant will be offered in a coupon obtainable in a shoe store. Discount coupons can be used in both related and unrelated businesses. This should be decided at a meeting of all the merchants.

Another approach is to have discount coupon booklets with special offers for every store. Each store has one or more coupons and the cost of printing is divided among everyone involved. These are free and are available to the public in all the stores, in the mall office, or from an information booth. Once again newspaper advertising should be used to alert the public to the existence of the coupon booklets.

Seasonal promotions can be fairly simple. Santa Claus will have a place to meet the children at Christmas, for example. And the Easter Bunny might be present during the Easter season.

Constant promotion is the key to success with a shopping center. By having the stores work as a cohesive unit when planning special events, more business will result for each store.

# 10

# Outdoor Advertising

Outdoor advertising is one of the more questionable forms of promotion. It is seen quickly, usually by a disinterested party whose mind is on the traffic, the weather conditions, the stacked new secretary in the low cut dress, or the best way to ask the boss for a raise. There is no time for more than a fleeting glance, so the impression must be strong or the advertising sign will not register at all.

The typical billboard—or "poster," as it is often called in the trade—comes in two forms. One is the painted bulletin that generally is 14 feet high and 48 feet wide. The other type is the poster panel that runs 12 feet by 25 feet.

Billboards are usually erected after careful studies of traffic and pedestrian flow. They are located where they can give advertisers the same type of saturation that is possible in magazines, newspapers, and the broadcast media. However, because of the short time they are viewed by passersby, they are seldom more effective than the 10-second television message. Therefore, it is important to use a number of billboards in various locations so that the message is seen frequently enough to take hold in the viewer's mind.

The amount of copy that can be used on a billboard is not related to the size of the space that can be used. Quite the contrary. In fact, many outdoor advertising experts feel that five words are the maximum number that should be used for effective billboard selling. Such a short message can be seen and grasped in the few seconds the sign has someone's attention.

There are only two points that can be conveyed by an outdoor advertisement—the name of the product and a reason to buy it. Any elaboration will not get read. The product name should be as large as possible and all letters should be at least a foot high to ensure legibility.

An outdoor advertisement is no place for subtlety. Never show a full-length figure of a person if a tightly cropped, giant head will have greater impact. Everything should be large and preferably in bold colors. Subtle shadings are for magazine advertisements that can be studied up close. A billboard is seen for seconds from a great distance. It either grabs the viewer or it fails completely.

Be wary of the way colored lettering is used. Red is the strongest color when it has the proper background. Red on white leaps at the reader but red on a dark background often disappears. The same is true with white letters on a red background.

Some billboards are becoming animated and a few are actually message centers. The animated billboard is usually what is known as a multivision unit. The boards have three or more different designs or changes in copy with each change appearing for a few seconds. Usually the parts of each message rotate in unison.

The message centers use lights to spell out information. Sometimes the message moves along the sign. Other times the words flash on and off until the full message is given. For example, one discount store tries to encourage people to have breakfast in their coffee shop by flashing a message in segments. It reads: "Bacon and Eggs." Then, "Hash Browns, Coffee." Then, "Special 99 Cents." The three segments take a total of perhaps 10 to 15 seconds. The sign is located near a traffic light where cars will be regularly stopping. After 10 in the morning, three hours after the breakfast special first was advertised, a product such as purses will be the advertised special. This ad will continue throughout the day, occasionally being changed so a lunch or dinner special can be promoted.

Another type of moving sign combines news of the day with a commercial message. This is usually located in a major business district such as the downtown section of the city. It is meant more for reaching pedestrians than drivers. Only during rush hour do drivers move slowly enough to see much of the sign.

Quality outdoor advertising requires the use of experienced personnel to prepare it. The medium is such that it uses a format radically different from all other forms of advertising. Unless someone has an understanding of this format and experience with its preparation, the advertisement may prove to be a wasted expense.

Whoever prepares the outdoor advertisement should produce renderings for your approval. This is not a do-it-yourself field, but you should exercise control over the final layout and copy.

Just how effective is outdoor advertising? It's hard to say. However, many of the studies indicate that businesses are often greatly helped.

For example, the food business can benefit from an outdoor advertising campaign when promoting a special sale or a new product. The repetitive sighting of the product keeps it in the buyer's mind when he or she enters the supermarket. Managers report both sales and product demand are much higher when billboards promoting the product are used than when just newspaper advertising and the broadcast media carry the message.

Companies successfully use billboards to introduce a new corporate logo. Politicians use billboards to keep their names in constituents' minds. Many voters cast their ballots because a name is familiar rather than because they know the candidate's stand on the issues.

Truly creative outdoor advertising will increase product awareness and sales. It can also increase a business's willingness to take on your product because the owner will feel sales will be supported by your strong outdoor campaign.

A variation of outdoor advertising is transit advertising. Bus and subway car advertising represent a major form of outdoor promotion in this country. Again, care must be taken in planning.

The outside of a bus is much like a billboard in terms of the way the public sees it. Such advertisements are generally considered "intersection" promotions. They can be effectively viewed only when the vehicle is stopped at an intersection. When it is in motion the message becomes a blur.

Interior advertisements are extremely effective. Mass transportation is regularly used by people going shopping; these people are thinking about spending money. They are also in a fairly fixed spot on the bus or subway. A limited number of advertisements will be in their line of sight and they may look at them repeatedly as they are in transit. This is often anywhere from ten minutes to a half hour. There is plenty of time to tell your story and you can use plenty of copy. Just be certain the lettering is large enough to be read at some distance.

The standard interior advertisement is 11 inches high by 28 inches wide. Variations include an almost square 22-inch by 21-inch design found on some new buses.

Advertisements must never be posted on a single bus. A large number must be used, the exact number varying with the size of the line. Transit companies have done studies on the number of advertisements needed for the greatest effect and can supply them much the same way that magazine ad departments have made demographic breakdowns of readers.

The same advertisement need not be used on all the buses when space is rented. You can have two or more different messages related to the same product line divided among the vehicles.

Some new buses offer a dramatic approach for night advertisements. They have lighted advertising sections across the top on each side of the bus. These are usually arranged two on each side with the space per ad being 12 feet across.

Advertisements to be lighted are made from materials such as vinyl on Plexiglass. Such materials allow the light to pass through. The signs are visible during the day just like other advertising on the outside of the vehicle. But at night they are moving beacons spreading your message through the otherwise darkened streets.

Transit space is rented for set periods of time with ads of certain sizes more popular than others. Before planning a campaign be sure to learn which space will be available at the time you wish to advertise. Many people rent from two to six months in advance. You should never expect to prepare a campaign until you know what size advertisements you can use.

The most effective sales approach is to use the theme and copy approach of ads in other media with the transit ads. By relating to one another in some way, the impact is greater in the public mind. A good example was the "Pepsi Generation" theme used by the Pepsi Cola Company for several years. This term and the image it conveyed could be seen in newspapers and magazines, on radio and television, as well as on billboards and transit ads. Each reinforced the other and the combined effect helped boost sales of the company's soft drinks.

If transit advertising will be promoting a product, make certain retailers in the area are aware of the campaign. Copies of the ads can be taken to show them what you are doing. This makes your line more desirable to them because they know there will be customer demand for the product.

Outdoor advertising can be effective as a regional tool. However, careful planning, consultation with expert specialists in your area, and simplicity of approach are essential to a successful campaign.

# 11

# Using Newsletters

Sometimes it seems that business people are snowed under with too much information. No matter what field of endeavor you are in, there are probably a dozen or more journals that in some way relate to your work. I know of one business person who receives sample copies or advertisements for 75 periodicals each month. But no one has the time to do so much reading. Even more frustrating is the fact that your particular area of interest might be confined to a single phase of the business you are in—a segment too limited to receive adequate coverage in traditional publications.

What is the answer? For many successful business people, it has been a subscription to one or more newsletters.

A newsletter is a 2- to 16-page capsule summary of news and information relating to one business, industry, nonprofit organization, or even a particular job area such as dry cell battery manufacture, biophysics, or space engineering. The newsletter distills essential information gleaned from the numerous sources available. A newsletter can enable a business person to learn the relevant information he or she would otherwise have to obtain through endless periodical reading. A newsletter can also serve to acquaint the public with the work of an organization in order to insure its continued support.

Newsletters are usually well read by their subscribers and very profitable for the people who produce them. Commercial newsletters, sold by subscription, often earn their publishers six-figure incomes. Noncommercial newsletters have enabled businesses to increase their sales and nonprofit organizations to increase the number and size of contributions they receive. It is likely that your business or organization could profit from the production of a newsletter.

Because newsletters are such valuable tools, let us explore how you or your firm could start such a publication. The initial expense is low and the ultimate returns usually far exceed the cost of even the newsletter that is sent without charge.

The first step in the production of a newsletter is to carefully examine the topic you are going to write about. It might relate to your field of business or to your specific organization.

For example, suppose you are attempting to promote a local hospital. The newsletter will be sent without charge to members of the community who have contributed money in the past, who are considered potential contributors, or who can be beneficial in some other way, such as the members of the press, radio, and television.

The hospital newsletter must serve a dual purpose. It must show what the hospital is doing for the public and why continuing support is needed. The newsletter might detail important medical breakthroughs achieved by staff researchers. It might tell of a free immunization program for children of low-income families. It might tell of a roving hospital trailer that takes skilled medical care to rural parts of the county. Or it might tell of a patient whose life was saved by recently purchased, specialized medical equipment.

The hospital newsletter tells the reader that money is being spent to provide community service. It also tells about the benefits that new contributions will bring to the public. Most people support such nonprofit organizations because of personal problems or needs. If the newsletter shows them how they or their loved ones might benefit, they are likely to contribute.

For example, a person who has kidney disease or knows someone so afflicted is going to be interested in supporting the purchase of a new kidney dialysis unit. A person whose child died of leukemia will want to support a cancer researcher working at the hospital. And someone who has had to take a child with a broken leg miles from home is going to support the building of a pediatric care wing in a nearby hospital.

Then there is the case of the business newsletter. One such communication device is the insurance company newsletter. This periodical, usually written in the home office but sent under an agent's name, might provide information relating to business and estate planning. It will have stories of new tax laws and other legislation of interest to the reader. It will also detail ways the company's offerings can help with retirement income, key man insurance, and related matters.

Another newsletter might be offered by an investment company. It would discuss financial trends, the stock market, money market, commodity futures, and other investment areas. It might be tied in with current company offerings or be a general information publication that barely mentions the company name.

Newsletters offered by businesses can be extremely soft sell. They can provide general information usable anywhere while still having greater impact than hard sell advertising.

For example, suppose a coin and stamp dealer decides to go after big spenders by starting an investor's newsletter. This newsletter will be issued by the company but will not promote the dealer's stock. Instead it will discuss such matters as what makes coins and stamps rare, how to select for long term growth, in-depth studies of long term gains recorded by different issues, ways to start an investment club, and other matters. The information could be used by anyone, working with any dealer in the country. However, without going into hard sell tactics or mentioning the writer's stock, the informational newsletter is going to gain more customers for the dealer than other forms of advertising are. The reason? The newsletter conveys the message that the writer is an expert in coin and stamp investment and, therefore, would be the best person with whom to do business. Other dealers might have better stock but they don't have greater knowledge. Or so the reasoning goes.

Sit down and decide what specifics your newsletter could cover. If the newsletter is for a nonprofit organization, it should stay with the organization's work and community benefits. If it is for a business, it must relate to the interest of your potential customers.

One note of caution. Earlier in this book I discussed internal publications for employees. Many times when an organization has such a publication, the newsletter produced for the general public is modeled along the same lines. It discusses employees and their activities instead of concentrating on the areas of interest of the readers. *A newsletter must always be written for the person to whom it is being sent.* Mary Money, noted philanthropist, doesn't care to read about Barney Blowhard, the Haven-Of-Rest Hospital's boiler room foreman who just celebrated 25 years with the institution. But she does care about Dr. Carlton Cardiac's development of a lifetime power source for heart pacemakers, because her husband has such a device and must be constantly on the alert for battery failure. Telling her about research that could effect her self-interest will get her money. Telling her about someone only other employees care about will get your newsletter tossed into the trash.

Similar problems arise with photographs. Newsletters must either contain interesting photographs with the impact of the old *Life* magazine features or they should have no illustrations at all. "Here is ramrod stiff Rodney Johnson receiving his 50-Year Service Pin from tense Fenster Feebush," is a typical, deadly picture approach that says nothing, bores the reader, and is a waste of space. If the pictures aren't eye-catching and of interest to the reader, they don't belong. People will read an interestingly written newsletter without pictures. However, they may discard the same newsletter if dull illustrations are used. The photographs are often the initial attraction for the reader. If they lack impact, he or she may go no further.

Once you decide upon your newsletter approach, you must decide whether the newsletter is to be issued for free or for money. If the newsletter is meant to provide general information about a business or a nonprofit institution, it is usually mailed without charge. It is a means of gaining customers and/or financial support. Its subject matter relates specifically to the group issuing the newsletter, so there will be no competitive publications to worry about. In a sense it is an aspect of your advertising, though far more subtle.

The alternative is to offer a newsletter for a fee. This time it will be only a secondary part of your business. The coverage will include information on a specific topic but with greater depth than just your firm's role in the field.

For example, a brokerage firm selling only stocks and bonds might produce a financial advisory newsletter covering a broad range of investment topics. It might discuss the money market, commodities, retirement plans, tax laws for investors, and other items of interest. Some of the facts mentioned will relate to the firm's services. Others will not. The newsletter is an investor service that gives important investment information involving far more businesses than just the firm publishing it.

If you are going to charge for a newsletter, you are going to place yourself in competition with other publishers. There may be one or more newsletters already serving the market that you wish to enter. It is essential that you first research the field to be certain you can compete.

The best approach to research is to go to the reference department of your public library. There you will find such volumes as *Ayer's Directory of Newspapers and Periodicals* and the *National Directory of Newsletters and Reporting Services,* among other references. A thorough study of these volumes will give you an idea of current competition, if any. You might also wish to get in touch with the Independent Newsletters Association, 621 National Press Building, Washington, D.C., 20004. This source can be of great value in helping you to launch your newsletter regardless of whether you are going to charge for it.

Once you know the competition you face, you must decide whether to continue with your publishing plans. You can be fairly certain that if there are more than five newsletters in your field, there is no sense in your attempting to start a new one for pay. The competition will be too great, according to experts in the field.

If there are fewer than five competitors, send for samples of their newsletters. This may be fairly expensive, but if you don't know what's being published you won't know whether there is a market for your concept.

There are exceptions to the five-newsletter rule, of course. Some newsletters are put out with inherent bias. They are produced by various associations that have certain messages to get across. They tell one side of an issue rather than providing objective information. They prosper because they are the only source readily available. An independent newsletter offering objective information covering all sides of the same topic can readily compete.

There is also the chance that your competition does not adequately cover special facets of the field you wish to write about. In the hobby and investment area, for example, a newsletter might promote gold and silver bullion trading as an investment. Your letter could discuss rare coins instead. Refining your original concept to fit a limited market can enable you to compete, regardless of the number of more general newsletters.

Once you have determined your topic you must make certain that there will be enough information available to ensure a continuous flow of material. To do this you are going to have to gather information as intensely as if you were actually writing the newsletter.

If you are going to be publicizing your own business or nonprofit organization alone, you are going to have to act as a reporter. It will be necessary to go from department to department, questioning employees about new developments that will effect the community at large. Nonprofit organizations will stress services, construction projects, and related matters. Businesses will stress whatever is of concern to their customers.

The newsletter being sold for profit is going to take a little more work. You cannot rely completely on your business. You must gather information related to the newsletter from every possible source. This will mean maintaining files of newspaper and magazine articles, speeches, press releases from manufacturers, and perhaps even corporate reports.

Once a month analyze the material received during the past 30 days. How many items can you pull from this recent material for use in your newsletter? Experts say that you must be able to glean at least 25 new developments your readers will want to know about in order to be certain you can fill a newsletter. Repeat this procedure once a month for three months. If the pattern is consistent and you always have adequate material, you have chosen a good topic.

All well and good. But how do you get such material?

There are numerous approaches. Perhaps the best way is to hire a clipping service that subscribes to a large number of periodicals relating to your field. Be certain to specify exactly what you are after, and be careful to warn the service that you do not wish to have them clip duplicate items from different periodicals. Often a wire service story will appear in 50 different newspapers and magazines. Unless you specifically tell the clipping service to avoid duplication, you will pay for the 50 clippings while receiving information worth a fraction of the price.

Another good approach is to write to the public relations' departments of all the businesses of value to your newsletter. *The Thomas Register* is one source for company names and addresses as well as key personnel. This regularly updated reference book, found in most libraries, is also a good source for names of possible newsletter recipients.

Once you are convinced the newsletter is possible, you will need to develop a mailing list. Names for a fee-paid newsletter can come from a number of sources. In addition to *The Thomas Register,* there are numerous references containing the names of people in different professions available at most large libraries. Next, determine if there are members of federal, state, or local governments who could benefit and check addresses for these.

Another source for names can be found with the various mailing list brokers. Such sources were discussed earlier, in the chapter on direct mail. Newsletters are very much like direct mail promotions and lists valid for one are likely to be valid for both.

The clippings and reports you have been accumulating are good sources for names. The companies and executives mentioned can form the basis for an additional list. As many as three names are often found in each clipping; annual reports can provide you with the names of numerous corporate executives. Naturally you will limit your contacts to those who can use your newsletter. A newsletter relating to accounting will be of interest to the comptroller, for example, but will probably have no appeal for the personnel director.

Be certain to check lists of associations as well. Again the library's reference division is a gold mine, though an abbreviated selection can be found in such common reference books as the annual *World Almanac* published by Newspaper Enterprise Association (NEA).

A newsletter that will be given without charge is not meant to make a profit. It is meant to improve community relations, gain new business for your corporation, and attract donations. But a newsletter for which you charge must reach a fairly sizable audience in order to be profitable.

Fee paid newsletters are likely to fail if you are not careful about several matters. First is the question of audience. Is it large enough to sustain the costs involved? Is your subject matter of specific value to the people you are trying to reach without their being able to get the same material as easily somewhere else?

Do you have adequate capital for promotion that will sustain you during the first year or two when losses are likely? And are you able to charge enough to meet costs and make a profit with the minimum audience you feel certain you can reach?

What costs will be involved? You are going to have to pay for paper, printing, mailing (both postage and envelopes), collating, stapling, typing, clipping service and subscriptions, telephone, heat, electricity and rent, if any, as well as office supplies. Many of these expenses will be slight. But they must all be determined in order for you to learn your average monthly cost.

The price you charge will vary with the market and the information you supply. The best rule of thumb is to charge whatever the market will bear. For example, if you publish a newsletter for oil company chief executives, $150 a year will not be too high if they can use the information in your newsletter. On the other hand, a newsletter aimed towards gas station owners must be far less expensive, perhaps a maximum of $25 a year, because of their limited capital. And it may be harder to justify that $25 than it is the $150!

The best approach is to figure your costs, determine the market size you expect to obtain—100 readers, 1,000 readers, or whatever—and then charge as much over your costs as you think the readers will pay. Keep in mind that it is easier to start a little high than it is to raise rates later on as your expenses climb. It is a wise idea to add 50 percent to your monthly expenses and earmark this money for promotion. Direct mail promotion is the only way you can ensure the eventual success of your business venture.

There are two approaches to newsletter format. The nonprofit organization and the business giving the letters away can use an informative style. Photographs can be liberally sprinkled throughout the two or more pages that will comprise the newsletter.

When you are out to make money from your newsletter, you must convince the reader that he or she is getting a bargain. The pages should be filled with hard news items—timely information that can be used immediately and that, hopefully, scoops more traditional news sources. No illustrations are necessary and the best way to prepare the news items is with typewriter type face. Using typewriter face instead of more commercial faces gives the newsletter an appearance of immediacy. The image is one of you sitting at your typewriter, working late into the night to get the latest information, then stuffing it into an envelope at the last moment, and rushing it to the subscriber. It's not an accurate image, I'll admit. But if the reader feels this kind of electric intimacy, he or she will be more likely to subscribe and resubscribe.

How long should your newsletter be? Keep it short enough so that when it is folded and placed in an envelope it can travel for the cost of a single first-class stamp. Self mailers are out because they do not seem personal. Since anyone can read them, the information is automatically downgraded in the mind of the recipient. A subscriber wants to think of the newsletter as a special, private source of information. And the more you charge, the more important this image becomes.

Usually 14-pound paper is effective. It holds up well and an average of 8 pages, 8 x 11 inches each, can fit into a standard envelope for the one-ounce charge. This gives you 16 sides of material, a good maximum figure for any newsletter.

The typewriter type face should be used only for news items. The masthead and other consistent forms should all have a professional look with quality type. After all, the general layout of the newsletter should look as though it is coming from a highly sophisticated authority with his or her hand on the latest information.

Never try to increase the number of items by reducing type size below standard pica or elite. If you make the material harder to read, every eyeglass wearer or would-be eyeglass wearer will become hesitant about continuing. Who wants to have to use a magnifying glass to read something? In fact, there are times when you might want to go to a slightly larger type face if your newsletter is going to a group such as the elderly, who may need such assistance to read it easily. Using large type for executives is self-defeating, though. They will think you are short on material and will be hesitant about subscribing.

Generally you will allow three inches at the top of the first sheet of your newsletter for the masthead. This should include the newsletter's title, address, telephone number, volume and issue number, date, and editor's name if desired. If there is a charge, the annual subscription rate should be included.

The rest of the page is for information presented either line-by-line or with the sheet divided into columns. Generally a ½-inch right-hand margin and a ¾-inch left margin is considered desirable.

Capitalize the first line of each story. This adds visual interest and helps to emphasize each item. Use double space between stories.

There are numerous ways your newsletter can be printed, but you want to go for the lowest possible cost while maintaining a quality appearance. Most printers feel that offset printing is the best approach. You can easily get competitive bids for this type of work. With offset printing you will type your newsletter, then have it photographed and made into a metal plate. The printing is done from that plate.

You should print your newsletter in fairly large quantities at first so that you have material for samples. Generally each additional 1,000 printed will cost you only a fraction of the cost for the first 1,000 copies. Ask printers about this.

Avoid using expensive coated papers and see what types of leftover 14-pound weight paper the printer might have from other jobs. Often printers have a few hundred sheets of multicolored odds and ends lying about that were charged to the person making the original order. These leftovers can be obtained very inexpensively for your needs. If you go this route, your 1,000 sheets might include 300 on red paper, 150 on blue, 400 on yellow, and so on. Since only one color will be going to any individual, the fact that multiple colors are used for your order will not look strange.

Mail no longer has an air mail rate so everything will be sent first class, or, if immediacy and a high subscription charge are warranted, by special delivery. Remember that you are trying to give the impression of timely, valuable material when you sell a newsletter. You cannot save money on postage without hurting your image. It is only when the newsletter is a promotional vehicle sent free of charge that you can make it a self-mailer and/or use second class rates.

Once you have started your newsletter you are going to have to start going after sources of information. Even the nonprofit organization's newsletter may have to contain material that cannot be found strictly from within the organization.

One approach is to attend seminars and conventions relating to the field of your newsletter. Take notes, make contacts, and be prepared to regularly keep in touch with acquaintances by telephone and letter. Sales literature, annual reports, press releases from the industry, government publications, copies of speeches, and even university or other academic research papers are all of value. Be certain to let public relations personnel know what you are doing so that they can send you pertinent information. Once you get on a few mailing lists, you will find your mailbox filling with brochures and other materials almost daily.

Obviously all this is going to take a little time and cost some money. However, if you want to make a profit from your newsletter it is well worth it. Even if you are making the newsletter a promotion vehicle whose cost is absorbed, it is still important that the material be meaningful enough for people to want to read it.

Take a hospital, for example. Suppose you want to discuss how the malpractice insurance problem affects your particular institution. You have immediate sources of information in the form of the staff doctors and the hospital's legal department and its insurance company. But you will also need to know recent and pending national legislation, approaches other hospitals have used when faced with this problem, and similar facts that can only come from outside sources. Phone calls will have to be made, letters written, and periodicals gleaned for the facts you need. Otherwise what you write will leave many questions unanswered and perhaps leave your reader with the idea that studying the newsletter was a waste of time. When that happens, the newsletter obviously loses its effectiveness as a promotion tool.

Or take the clothing store owner who wants to send a quarterly newsletter on fashion trends to regular customers. The newsletter must contain information on what people are wearing in the major fashion centers, such as New York, Paris, and London. It will need quotes from authoritative sources such as *Women's Wear Daily, Vogue,* and numerous other specialty and general interest publications. The reader must be convinced to change or add to his or her wardrobe, and that is going to take more than just an announcement that the store is featuring a new line of clothes. The newsletter must convince the buyer, with specific examples, that fashion trends will pass the person by if new clothing is not purchased.

Be certain to subscribe to trade journals relating to your field or utilize a clipping service that regularly reads them. Your local library has reference guides to the various trade journals and business publications that can be of assistance. Often by reading the entire magazine you can get leads to new sources of information, potential newsletter subscribers, and advertisements for products you might wish to report.

Naturally you will need to subscribe to rival newsletters should they exist. Sometimes you will get leads from them. Other times you will want to drop an item when you have been "scooped." But always you must be aware of what the competition is doing.

Your readers can be sources of information once you get going. Periodically survey the readers by mail, enclosing postage paid return envelopes for their replies. Question them about new developments with which they are involved. Ask if there are areas they want to see discussed or covered in greater depth. The more the reader feels you are serving his or her interests, the more likely the person is to resubscribe.

Middle management personnel are also good sources of information. They do not feel the need for secrecy that top people often do and they may have more time for talking with you. They are also interested in advancing their careers, so the chance to be quoted may please them.

At this point a word about quoting is in order. When a newsletter is a free promotion vehicle, there is seldom any problem with quoted materials. The information is invariably favorable to the business, so no one among the top brass will mind. However, this may not be the case with the fee paid newsletter.

A fee paid newsletter is objective, at least in theory. You may wish to quote someone concerning an industrial cover-up of a potential health hazard or some equally serious charge. The person cooperating could be fired and perhaps blacklisted in the industry. Therefore, whether or not you quote by name could make a difference in some of your news sources.

Most fee paid newsletter editors find that names should be used only when the person being quoted gives his or her approval. Alternatives to direct quotes are phrases such as, "Experts in the industry have found," "According to reliable sources in the field," "Officials tell us," or any other approach that does not indicate the specific person involved. Naturally if a company has just one research scientist, a line such as, "Researchers have informed us" is the same as giving the person's name.

Sometimes you will want to rewrite a press release so that it sounds as though you are initiating a story, not just passing it on. For example, suppose the Wing-And-A-Prayer Airplane Manufacturing Company sends you a release stating, "President Lance 'Lucky Lindy' Brittlehoffer of Wing-And-A-Prayer Airline Manufacturing Company is proud to announce the development of the Connie Commuter Special, a new twin engine, four passenger airplane named for his wife. The plane is designed to take off and land on a space as short as the typical home driveway. It is meant for going to and from suburban shopping centers when the family car is being used for other purposes. It is fast, lightweight and easy to fly. Its $175,000 price makes it within reach of almost everyone . . . ."

You want to mention this item in your newsletter but you want your readers to think they are getting an exclusive from your special sources. Instead of quoting the release, you write something to the effect: "The *Aviation Newsletter* has just learned that Wing-And-A-Prayer Airplane Manufacturing Company will shortly release its latest product, the Connie Commuter Special. According to our sources this aircraft can take off and land in a space as short as the typical home driveway. It is meant for short trips to and from suburban shopping centers."

Note how the slight switch in emphasis makes it seem as though you are telling an unreleased fact. Everything you say is correct. The *implication* is that you got the information from a secret source well in advance of the general public. Just make sure it's not something everybody else already knows.

You may wish to add visual emphasis to different parts of your newsletter. This can be done by underlining some of your copy, either to call attention to a main point or to emphasize some facet of the text. For example, you might prepare the following item:

"An increasing number of money managers are having their clients liquidate their stock holdings and transfer their funds to rare coins. <u>Rare gold has increased in value 25% per year</u> the past several years. <u>Rare silver coins have doubled in value</u> every five years. Money managers say they are proving to be one of the <u>best hedges against inflation</u> when selected for rarity, condition, and collector interest rather than just intrinsic worth."

Note how key sections are underlined to provide emphasis and to feature important points. Underlining can also be used in place of capitalizing the first line of each item.

The timing of your newsletter can be important. If the newsletter is free and sent quarterly or over some equally long period, varying the day it is prepared will not matter too much. However, when you charge a fee, your subscribers are going to expect to receive it at definite intervals. If they get it on Monday one week, the next issue must also arrive on Monday. You must organize yourself so you can maintain an exact schedule.

You will need to have all your basic tasks planned before you start the newsletter. Arrange for a printer and learn what schedule you can count on. If the printer says, "We try to give you three-day service," this is not good enough. You need to know the *maximum* time the printing could take so you can plan around that. Your order will probably never be so large that the printer is willing to drop everything for you. Therefore, you must be prepared for the longest possible delay.

Line up professional typists unless your business staff can handle this chore. If you are using free-lance typists, you should have at least two on whom you can rely. One of the typists could become ill or have another assignment. You need to know there will always be someone who can translate your scratchings into readable copy.

If at all possible, a year's supply of envelopes should be ordered at one time. This is also a good idea for paper stock, undated sales promotion letters, and similar items. The more you buy at any one time, the less the cost for handling the order and the better the price break. The only exception will be if your printer can give you a substantial discount for taking leftover paper in a size and weight you will want.

Once everything is set, develop a work schedule for yourself based on the printer's time, mailing time, and frequency of publication. You might publish every week, having from five to seven days with which to work. Or you might publish every two weeks or even monthly, the latter situation giving you at least 20 working days.

How you arrange your schedule will be personal. However, a breakdown of your needs might be as follows:

1. Gather and organize news.
2. Write general news.
3. Write last minute news.
4. Take copy to typist; be certain of same day return.
5. Take typed material to printer.
6. Address envelopes.
7. Get newsletter from the printer; fold, stuff, and seal the envelopes and take them to the post office.

A fee paid newsletter must be promoted just like your business and product. You can use all the direct mail advertising techniques discussed earlier in the book. In addition, you might add a promotion incentive such as a free binder or a free annual index for which there is normally an additional fee.

Promotional letters can be sent either by themselves or with sample copies of the newsletter. I prefer the latter approach for it is difficult for the client to envision what you are going to be offering. After all, in theory your newsletter is going to be filling a void. It will be unique.

There is nothing with which the person can compare it. If he or she receives a promotion piece without a sample, it may seem like yet more literature for which there will be no time. But when a sample is included the person will realize how valuable it will be.

What sort of return should you expect from you selling efforts? Most newsletter experts say that when a fee is charged, you can hope to receive only 5 favorable responses from every 100 promotion pieces you mail. Therefore, you are going to have to do substantial mailing in order to gain enough subscribers to make a profit.

You may wish to send your newsletter to columnists and other members of the press. Sometimes the newsletter will be of interest to the daily papers. Other times it is of interest only to specialty publications. In either case, sending the newsletter to these markets without charge could get you valuable write-ups.

If you are working for a nonprofit organization, send the material to the press at the same time you send it to everyone else on your mailing list. However, if you charge, wait two or three days. You want your paying customers to feel they have an edge over everyone else when you provide them with news. If they think they can read the same material in the paper, there is no reason for them to send you their money.

The fee paid newsletter must be promoted just like any other product. In addition to direct mail, you might advertise in trade journals and offer the newsletter at conventions. Often direct selling to interested specialists at conventions can result in the greatest return for the least expense.

Naturally you will need to maintain your subscribers over the years. Most experts feel that renewal notices should be sent from three to six months in advance of renewal time. A new notice should be sent each month, perhaps with special offers. There might be a bonus discount, or perhaps a free binder, with a two- or three-year renewal.

Some newsletter publishers feel that if all else fails, a telephone call to a subscriber who has failed to respond to a number of notices may result in a reorder. *Changing Times* magazine, published by Kiplinger, famous for its newsletters, has personnel call subscribers who took advantage of trial offers. They attempt to get the renewal through the telephone offering of a special price, and their results are excellent. Most experts feel that 35 percent of all the people who refuse to renew when approached by mail will subscribe again if contacted by telephone.

Whether or not such figures will hold true in your case, the evidence seems to indicate that it would be worth the expense of trying telephone calls. You will be able to quickly determine whether or not the cost is beneficial or just a drain on your profits.

The biggest problem facing the fee paid newsletter publisher is unauthorized duplication. Office copying machines are used to spread a single issue of the newsletter to everyone in a business who might be interested in the contents. Instead of a dozen or more subscriptions being sold to the staff, you sell one and it is duplicated for those who are interested. This is costly to you and can make the difference between your newsletter turning a profit and its failing to break even.

There is no way to keep the public completely honest. At one time ink could be selected in a color that would not reproduce on the typical copier. But companies are obtaining copiers that can handle all colors, so such a precaution is usually meaningless.

The alternative is to mark the newsletter so that copying is greatly discouraged. This means placing strongly worded warnings in fairly large type so that they are readily visible on every page. Phrases that might be used include:

"Contents of this newsletter may not be published or duplicated in any form."

"This newsletter may not be copied or reproduced in any manner without the written permission of the publisher."

"Duplication of this newsletter in any manner is expressly forbidden."

"This newsletter is meant for the eyes of our clients *only!* Duplication in any manner without written permission from the publisher is expressly forbidden."

"Duplication of this newsletter is strictly forbidden! $100 will be paid for information concerning any unauthorized duplication."

When sending a newsletter to the members of the news media, an accompanying note may give the recipients the right to reproduce or quote sections of the newsletter.

Your newsletter readers should be regularly surveyed to learn who they are, their general income level, occupations, marital status, and as many other personal areas as possible. Such questionnaires should include return envelopes. It should be clear that they need not be signed since the information is of a personal nature and may be embarrassing to some subscribers.

It can also be a help to survey potential readers concerning the charge for the newsletter and even the contents. Before printing that first issue, work out a list of at least 1,000 possible subscribers. Then, before sending sample newsletters and your subscription appeal, randomly contact at least 25 percent of your list. Ask if they would be interested in the newsletter concept you have developed. Explain the frequency you have in mind and ask what they would be willing to pay to subscribe. Give them specific dollar amounts. Be certain that the minimum figure mentioned is one that will enable you to make a profit with the minimum number of subscribers. Once again a self mailer, stamped, self-addressed envelope, or similar reply device is essential.

Newsletters take a great deal of time and effort to launch, though costs are minimal compared with almost all other types of publications. For the nonprofit organization or the business sending them free of charge to customers, they are a way of reaching interested individuals in an effective manner. They enable you to tell your organization's story and ensure continued support.

When you launch a fee paid newsletter you are going to receive double benefits. The first benefit is the income derived from the newsletter. A good newsletter, carefully written and extensively promoted can bring in profits in the upper five figures within a fairly short period of time. The cost of production, including the writer's time, is easily met and your company has an additional source of revenue.

The second benefit is the interest such a newsletter generates for your business. A fee paid newsletter must be general in nature, even providing information that may be more beneficial for other firms. For example, the brokerage firm newsletter may have to advise its readers that stocks will not yield the best results during certain periods of economic recession. It may have to advise investing in areas handled by other companies, an apparent contradiction in concept since the newsletter should be helping one's business.

In reality the fact that your company, from time to time, recommends other businesses through its newsletter actually builds your concern. People look at your firm as being honest, objective, and having the client's best interest at heart. They feel that your firm is concerned about them, not merely interested in making a profit. They develop an intense loyalty and will often ignore your advice when you suggest dealing with someone else.

The same is true when you supply general information. Earlier I mentioned the example of the dealer in rare stamps and coins who tells his newsletter readers how to spot quality investment material wherever it is located. This information is of such value that the reader feels the dealer is concerned about him. When he or she is ready to spend money, the dealer issuing the newsletter is consulted; the newsletter has generated the idea that the dealer is an expert in the field and is completely honest.

Newsletters are excellent promotional tools. If you are not already producing one, it will be well worth your time to consider this method for advancing yourself, your product or your business.

# 12

# Printing

This chapter will give you a general understanding of the types of printing. I will not go into great detail since costs and services vary from area to area. It is important for you to learn what is available in your community. Specific cost cutting methods (such as using a printer's leftover paper when it is the proper weight and quality) have already been discussed. Always keep in mind that quality should be your first consideration, followed closely by cost. But remember that there are many inexpensive printers taking the trouble to produce high quality work and some fairly expensive printers who tend to be rather careless at times.

There are several different methods printers use to reproduce your advertisements, newsletters, etc. One of the most common is known as offset printing. It is also called lithography, photo-offset, offset-lithography, and Multilith, the latter being the trade name of a specific type of offset printing.

When you use offset printers, you bring in the material you want duplicated in the form in which it is to be duplicated. The material is properly laid out, the type is set in the style and position you want, and everything is in order before you arrive. All that will be missing are the illustrations, though the spaces where the artwork is to go have been prepared.

The printer photographs this completed layout, known in the trade as a "dummy." The illustrations to be used are photographed separately from the text.

The photographic image is transferred from the negative to a metal plate that is chemically treated to react to light. The sections of the plate on which the printed matter or illustrations have been recorded will accept ink. The areas that have been struck by light will not.

Next, the specially made metal plate is mounted on a cylinder. A blanket of ink rolls across the plate, leaving ink only where the printed matter was transferred. Then a rubber blanket rolls across the inked plate, taking the impression of the printed matter. When the rubber blanket rolls across the paper, your pictures and/or text will be printed. This process received its name because the material is "offset" from the plate to the blanket to the paper.

Naturally I have greatly simplified this process, but it will give you a general idea about what is involved. It can handle color or black-and-white and is excellent for reproducing line drawings. It does not reproduce photographs as well as other methods, however.

The cost of offset is quite low if you can supply everything to the printer. For example, if you are preparing a newsletter in typewriter face, the printer can reproduce by offset quite cheaply. However, if the printer must handle layout and special typesetting for you, this gets a little more expensive. The printer handling everything makes the layout to be photographed, sets the proper type, makes a sample or "proof," and then photographs that for the offset plate.

A second type of printing is known as letterpress. This is the oldest form of commercial printing known to man. It is what the first movable presses used.

With letterpress printing the ink is applied directly to the face of the type. Then the type is placed against the paper, leaving an impression. Specialized type faces and oversized type for headlines might be set by hand. The rest of the printing type usually is set by machine.

Letterpress printing does an excellent job of printing full color photographs and illustrations—technically known as "four color" illustrations. Black-and-white photographs do not print quite so well and usually are first made into a plate by a method known as photoengraving.

Another type of printing is rotogravure, also known as roto or gravure. This is one of the best means for reproducing photographs. Again a metal plate is used but this time the image is actually etched into the plate. The deeper the etching, the greater the amount of ink absorbed. The shading of a photograph will be determined by the depth of the etching.

Rotogravure printing allows for extremely high quality reproductions and for consistent reproductions when millions of copies are made. This is why expensively printed magazines and catalog houses are likely to use this method. Many newspapers use such an approach with a locally produced Sunday magazine in order to offer their readers especially fine photo coverage.

You are not likely to have use for rotogravure printing unless you are a major retailer. Should you wish to promote through the pages of a magazine using this printing process, the illustrations and text provided should be in the same form as they would be if you were supplying material for offset printing.

Low budget printing of small orders, generally under 500, can be accomplished with a mimeograph machine. The material to be reproduced is typed, drawn, or hand-lettered on a mimeograph stencil; this stencil is porous and coated with a chemical that will not allow it to hold ink. The typing creates holes in the shape of letters that will pick up ink. Then the stencil is wrapped around an inked drum, the drum is rolled over the paper, and the ink passes through the holes. The written material is transferred exactly and the quality can be almost as good as with offset printing. Unfortunately this is a poor method for use with illustrations. Obtaining good reproduction of artwork can be more expensive than you would wish.

Some businesses feel it is wise to buy a new or used mimeograph machine for use on small jobs. However, most experts feel that the cost of the machine is such that unless there is reason to use it regularly, you will probably come out ahead letting printers handle the job.

Paper types should be explained by a printer so that you can decide what will be most effective. Most quality work is done on bond or "book" paper. The difference is mostly in the page size and should be discussed with the printer in relation to your specific needs.

Paper merchants can save you money but only when you are buying in tremendous quantities. Generally it is cheapest to buy your paper directly from the printer, whose large orders usually result in a lower price than you could hope to gain on your own.

Always try to prepare circulars, newsletters, and similar items on paper that is of a standard size. If there is any trimmed waste it will cost you money. Standard pages are usually quite large but can be cut to the size desired. Again your printer will guide you.

Different thicknesses of bond paper weigh less than book paper. Sixteen-pound bond paper, for example, a weight you are likely to use for promotion pieces that must take some abuse, is equivalent to 40-pound book paper. Sales literature made into pamphlets, catalogs, etc. will usually use 20-pound and 24-pound bond paper or 50-pound to 60-pound book paper.

Envelopes are generally made from paper similar to that used for circulars and related items. The heavier the weight, the more abuse it can take; 20-pound and 24-pound envelopes are standards. The heavier 28-pound is meant for mailing catalogs and other heavy items. A paper such as 13-pound is meant for handling lightweight, overseas airmail letters.

Envelopes, unlike paper, are often best purchased independently from the manufacturer or jobber. These should be bought in great quantity with 5,000 considered a "small" order. If you can buy so that you meet your needs for a year, you will probably be making the most practical purchase possible.

What should you expect from your printer? Beyond service, quality, reliability, and honesty (check each printer with your Better Business Bureau), there are a few things you need to know.

All the preparatory materials used for the production of your printing order are considered the property of the printer unless otherwise stated *in writing*. This means plates, artwork, and all other items.

The printer will supply you with proofs of your work, the form of which will vary with the printing method used. However, in every case you are expected to check the proof against the original copy. When you approve of each page, mark it with an OK. This is the printer's go ahead to begin production.

One word of caution! When you read your proofs you may suddenly decide that your language could have been better, your layout slightly different, and other areas changed. If these changes will drastically alter the effect of the material for the better, by all means make them. But if they are fairly minor and your only reason for making them is that you tend to be a perfectionist, restrain yourself and go with the copy as originally prepared. Every change you make is going to cost you money; perfectionism could easily double the expenses for the job.

If you need to cancel a printing order, expect to pay for work done up to that point. If you are going to eventually order additional printing identical to what you are having done, tell the printer so that the plates, etc. can be saved.

Printers generally charge for all their services. This includes the time for obtaining paper and the cost for storage after an agreed upon time—usually 30 days. Each step of the printing process is charged to you. This happens regardless of whether or not the final bill is itemized.

If you make an error, you pay for it. If the copy is wrong when the job is completed but it matches the proof you okayed, you are going to pay the bill for the additional work. The printer accepts responsibility only for his or her own mistakes.

How do you find a printer? Look in the Yellow Pages as well as the classified advertising in newspapers. Check the firms through the Better Business Bureau; then visit the shops, discuss your work, and view samples of similar jobs the printer has handled for others. When quality and cost meet your standards, give the printer your business. Let the person know that your orders may be larger in the future, and reward any breaks you are given with loyalty. However, each time you must have work done with a different printing process than the one your printer has been regularly using for you, check competitors as well. A printer who is a genius with letterpress may not be competitive with offset, for example.

Remember that what you have printed represents you, your product, or your business. A little caution can be extremely important.

# Index

## A

Advertising, as a public information source, 69-71, 86-87
Advertising agency fees, 81-82
American Federation of Musicians (AFM), 82
American Federation of Television and Radio Artists (AFTRA), 82
Artwork, 107-8. *See also* Illustrations
Audience selection, 11-12, 14, 53, 106-7, 112-13, 119, 158
Automotive section, newspaper's, 3
AutoTyper, 121-23, 127-28, 149
*Ayer's Directory of Newspapers and Periodicals,* 199

## B

Beaudry, Lee, 85-88
Billboards, 189-93
  moving signs, 190-91
  transit advertisements, 191-93
Book Clubs, 112-13
Book section, newspaper's, 3
Business section, newspaper's, 3

## C

*Changing Times,* 209
Charity drives, 135-71
  board of directors, 145
  bonuses, 148, 149-50
  crisis situations, 168-71
  direct mail, 146-49, 156
  donor files, 142-43, 143-44, 148, 155

follow up, 149
fund raising, 140-66
   letters, 156
   media publicity, 158-65
   newsletters, 142, 143, 155, 195-212
   spokesman, 136
   staff morale, 157-58
   telephone solicitations, 165-66
   volunteers, 144, 145-46, 147
Christmas seals, 150
Clip book, 107-8
Commercial artist, 107
Commercials. *See* Radio advertisements; Television advertisements
Comparison advertising, 103-4
Computerized mailings, 119-23
Construction promotion, 12-13, 45-46
Convention exhibits, 116-17, 182-83
Copywriting, 23-24, 91-107, 123-25, 128-30
   body of ad, 98-102
   headline, 92-96, 99-100, 106
   illustration, 97-98, 107-8
   layout, 107, 108
   positive approach, 92-93, 95-96
   type specifications, 96, 101, 102, 108
Crisis situation contributions, 168-71

**D**

Direct mail advertisements, 111-31, 146-49, 156, 171
   computerized mailings, 119-23
   copywriting, 123-25, 128-30
   costs, 114, 122, 127, 129
   follow up, 129-30
   mailing list sources, 112, 115-20; seeded lists, 118
   multipiece mailings, 126-27
   paper quality, 128
   replies, 126-27
Direct Mail and Marketing Association, 118
"Direct Mail List Rates and Data," 115
Donor files, 142-43, 143-44, 148, 155

**E**

Easter seals, 150
Endorsement advertisements, 104-5, 124-25, 133
*Engineering News-Record,* 12
Envelopes, 216
Exhibit booths, 116-17, 182-83

**F**

Fair share approach, fund raising, 142
Film for commercials, 80-81
Fund raising campaigns, 122-23, 124, 138, 140-66

**H**

Housing and Urban Development, Department of (HUD), 11
*How to Win Friends and Influence People* advertising campaign, 95-96

## I

Illustrations, 97-98, 107-8. *See also* Photography, advertising
  magazines, 31, 97-98, 107-8
  newsletters, 198
Independent Newsletters Association, 199

## K

Keying the advertisement, 109, 131-32

## L

Layout and design, 96, 101, 102, 107, 108, 203-4, 207
Letterpress printing, 214
List broker, 117-18, 201

## M

Magazine advertisements, 4-5, 76-77
  copywriting, 91-107
  feature articles, 13, 164
  free publicity, 45-53, 132-33
  general interest publications, 4, 47-48, 50
  illustrations, 31, 97-98, 107-8
  monthlies v. weeklies, 5, 125
  press releases, 26
  query letters, 51-53
  special interest publications, 4, 47-48, 50, 132-33
  testing, 108-10
  timing, 114
  type specifications and layout, 96, 101, 102, 107, 108

Mailing lists, 112, 115-20, 201, 209-11
  brokers, 117-18, 201
Mail order, 131-32
Mail rates, 127, 204
Mimeograph, 215

## N

*National Directory of Newsletters and Reporting Services,* 199
*Nation's Cities,* 13, 46
Newsletters, 142, 143, 155, 195-212
  business promotion tool, 197-201
  costs, 202
  gathering information, 204-7
  illegal reproduction of, 210
  illustrations, 198
  layout and design, 203-4, 207
  mailing lists, 201, 209-11
  nonprofit organization promotion tool, 195-97
  scheduling, 207-8
Newspaper advertisements, 1-3, 14. *See also* Press releases
  articles, 12-13, 14-15, 16-18, 162-64, 167-68
  copywriting, 91-107
  coupons, 1-2
  created news, 18
  illustrations, 107-8
  selecting space, 2-3, 162
  testing, 108-10
  timing, 15-16
  type specifications and layout, 96, 101, 102, 107, 108
*New York Times,* 164

Nonprofit organization promotions, 135-71
  board of directors, 145
  bonuses, 148, 149-50
  direct mail, 146-49, 156
  donor files, 142-43, 143-44, 148, 155
  follow up, 149
  fund raising, 140-66
  letters, 156
  media publicity, 158-65
  newsletters, 142, 143, 155, 195-212
  press kit, 137-40, 145, 165
  spokesman, 136, 154
  staff morale, 157-58
  telephone solicitation, 165-6
  volunteers, 144, 145-46, 147

O

Offset printing, 213-14
Outdoor advertising, 189-93
  moving signs, 190-91
  transit advertisements, 191-93

P

Paper quality, 128, 203, 204, 213, 215-16
Photography, advertising, 29-34, 97-98, 150-54, 198
  reproduction, 214, 215
Political campaign advertising, 13, 14-15, 32-33, 37, 42-43, 44, 48-49, 50, 106-7, 113, 124, 125
Postal rates, 127, 204

Preemptible commercials, 77
Press conferences, 35-47, 169
  preparation, 38-44
  timing and effectiveness, 36-37
Press kits, 137-40, 145, 165
Press releases, 18-35, 44
  announcements, 19-20, 25, 162
  columnists, 21, 27-29
  forms, 34-35
  illustrations, 29-34
  selecting an editor, 22, 24, 26
  timing, 21-22, 24, 26, 171
  writing, 23-24
Printing, 204, 207-8, 213-17
  letterpress, 214
  mimeograph, 215
  offset, 213-14
  proofs, 214, 216-17
  rotogravure, 215
  split runs, 109-10, 131, 132
Public service programs and announcements, 136-37, 160
"Puff" piece, 47

R

Radio advertisements, 5-7, 84
  classical stations, 7
  costs, 81-82, 83
  country-western stations, 7, 62
  FM stations, 7
  middle-of-the-road (M.O.R.) stations, 6-7
  news releases, 26
  producing, 74, 84-89
  rock stations, 7, 62
  talk shows, 5-6, 7, 55-66, 159-62; preparations, 61-66

## Index 223

Real estate section, newspaper's, 3
Religious organization promotions, 136, 142-43, 166-68
Residuals, 82
Rotogravure printing, 215
Run of schedule clause, 77-78

### S

Screen Actors' Guild (SAG), 82
Seeded lists, 118
Shopping center promotions, 185-88
    coordinate sales, 187-88
    special events, 186-87
Split run printing, 109-110, 131, 132
Sports section, newspaper's, 3
Storyboard, 80, 83

### T

Teaser, 128-29
Telephone, use of, 44-45
    solicitations, 165-66, 209-10
Television advertisements, 7-10
    buying time, 77-78
    cable television, 9
    costs, 81-82, 83
    educational stations, 8
    network stations, 8
    news releases, 26
    news spots, 66
    nonnetwork stations, 8-9
    photographs, 31
    prime time, 8
    producing, 74-84

talk shows, 9-10, 55-66, 158-59;
    preparation, 61-66
UHF stations, 9
Testing advertisements, 108-10, 114
*Thomas Register, The,* 201
Transit advertisements, 191-93
"Turn-key" housing, 11, 13
Type specifications, 96, 101, 102, 107, 108

### U

United Way promotion, 137, 142, 146, 161, 164

### V

Video disc players, 179
Videotape, 80-81, 179
Volunteers, 144, 145-46, 147

### W

Window displays, 173-83
    animated, 176-77
    audiovisuals, 178-80
    colors, 177-78
    institutional displays, 175
    lighting, 180, 181
    live demonstrations, 180-81
    security, 181-82
    theme, 175-77
Wire services, 29, 47
Women's section, newspaper's, 2-3
*World Almanac,* 201
*Writer's Market,* 51